Fiscal Policy

AF793259

Şebnem Tosunoğlu, Süleyman Kasal (eds.)

Fiscal Policy

Navigating Today's Challenges

PETER LANG
Berlin · Bruxelles · Chennai · Lausanne · New York · Oxford

Library of Congress Cataloging-in-Publication Data
A CIP catalog record for this book has been applied for at the Library of Congress.
Library of Congress Control Number: 2025001407

Bibliographic Information published by the Deutsche Nationalbibliothek
The Deutsche Nationalbibliothek lists this publication in the Deutsche Nationalbibliografie; detailed bibliographic data is available in the internet at http://dnb.d-nb.de.

ISBN 978-3-631-92372-6 (Print)
E-ISBN 978-3-631-93515-6 (E-PDF)
E-ISBN 978-3-631-93516-3 (E-PUB)
DOI 10.3726/b22745

© 2025 Peter Lang Group AG, Lausanne (Switzerland)
Published by Peter Lang GmbH, Berlin (Germany)
info@peterlang.com

All rights reserved.
All parts of this publication are protected by copyright. Any utilization outside the strict limits of the copyright law, without the permission of the publisher, is forbidden and liable to prosecution. This applies in particular to reproductions, translations, microfilming, and storage and processing in electronic retrieval systems.

This publication has been peer reviewed.

www.peterlang.com

Indice

Examining Tax Penalties in Views of Taxpayers and Tax Officials: A Phenomenological Study*

Mustafa Erkan ÜYÜMEZ[1] *& Ali Osman YILMAZ*[2]

1 Introduction

States impose certain sanctions to collect taxes in full and on time. Taxpayers who do not comply with their tax obligations may be subject to tax penalties. Tax penalties may vary according to the nature of the unlawful act. In case of a minor violation, only a financial penalty is foreseen. On the other hand, there are more severe tax sanctions in the case of an act that is considered a serious violation committed against the social order. Tax penalty procedures for taxpayers are carried out by the tax office. In this context, it is thought that there is a need for qualitative research on the evaluations of taxpayers and tax officials about tax penalties and related practices. The subject of this study is the evaluations of taxpayers and tax officials about tax penalties and practices. The main purpose of this study is to determine the evaluations of taxpayers and tax officials regarding tax penalties and the reflections of tax penalties on taxpayers. In this study, phenomenology, one of the qualitative research designs, was utilized. In this context, it will be tried to determine how the participants understand tax penalties and practices. Afterwards, the research findings will be presented within the framework of themes.

2 Conceptual Framework

2.1 Tax Penalties

Tax penalties are sanctions for crimes committed against the state treasury. Tax penalties are divided into two as fiscal penalties and penalties in the

---

* It was presented orally at the 2nd International Congress on Economics and Administrative Sciences (June 09–11, 2021, Bishkek/Kyrgyzstan) and its text was presented in Summary Book of the Congress with ISBN: 978-625-7813-82-2

1 Prof. Anadolu University, Faculty of Economics and Administrative Sciences, Department of Public Finance, meuyumez@anadolu.edu.tr, ORCID ID: 0000-0001-7567-3486

2 Assist. Prof. Karabük University, Safranbolu Ş.Y.D. Vocational School, Department of Accounting and Tax aliyilmaz@karabuk.edu.tr, ORCID ID: 0000-0001-7758-1323.

context of criminal law (Öncel, Kumrulu & Çağan, 2013:209–210). This distinction is based on the following. Some of the unlawful acts constitute a serious violation against the legal order. The other part is in the form of minor violations. Acts considered as gross violations are referred to as crimes. Actions considered as minor violations are defined as misdemeanors. Due to this distinction between the acts, tax penalties are differentiated. In tax misdemeanors, the public nature of the tax is taken into consideration. In tax crimes, tax penalties vary due to the public nature of the tax as well as inconvenient situations for the social order (Akdoğan, 2023:149–150). Penalties for tax misdemeanors are monetary (administrative fines). The penalties for tax offenses consist of imprisonment and judicial fines (Karakoç, 2012:477). Tax misdemeanors are offenses of a fiscal nature. The authority that imposes such penalties is the tax administration. Such penalties aim to protect the economic order, social order, and public morality. Fiscal offenses consist of tax loss penalties and irregularity penalties. Tax loss offenses arise in the event of tax loss. Irregularity offenses are non-compliance with the formal and procedural provisions of tax laws (Ortaç & Ünsal, 2022:252–255).

Crimes that bind the liberty consist of tax evasion offense, violation of tax privacy offense and the offense of conducting private affairs of the taxpayer. For these offenses, there is a financial penalty (monetary penalty) in the tax procedure law and imprisonment in the context of criminal law (Oktar, 2018:384).

2.2 Taxpayers and Tax Officials

The taxpayer is defined in many ways in the literature. A taxpayer is a person who must pay a certain amount of tax to the public administration (Öncel, et al. 2013:71). In the Tax Procedure Law, a taxpayer is a natural or legal person to whom a tax obligation arises according to the tax laws (T.P.L., Art. 8)[3]. A taxpayer is a person who is obliged to fulfill material and formal responsibilities. The main rule in the fulfillment of tax obligations is the realization of the obligations by the taxpayers. In addition, due to some economic, administrative, and legal reasons, some formal tax duties are fulfilled by tax responsibles (Ortaç & Ünsal, 2022:94). The tax responsible is

---

3 https://www.mevzuat.gov.tr/mevzuat?MevzuatNo=213&MevzuatTur=1&MevzuatTertip=4

the person who is responsible to the tax office in terms of tax payment and formal duties (Bülbül, 2022:136).

Another concept related to the research is tax Tax officials. The tax administration is the administration that carries out all the work and transactions related to taxation according to the current tax legislation (Taşkan, 2019:143). Taxation procedures are generally carried out under the roof of revenue administrations. Revenue administrations can organize their employees and other resources in different ways to collect national revenues. Traditional organizational structures can be designed according to tax types, taxpayer types, and functions (such as audit, debt collection) (Kahriman, 2016:234). In today's organizational structures, administrations such as Her Majesty's Revenue and Customs (HMRC) have transformed into a customer-oriented organizational structure[4]. Tax administrations may differ according to each country's administrative structure, legal structure, and tax system. For example, the Revenue Administration (Revenue Administration)[5], Internal Revenue Service[6], General Manegement of Taxes (Direction Generale des Impots/DGI)[7], Federal Ministry of Finance (Bundesamt für Finanzen)[8], and Federal Tax Service of Russia (ФНС Россиии)[9], tax officials follow taxation procedures in different units according to their job descriptions. Tax officials can be defined as public employees with different titles depending on the unit and the type of employment, who follow the work and procedures related to tax transactions according to the organizational law or legislation.

3 Literature Review

Tax penalties can be defined as control mechanisms designed to ensure that taxpayers fulfill their material and formal obligations. When the literature is examined; it is seen that studies using mainly quantitative

4 https://www.gov.uk/government/publications/hmrc-organisation-chart/organisation-chart
5 https://www.gib.gov.tr/kurumsal/organizasyon-semasi
6 https://www.irs.gov/pub/newsroom/marketing/internet/irs-organization-chart.pdf
7 https://www.impots.cm/fr/organigramme
8 https://www.bundesfinanzministerium.de/Content/DE/Downloads/Ministerium/organigramm.pdf?__blob=publicationFile&v=8
9 https://www.nalog.gov.ru/rn77/about_fts/fts/structure_fts/

methods are quite common. However, it is seen that studies using qualitative research methods on tax penalties have started to increase in recent years (Güngör Göksu & Saruç, 2012; Saad, 2014; Gencel, 2015; Bişgin, 2018; Yılmaz, 2019).

Looking at the literature, it is seen that many studies have been conducted on the behavior and attitudes of taxpayers. In general, these studies include determinations and evaluations on tax crimes and penalties (Muter, Sakınç & Çelebi, 1993; Yeniçeri, 2004; Çiçek, 2006; Yılmaz & Şeker, 2007; Tuay & Güvenç, 2007; Çiçek, Karakaş & Yıldız, 2008; İpek & Kaynar, 2009; Alp & Töngür, 2018; Akbelen & Aydın, 2019). In some other studies, it is seen that tax crimes and penalties are studied as the main subject of study (Aslan, 2008; Kovancılar & Demirdizen, 2010; Şanver, 2017; Bahşı, 2019; Ateşağaoğlu, 2019).

In the literature, many studies have been conducted on the effectiveness of tax penalties. According to these studies, there are results that the sanction power of tax penalties is not effective (Muter, Sakınç & Çelebi, 1993:14–20; Yeniçeri, 2004; Tuay & Güvenç, 2007:62; Yılmaz & Şeker, 2007:56; İpek & Kaynar, 2009). In addition, some studies have concluded that tax penalties are effective (Aslan, 2008:357). In some studies, it has been determined that tax penalties have no positive or negative contribution to tax payment (Çiçek, 2006; 113). In some studies, it has been concluded that sanctions in the form of imprisonment will increase the effectiveness of tax penalties Tuay and Güvenç, 2007:66, Şanver, 2017:104). In some studies, it has been found that factors such as financial restructuring laws (tax amnesties), reconciliation and frequency of tax audits negatively affect the effectiveness of tax penalties (Yeniçeri, 2004; Bahşı, 2019:92).

The main purpose of this research is to determine the evaluations of taxpayers and Tax officials regarding tax penalties and the reflections of tax penalties on taxpayers. In this context, answers to the following research questions were sought.

1. How do taxpayers make sense of tax crimes and penalties?
2. How do taxpayers evaluate the effects of tax penalties on the taxpayer?
3. How do tax officials evaluate the effects of tax penalties on the taxpayer?

4 Methodology

In this study, phenomenology, one of the qualitative research designs, was used. Phenomenology is a study aimed at uncovering and developing lived experiences and ways of understanding these experiences (Marshall, & Rossman, 2006:104). The phenomenological design focuses on phenomena that we are aware of but do not have a detailed understanding of. With the phenomenological design, it is tried to reveal how the studied event is understood and perceived (Yıldırım & Şimşek, 2008:72). In this study, it was tried to determine the evaluations of taxpayers and tax officials regarding tax penalties in the context of their opinions, how they make sense of tax penalties and the reflections of tax penalties on taxpayers. In this study, the views, experiences and evaluations of taxpayers and tax officials on tax penalties are analyzed.

4.1 Participants

Purposive sampling methods are used in qualitative research. Purposive sampling methods allow the selection of information-rich situations for in-depth studies. Maximum variation sampling method selects cases from a certain range of diversity. It examines common patterns from a wide variety (Glesne, 2015:59–61; Flick, 2011:28). In this study, maximum variation sampling was used to determine the participants. The participants of this study consisted of taxpayers and tax officials. Taxpayers are six businessmen who have their head offices in Ankara/Türkiye and are engaged in commercial activities in different sectors. Tax officials consist of 5 tax office managers, assistant managers, and revenue specialists working in tax office directorates located in Ankara. The total number of participants is 11.

4.2 Collection Tools and Data Collection

The main data collection tool in phenomenological studies is the interview (Flick, 2011:78). Phenomenological interviewing is a special type of in-depth interviewing. The strength of phenomenological interviews is that they allow the researcher to focus on explanatory situations in the interviews. This data collection tool allows the researcher interaction, flexibility, and in-depth knowledge to identify experiences and meanings of phenomena (Marshall, & Rossman, 2006:105). In the phenomenology design, semi-structured interview forms were used in this study to obtain more detailed information about the phenomena that we are aware of but cannot fully grasp.

A comprehensive literature review was conducted while creating the interview forms. The draft interview questions created after the literature review were evaluated by field experts. A pilot study is required to test the interview questions (Silverman, 1993:148). Pilot study is important for the consistency of the interview forms and the researcher (Türnüklü, 2000:550). The interview forms were finalized by conducting a pilot interview. Then the interviews were started. In this study, interviews with participants were conducted between 01/05/2020 and 02/20/2020. A letter of commitment regarding ethical rules was presented to them before the interview. Consents of the participants were obtained for voice recording in the interviews. Within the scope of the research, a voice recorder was used to prevent data loss. During the research process, data collection tools such as research diary, pre interview diary, and post interview diary were also utilized. Thus, attention was paid to data diversification for the richness and consistency of the data.

4.3 Data Analysis

In phenomenological research, data analysis is about identifying experiences and meanings. In this context, content analysis involves conceptualizing the data and creating themes. The results are conveyed in a descriptive way and there are many direct quotations (Yıldırım & Şimşek, 2008:75). In data analysis, the coding of data proceeds in the form of classification-definition and definition-classification. Data analysis consists of examining, classifying, and recombining evidence to draw conclusions (Glesne, 2015:268–271).

Content analysis was used in the data analysis of this study. The process of content analysis of qualitative data is inductive in form. The main purpose of content analysis is to reveal the concepts that can explain the collected data and the relationships between them. In content analysis, concepts and themes are tried to be discovered by examining the data in depth. In this process, firstly, the data are defined, then similar data are brought together under certain concepts and themes, organized and interpreted in a way that readers can understand (Tracy, 2013:194–195).

After the interviews were completed, the voice recordings were transcribed. In data analysis, the data were first subdivided (coded). The concepts identified in the content analysis and those related to each other were grouped under certain themes. Expert opinions were taken in coding and thematization studies. Thus, themes pointing to a general phenomenon were revealed. In the study, direct quotations were used to illustrate the important points of the findings.

4.4 Credibility, Transferability, Consistency and Verifiability

In qualitative research, some measures need to be taken to transfer the research phenomena in accordance with the nature of qualitative research. Through these measures, it is tried to ensure credibility, transferability, consistency, and confirmability in qualitative studies (Yıldırım & Şimşek, 2008:254–255: Gibbs, 2008:93–98: Creswell, 2009:190–191). In this context, to ensure credibility (internal validity), long-term interviews, data triangulation, in-depth information collection and expert review were conducted. Within the scope of transferability (external validity), detailed description and purposive sampling were utilized in this study. Direct quotations were included in the study. To ensure consistency (internal reliability), interview questions were prepared in accordance with the qualitative research method. The questions were tested with a pilot application. Then, the questions were renewed with the evaluation of field experts. To ensure confirmability (external reliability) within the scope of the research, a voice recorder was used in the interviews. Thus, data loss was prevented. The research diaries, interview diaries, and research notes kept during the research process enabled the experts to follow the stages of the study. The evaluations of field experts were taken in the coding and thematization process. As a result of these studies and evaluations, it was determined that the data analysis process of the research had integrity.

5 Findings

In this study, three main themes were reached because of the content analysis conducted on the data obtained through interviews with the participants and other data collection techniques. These themes are as follows:

- Taxpayers' Tax Penalties and Procedures (Liabilities) Information
- Deterrence of tax penalties
- Reflection of tax penalties on taxpayers

5.1 Taxpayers' Tax Penalties and Procedures (Liabilities) Information

The first theme of this study is "taxpayers' level of knowledge about tax penalties and transactions (liabilities)". In the answers given by the taxpayers participating in the study to the question of whether they know about tax crimes; taxpayer 1 stated that "he does not know what constitutes a tax crime", while the other taxpayers stated that "… they do not know everything, they learn what constitutes a tax crime when something happens to them…" In addition, they stated that they learn about tax crimes from their sworn financial advisors.

In addition, when we asked them to list the tax crimes they knew about, they gave the following answers: "…tax loss…, … issuing false documents, selling without an invoice, not paying tax on time…, … not reporting declarations on time…, … irregularity penalties, not issuing the delivery note on time, not writing certain elements on the delivery note…, … covert profit transfer, VAT transfer between companies…, … hiding profit…, covert interest payment, tampering with documents…, … all kinds of actions that will cause tax loss."

Within the scope of the research, it has been determined that some taxpayers know the difference between tax offenses and tax crimes. It has been determined that owners of large-scale companies have more information about tax crimes and penalties. Some taxpayers stated that their certified public accountants informed them about tax penalties.

Some taxpayers stated that the amount of tax penalties they incurred due to inadvertent mistakes was high and that this situation was unfair. Some taxpayers attribute this situation to the fact that the tax administration is disconnected from business life. They attribute this to the lack of coordination and communication between the tax administration and the private sector. Taxpayer 6 stated that there is a disproportion between the situations that cause tax loss and tax penalties due to formal obligations (procedural errors).

Participating tax officials stated that the level of knowledge about tax crimes and penalties varies according to the level of institutionality of the companies. Tax official 1 stated that "…all taxpayers know that there is a penalty if the document is not prepared. But they do not know the amount of the penalty." tax official 4 stated that taxpayers are generally knowledgeable about tax crimes and penalties and are conscious about their tax liabilities. Participating tax official 3 made the following assessment about taxpayers operating in the service sector: "…the reason they are penalized is that they generally prefer the tax penalty between the amount of the penalty and paying tax…, … taxpayers make an income-expense comparison [benefit-financial analysis], and since their daily turnover is high, they risk the penalty of not complying with the document system…" Tax official 2 stated that "instead of paying a high amount of tax now, tax audits are not being done enough, I will continue this activity until it is my turn to be audited - until I am detected, I do not see many people around me who have been detected, let's evade taxes, nothing is being taken from anyone anyway, we will not be charged tax or fines either." Another tax official stated that "taxpayers do not consciously fulfill their tax obligations because the tax audit rate is at a low level of 1–2%."

According to the research data, the level of taxpayers' knowledge on tax transactions is directly proportional to the level of institutionalization of their firms. It has been determined that owners of small-scale firms do not have sufficient knowledge about tax liabilities. It can be said that taxpayers mainly fulfill their responsibilities according to the guidance of their financial advisors.

Regarding the tax penalties applied to tax offenses, it has been revealed that taxpayers have basic information about irregularity, special irregularity, smuggling penalties, and that there is a perception that the penalty rates are generally applied as one and three times, and although a taxpayer does not know the concept of misdemeanor and crime, it has been revealed that he is aware of the distinction that the penalty is imposed by the tax offices and the crime is transferred to the prosecutor's office.

It can be said that taxpayers know what tax penalties and offenses are in general terms with the size of their companies and the experience of having received some penalties.

Although taxpayers have knowledge on basic tax issues, they can afford the tax penalties they will be subjected to if they are caught due to the low rate of detection of their transactions contrary to the legislation by the tax administration. According to the scale of taxpayers, it can be stated that they need continuous education and information about their tax obligations and responsibilities.

5.2 Deterrence of Tax Penalties

The second theme of the research is "deterrence of tax penalties". According to the evaluations of the participants, some administrative practices and sanctions are more effective than tax penalties. Participants stated that the "Special Principles[10]" imposed by the Ministry of Finance on companies that issue counterfeit documents and that have exchanges with companies that use these counterfeit documents is a more deterrent sanction than a monetary penalty. The reason why this administrative practice is more effective than tax penalties is that companies are exposed to loss of turnover and customers because of taxpayers being subject to "special basis provisions". In addition, one of the participants, taxpayer 2, stated that taxpayers pay attention to their obligations due to the condition of not having a debt to the tax office for his company to participate in public tenders. He also stated that they pay more attention to tax debts than even the wages of their employees. Here, it is revealed that not having any debt to the tax authorities as a condition for participating in public tenders is a more effective sanction than imposing a tax penalty on the taxpayer.

The common aspect of the answers given by taxpayers in the questions we asked about the effectiveness of tax penalties is primarily the failure to register everyone rather than the amount and rate of tax penalties. It is stated that taxpayers should be registered, and control should be ensured. There is unfair competition between registered and unregistered workers in the market. It was also stated that the state suffers from this informality. According to all participants, tax penalties are not deterrent for unregistered taxpayers. Therefore, it can be said that tax penalties have a sanction for registered taxpayers.

On this issue, Taxpayer 3 stated, "People working unregistered do not care about tax penalties anyway. They do not pay their taxes; nothing changes for these people." Taxpayer 4 stated, "...registered and unregistered compete, registered employees are more under control, and it happens to registered employees. Nothing happens to unregistered employees..."

---

[10] https://www.mevzuat.gov.tr/mevzuat?MevzuatNo=19631&MevzuatTur=9&MevzuatTertip=5 The purpose of the provisions titled Special Principles in Section IV/E of the Value Added Tax General Implementation Communiqué is to investigate the accuracy of taxpayers' Value Added Tax returns. It is to prevent unfair tax refunds by identifying unreal VAT amounts.

Taxpayer 5 stated that tax rates should be looked at before tax penalties. He emphasized that the reasons why people go outside the system should be investigated. He stated that the reason for the increase in informality is the high tax rates and the fact that the tax is not spread to the bottom in a fair manner. They stated that these two problems should be solved first and then the system should be redesigned. They argue that tax penalties should be applied in certain limits and steps. They stated that a distinction should be made between taxpayers who fulfill their obligations continuously and regularly and those who work off the books. To increase the deterrence of tax penalties, they stated that the amount of the penalty should be determined in direct proportion to the amount of unfair earnings.

In addition, it can be said that all participants agree that the most effective tax penalty is a "sentence of imprisonment". In addition, since the initiation of seizure procedures due to tax penalties and debts and the blocking of bank accounts negatively affect the taxpayer's commercial activity, such measures are more effective than tax penalties. However, taxpayer 6 (who is the owner of a large-scale company) stated that tax penalties are not in a way to reduce the commercial activity of the taxpayer. According to this person, both the taxpayer and the state should be kept alive, and collection should be made without killing the taxpayer.

Taxpayers generally stated that they are afraid of the implementation of penalties. Participating taxpayers stated that they are "...afraid of falling into a situation like having a criminal record..., ...their credibility will decrease in the eyes of banks and partners..., ...they are afraid of the question marks that may arise about their companies in terms of shareholders or those who want to be partners in their companies..." The reason they are particularly afraid of being penalized is that the Ministry of Finance will put them in a different category when evaluating them if they receive a tax penalty, they will fall into a situation like having a criminal record, and their credit will end. Taxpayer 3 stated that they are afraid of the disclosure of commercial information about their company during the investigation, and they are afraid of the question marks that may arise about the company in terms of banks and credit institutions, shareholders or those who want to be partners. Taxpayer 4 stated that "my psychology is damaged, I did not sleep for a week, my health is damaged."

Within the scope of this theme, tax official 1 stated that receiving a penalty does not have much effect on paying subsequent taxes on time, as the importance of paying taxes is not recognized by the society in general. Tax official 3, on the other hand, stated that small-scale taxpayers with limited income are more careful after the penalty and learn from this situation. On the other hand, taxpayers with high turnovers stated that the fines imposed did not make sense for them since they did not record high amounts of income.

Tax officials 2 stated that taxpayers do not care about the fines imposed. In addition, he stated that "...what can they do, what do I have that they will take, the most you can do is throw me in jail, what do I have, are you going to take my life, are they going to take my life, and walk away..." It can be said that if the taxpayer does not have the ability to pay, the effect of tax fines is considerably reduced, and therefore the ineffectiveness of tax fines emerges.

Tax officials 4 stated that tax loss fines are more deterrent than irregularity fines. It is understood that the main reason for this is that the irregularity fine amounts are relatively lower.

According to Tax officials, taxpayers continue to use false documents due to the low tax audit rate, and that there is no sanction for these people due to the high tax penalties. Another tax officials stated that "the perception that tax evasion is a bad thing has disappeared in society, and in fact, in our society, the crime of tax evasion is seen as something to be proud of...". It has also been determined that frequently enacted tax amnesty (financial restructuring) laws negatively affect the sanction power of tax penalties.

According to the research data, taxpayers are aware that they are less likely to be detected due to the low tax audit rates. It is concluded that as the frequency of tax audits increases, the effectiveness of tax penalties and taxpayers' compliance increases. In general, it has been determined that tax compliance of small-scale taxpayers increases because of the tax penalties they face. On the other hand, it has been revealed that taxpayers who receive very high amounts of tax penalties may not increase their tax compliance, but on the contrary, tax non-compliance may increase. In some segments of the society, it can be said that tax evaders or those who do not pay their taxes in full constitute a bad example, and that those who pay their taxes on time and in full are viewed unfavorably.

5.3 Reflection of Tax Penalty Practices on Taxpayers

The final theme of the research is "the reflection/impact of tax penalty procedures on taxpayers".

Reactions of taxpayers during the notification of the penalty

According to the tax officials among the participants, when taxpayers are subject to a high tax penalty, they "become very stressed and aggressive, they see tax official as enemies, you did it, you did it" and make accusations such as during the notification of the tax penalty.

Reactions of taxpayers during the payment of the tax penalty

Some tax officials stated that the taxpayer; "...was unfairly penalized...", "...sufficient investigation was not carried out, very high penalties were taken from him...", "...was victimized due to mistakes made by another taxpayer with whom he had commercial activities...", "...objected and complained that it was not his fault, the penalties were high..."

According to some tax officials, taxpayers "come to tax offices as places that impose unnecessary and unnecessary fines" and come with prejudice and fear, "the number of taxpayers who come feeling guilty is usually very few", "they do not accept the fine", "some taxpayers are shameless", "they continue to be shameless", "they have become accustomed to this situation", and "they do not have feelings such as shame and feeling bad".

According to some tax officials, taxpayers "see tax offices as places where unnecessary and unnecessarily fines are imposed" and come with prejudice and fear, "the number of taxpayers who come feeling guilty is usually very few", "they do not accept the fine", "some taxpayers are shameless", "they continue to be shameless", "they have become accustomed to this situation", "they do not feel ashamed or bad". Some taxpayers stated that tax officials treat them as 'tax evaders' as people who are trying to create employment and produce. Some taxpayers see tax offices as places where unnecessary and unnecessarily fines are imposed on them, and taxpayers are punished.

According to the research data, it was determined that tax compliance of small-scale taxpayers increased in terms of the effect of tax penalties on taxpayers' fulfillment of their obligations. It has been determined that tax compliance may be lower for taxpayers with high turnover. In addition, it has been determined that some small-scale taxpayers reacted as "I do not have any assets, what can you do?". Here, it can be said that tax penalties may not influence tax compliance if the taxpayer does not have the ability to pay. It can be said that for the penalties to influence the taxpayer, the taxpayer must have a minimum payment capacity.

Acceptance of tax penalties and its repercussions

Some taxpayers who participated in the research stated that the tax penalty did not have any effect on them because they did not accept it. Some taxpayers stated that the tax penalties that they were subjected to inadvertently or unjustly while carrying out their commercial activities demoralized them, negatively affected their psychology, discouraged them from doing business, deteriorated their health, and made them feel bad towards their children and relatives.

Taxpayer 3 stated that there is no escape from paying taxes and that they are aware that the state will collect tax receivables even if it is late. Some taxpayers think that tax evaders should be terminated and prevented from doing business. On the other hand, some taxpayers stated that economic penalties should be imposed for tax penalties. Some taxpayers stated that the imposition of tax penalties that bind them to life imprisonment leads some taxpayers to use illegal means to reduce the risk of such penalties. In response to the risk of tax penalties, they may transfer movable and immovable property registered in their name to other persons. Sometimes they carry out their commercial activities through others. According to the research data, it can be said that malicious or dishonest taxpayers can use illegal ways. On the other hand, taxpayers with sufficient tax awareness do not prefer illegal ways.

Reflection of tax penalties on liabilities and solutions

The common view of the participating taxpayers is that tax penalties contribute positively to the fulfillment of obligations. Tax office employees stated that no matter how much the taxpayers react, they try to pay the tax penalty debts. It was shared that they benefit from alternative ways such as using the reconciliation process, benefiting from tax amnesty laws, postponement and installment opportunities of tax debt. Some taxpayers stated that if they are confident, they do not pay their tax penalty debts and file lawsuits in tax jurisdictions. According to the research data, it can be said that taxpayers value judicial remedies according to the possibility of losing the tax case.

6 Conclusion

According to the results of the research, it is determined that the tax penalties applied in Türkiye are not effective enough to collect taxes and to prevent the recurrrence of tax crimes. It can be said that taxpayers mainly fulfill their responsibilities according to the guidance of their financial advisors. It has been determined that especially certified public accountants inform the taxpayers. It can be said that the level of taxpayers' knowledge of tax transactions is directly proportional to the level of institutionalization of enterprises and the size of the enterprise. In addition, it can be said that tax audits also contribute to taxpayers' knowledge about tax penalties. As a result, it can be stated that taxpayers need continuous education, information and guidance on their tax obligations and responsibilities according to their scales. After informing taxpayers about their obligations, tax audits should become periodic, or the frequency of audits should be increased. Thus, taxpayer compliance can be increased.

Within the scope of the deterrence of tax penalty's theme of the research, it has been determined that the tax penalties applied in Türkiye are not effective enough in terms of collecting taxes and preventing the repetition of tax offenses. It can be said that tax penalties are not deterrent enough. To increase the deterrence of tax penalties, it can be stated that the frequency and effectiveness of tax inspections should be increased. However, it is seen that the sanctioning power of the penalties that bind the freedom is high. On the other hand, some administrative practices (such as taxpayers being subject to a special provision regime[11], ineligibility to participate in public tenders) have been found to be more effective sanctions than tax penalties. These administrative practices directly affect the business volume and sales of taxpayers. In addition, it can be said that these administrative practices are more effective than tax penalties because they negatively affect the reputation of the firm in the eyes of banks, financial institutions, shareholders, shareholders and the public.

---

[11] The purpose of the provisions titled Special Principles in Section IV/E of the Value Added Tax General Implementation Communiqué is to investigate the accuracy of taxpayers' Value Added Tax returns. It is to prevent unfair tax refunds by identifying unreal VAT amounts

Another factor that negatively affects the effectiveness of tax penalties is unfair competition caused by unregistered persons. Taxpayers think that they are penalized for working under the records. It can be stated that this situation may lead taxpayers to engage in unregistered activities. This situation may have a negative impact on the tax compliance of honest taxpayers. Within the scope of this theme, it has been determined that reducing unregistered activities and auditing unregistered businesses will have a positive effect on tax compliance

According to the results of the research, it can be said that taxpayers perceive tax offices as public administrations that unfairly impose tax penalties and do not distinguish between error and fraud (cheating). In the whole process from the notification of tax penalties to the collection stage, it has been determined that many taxpayers are very affected by this situation, lose their health from time to time, react against the tax administration at the level of rebellion, and are disturbed by being treated as tax evaders. However, it has been determined that tax penalties may not have much effect on some taxpayers, including psychological effect.

In general, although taxpayers react to tax penalties, it is determined that they seek ways to pay tax penalties. It has been determined that they benefit from alternative payment methods such as benefiting from the reconciliation institution, benefiting from tax amnesty laws, postponement of tax debt and evaluation of installment opportunities. However, tax amnesties should not lead to an increase in unregistered activities. At the same time, it should be prevented from turning into a tool for taxpayers to avoid tax inspections.

Bibliography

Akbelen, Z., & Aydın, Z. B. (2019). Vergi Afları ve Vergilemede Adalet Algısının Vergi Uyumuna Etkisi: Bursa İli Örneği. International Journal of Social Inquiry, 12(2), 409–437. https://doi.org/10.37093/ijsi.658995

Akdoğan, A. (2023). Vergi hukuku ve Türk Vergi Sistemi, (16th Ed.). Gazi Bookstore.

Alp, B., & Töngür, Ü. (2018). Vergi Dairesi Başkanlığı Çalışanlarının Vergi Algıları: Antalya Örneği. Akdeniz İİBF Dergisi, 18(38), 151–172. https://doi.org/10.25294/auiibfd.492743

Aslan, M. (2008). Türk Vergi Sistemindeki Cezaların Etkinliği, Maliye ve Hukuk Publications.

Ateşağaoğlu, E. (2019). Vergi Mahremiyetinin İhlali veya Sırrın İfşası Suçunu İşleyenler Hakkında Uygulanması Gereken Ceza Hukuku Hükümlerinin Değerlendirilmesi. Maliye Araştırmaları Dergisi, 5(1), 21–38.

Bahşı, S. (2019). Vergi Kaçakçılığının Nedenleri. İzmir YMMO Dergisi, 1(2), 89–95.

Bişgin, A. (2018). An analysis of the interaction between the accounting professionals and taxpayers in the context of tax compliance in Turkey. (Unpublished doctoral dissertation). Eskişehir: Anadolu University, Institute of Social Sciences

Bülbül, D. (2022). Devlet maliyesi, (5th Ed.). Dizgikitap Publications.

Creswell, J. W. (2009). Research design: qualitative, quantitative and mixed methods approaches, Thousand Oaks, CA: Sage Publications Inc.

Çiçek, H. (2006). Psikolojik ve Sosyal Yönden Yükümlülerin Vergiye Karşı Tutum ve Tepkileri (İstanbul İli Anket Çalışması), İSMMMO Issue no:65.

Çiçek, H. Karakaş, M. & Yıldız, A. (2008). Güneydoğu Anadolu Bölgesi'nde Vergi Yükümlülerinin Vergiyi Algılama ve Tutum Analizi: Bir Alan Araştırması, Maliye Bakanlığı SGB Publications 2008/381.

Flick, U. (2011). Designing qualitative research, SAGE Publications Inc.

Gencel, U. (2015). Türkiye'de Vergiye Bakış Metaforik Bir Analiz, Ekin Publications.

Gibbs, G. R. (2008). Analyzing qualitative data, London: Sage Publications Ltd.

Glesne, C. (2015). Nitel araştırmaya giriş, (Trns.) Ersoy A. & Yalçınoğlu P., (5th Ed.). Anı Publications.

Güngör Göksu, G. & Saruç, T. (2012). Türkiye'de vergiye uyum: mülakat çalışması. Mevzuat Dergisi, Sayı: 176, 1. https://www.mevzuatdergisi.com/2012/08a/01.htm

İpek, S. & Kaynar, İ. (2009). Vergiye Gönüllü Uyum Konusunda Çanakkale İline Yönelik Ampirik Bir Çalışma, Celal Bayar Üniversitesi İ.İ.B.F. Yönetim ve Ekonomi Dergisi, 16(1).

Kahriman, H. (2016). Vergiye Gönüllü Uyum Çerçevesinde Türkiye'de Gelir İdaresinin Organizasyon Yapısı Üzerine Bir Değerlendirme. Ekonomik Ve Sosyal Araştırmalar Dergisi, 12(1), 229–250.

Karakoç, Y. (2012). Genel vergi hukuku, (6th Ed.). Yetkin Publications.

Kovancılar, B. & Demirdizen, Ö. (2010). "Türk Vergi Suç ve Ceza Sistemine İlişkin Algılamalar (Manisa İli Örneği)", Vergi Dünyası, (349).

Marshall, K. & Rossman, G. B. (2006). Designing qualitative research, Sage Publications Inc.

Muter, N., Sakınç. S. & Çelebi, K. (1993). Mükelleflerin Vergi Karşısındaki Tutum ve Davranışları Araştırması: Manisa İli Anket Çalışması, http://www2.bayar.edu.tr/iibf/maliye/sureyya_sakinc/docs/yayinlar/mukelleflerin_vergi.pdf

Saad, N. (2014). Tax knowledge, tax complexity and tax compliance: taxpayers'view, Social and Behavioral Sciences, 109 (2014) 1069–1075/ 2nd World Conference On Business, Economics And Management.

Silverman, D. (1993). Interpreting Qualitative Data: Methods for Analysing Talk, Text and Interaction, Sage Publications Inc.

Tracy, S. T. (2013). Qualitative Research Methods Collecting Evidence, Crafting Analysis, Communicating Impact, Wiley-Blackwell Publications.

Oktar, S. A. (2018). Vergi hukuku, (13th Ed.). Türkmen Bookstore.

Ortaç, F. R. & Ünsal, H. (2022). Vergi Hukuku (Genel Hükümler), Seçkin Publications.

Öncel, M., Kumrulu, A. & Çağan, N. (2013). Vergi hukuku, (12th Ed.). Turhan Bookstore.

Şanver, C. (2017). Türk Vergi Sisteminde Vergi Kabahat ve Suçlarına Uygulanan Yaptırımların Caydırıcılığı Araştırması. Yönetim Bilimleri Dergisi, 15(29), 91–106.

Taşkan, Y. Z. (2019). Vergi hukuku, (2nd Ed.). Adalet Publications.

Tuay. E. & Güvenç, İ. (2007). Türkiye'de Mükelleflerin Vergiye Bakışı, GİB Issue No.51.

Türnüklü, A. (2000). Eğitimbilim araştırmalarında etkin olarak kullanılabilecek nitel bir araştırma tekniği: görüşme. Kuram ve Uygulamada Eğitim Yönetimi, (24), 543–559.

Yeniçeri, H. (2004). Beyan Esasına Dayanan Vergilerde Vergi Kayıp ve Kaçaklarının Psikolojik Nedenlerinin Tespitine Yönelik Bir Araştırma, E-Yaklaşım, (11).

Yıldırım, A. & Şimşek, H. (2008). Sosyal bilimlerde nitel araştırma yöntemleri, (6th Ed.). Seçkin Publications.

Yılmaz, A. O. (2019). Problems and Solution Proposals in Tax Audit: A Case Study of Turkey. (Unpublished doctoral dissertation). Eskişehir: Anadolu University, Institute of Social Sciences.

Yılmaz, B. E. & Şeker, M. (2007). Vergiye Karşı Tepkiler: Mükellef Davranışları (İstanbul Örneği), İSMMMO Issue No 86.

https://www.gov.uk/government/publications/hmrc-organisation-chart/organisation-chart (15/06/2024)

https://www.gib.gov.tr/kurumsal/organizasyon-semasi (15/06/2024)

https://www.irs.gov/pub/newsroom/marketing/internet/irs-organization-chart.pdf (15/06/2024)

https://www.impots.cm/fr/organigramme (15/06/2024)

https://www.bundesfinanzministerium.de/Content/DE/Downloads/Ministerium/organigramm.pdf?__blob=publicationFile&v=8 (15/06/2024)

https://www.nalog.gov.ru/rn77/about_fts/fts/structure_fts/ (15/06/2024)

https://www.mevzuat.gov.tr/mevzuat?MevzuatNo=213&MevzuatTur=1&MevzuatTertip=4 (05/06/2024)

The Concept of Construction in the Turkish Tax System and Taxation of Construction Works

Canatay HACIKÖYLÜ[1]

1 Introduction

Some tax liabilities that may arise in the sale and lease of an immovable property are frequently included in studies in the literature. However, one of the main factors that affects the taxation of the income to be obtained because of the sale of the immovable property is the material and formal tax liabilities during the construction phase of the immovable property. Especially in construction works that last for more than one year, there are special regulations in the tax laws in the formal sense. However, the status of the income obtained from the sale of the immovable property in the face of tax laws varies according to the type of construction of the immovable property, and the income obtained may be subject to different taxes.

The construction sector is one of the leading sectors of the economy, providing employment to a large number of businesses associated with many sub-sectors. All types of activity in the construction sector include complex and multifaceted relationships (Tokat, 2010:62). The legal regulations concerning this sector are quite comprehensive, complex, and specialised. In construction activities, starting from the procurement and acquisition of the land where the immovable property will be located, the construction, completion, and sale of the building are issues that concern the fields of accounting and law, as well as tax laws. These issues are often not easily understood by local/foreign real and legal persons. In the construction and real estate sectors, especially, the lack of full knowledge of taxation processes causes these people to face a few negative consequences.

As a result of the growth in the construction and real estate sectors in Türkiye since the early 2000s, the number of domestic and foreign companies operating in these sectors has increased. Parallel to this increase, it would not be wrong to say that the basis of the problems between these companies,

1 Anadolu University, FEAS, Department of Public Finance, chacikoylu@anadolu.edu.tr, ORCID-ID: 0000-0002-8853-6461

each of which is a taxpayer, and the tax administration is that the taxation processes are not fully known (Hacıköylü, 2012:25).

Within the Turkish legal system, the concept of construction is defined in different ways in various legal regulations. Unlike the concept of immovable property, the concept of construction is not defined in tax laws. However, in terms of taxation differences, the types of construction are subject to a binary distinction in the relevant literature as private constructions and contractual constructions. Again, in terms of some other taxes, especially income tax, taxation differences can be divided according to the stages of construction and sale of immovable property. However, in this study, taxation processes, which are comprehensive and complex within the framework of these distinctions, have been tried to be addressed in general terms for the construction phase of the immovable property.

2 Construction Concepts and Types of Construction in terms of Taxation

Although the concept of construction is not included in the tax laws, it is expressed in different ways in the Zoning Law No. 3194 and Public Procurement Law No. 4734 and similar regulations. Before explaining the types of construction in terms of taxation differences, a better understanding of the issue will be provided to explain the concept of a construction enterprise, which is an important element in terms of the taxation process. A construction company is defined as an organisation that constructs on its own behalf, for its own account, or for others through contracting. Even if construction enterprises are established as private construction enterprises and construction contracting enterprises, those established as construction contracting enterprises may carry out private construction works and contracting works. Enterprises that perform various works together or perform construction works spread over numerous years face different processes in terms of accounting and tax practices (Türüng, 2006:6). Under the Turkish Civil Code, construction works are divided into two categories: movable constructions and immovable constructions. Movable constructions are defined as huts, kiosks, gazebos, sheds and similar light structures built on someone else's land in a non-permanent manner. On the other hand, immovable structures are structures that are built by human hands-on land (on land/land) to stay permanently and have economic value (Kızılot, 2008:3). Although there is no distinction in the tax laws as in the Civil Code, a distinction is seen in terms of the taxation differences of construction works and enterprises. Accordingly, in terms of tax laws, construction types can be divided into two types: private constructions and contractual constructions.

In terms of the Turkish legal system and financial legislation, there are some differences between the construction of immovable property by a contractor on his own behalf and account and selling it in independent sections and the construction of immovable property on behalf of another person in the form of a contract. The similarity is that, in both cases, an immovable construction is in question.

A person who constructs a building on his own behalf and on his own account and sells it in independent sections undertakes the construction spontaneously for the purpose of selling it. In contract construction, construction is carried out on behalf of a business owner. In construction on one's own account, the main element of the contract is the goods and materials. The wage or price given is the equivalent of the goods and materials. Labor is the second element. On the other hand, in construction by contract, the main element of the contract is labor. The wage or consideration given is equivalent to the labor of the builder. Even if the materials and goods are provided by the contractor, they are the second element. Again, there is no process such as the transfer and assignment of ownership of the construction to the owner at the end of the contract work. On the other hand, for the transfer of ownership to the buyer in the construction carried out on its own behalf and account, it is obligatory to issue an official deed and carry out registration procedures at the land registry office (Kızılot, 2008:302).

Construction works carried out for the purpose of building and selling buildings on one's own behalf and account are financially costly, and taxation processes are quite complicated, starting from the way the land is acquired, starting construction and licencing, the cost of construction and inspection processes, the sale of independent sections of the completed construction, and the delivery of housing/workplaces to landowners in return for land. Construction and repair works spread over numerous years, on the other hand, have more complex characteristics due to the income generated and the related efforts to stabilise the income. Although construction and repair works are considered commercial activities and commercial earnings in terms of the nature of the activity and the income elements obtained, such as the construction of buildings on one's own behalf and account and construction for the purpose of selling them, they have some fundamental differences in terms of taxation compared to build/sell type construction works. For these reasons, different regulations are included in Income Tax Law No. 193 for contracted construction and repair works in the form of contracting, compared to other works that are considered commercial earnings. As a matter of fact, according to the provision in the said law, whether the construction and repair works are carried out by real or legal persons, the taxation processes are subject to special regulations regardless of this issue (Tokat, 2010:62).

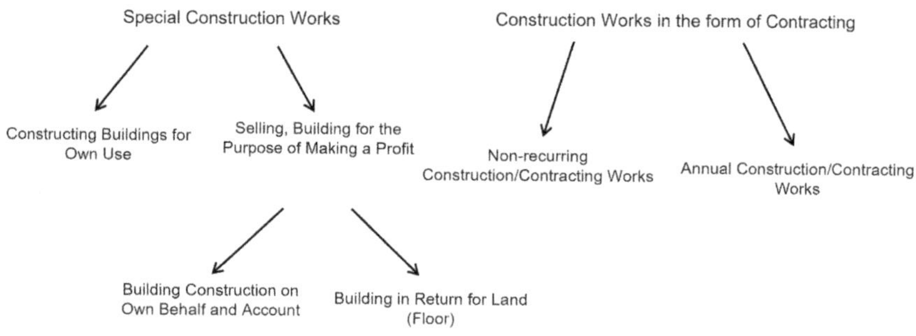

Fig. 1: Types of Construction in terms of Tax Laws.
Source: Figure prepared by us.

3 Taxation in Private Construction Works

Private construction works are defined as construction works carried out on one's own land for one's own needs without the purpose of building and selling buildings in independent sections on one's own behalf and account and without the purpose of selling. Following this definition, in terms of taxation differences, private construction types are divided into three types: construction works on own land/plot without the purpose of selling, construction works on own land/plot without the purpose of selling, construction works for the purpose of selling by constructing buildings on own behalf and account (build/sell works) and construction works in return for land (flat).

In private construction works, the sale of independent sections is usually done before the construction is complete. Another feature of this type of construction work is that construction work can last for more than a year. In this case, the timing of the taxable event and taxation processes gain importance (Çankaya, 2003:388).

Generally, it is considered that the tax generating event in private construction works is realised with registration at the land registry office. However, even without the registration process, construction companies sell the independent sections they are building with a special contract or a sales promise agreement while construction is in progress. However, as soon as the construction is made available to the buyer, it is deemed to have been delivered, and the sale is deemed to have been realised in tax terms. The profit or loss obtained from private construction works is determined on the basis of sales during the year. Whenever private construction enterprises sell the independent sections they produce, the positive difference between the production cost and the sales price is taxed as a commercial gain in the period in which the sale is realised and declared as the income of that year. Similarly, for sales made during the construction phase, the entire sales price should be recognized as sales revenue in the year in which the construction is completed and the turnkey delivery is made (Şenlik, 2011:144–145).

3.1 Taxation on Construction Works for Own Use

Since construction is a production activity, it is in principle subject to the provisions of the Income Tax Law on commercial income (Pur, 2006:167). In Article 37 of the Income Tax Law, commercial income is defined as "the income arising from all kinds of commercial and industrial activities", and in the fourth paragraph of the same article, it is stated that "those who are continuously engaged in the purchase, sale, and construction of real estates are subject to tax".

When we look at the issue from an income tax perspective, the taxation of immovable properties can be divided into two according to the construction and sale stages of immovable properties. This distinction is particularly important in terms of private construction works, and these two elements should be evaluated separately in terms of taxation. Firstly, an immovable property in the construction phase will be evaluated within the framework of commercial income provisions, and if there are certain elements (capital element, continuity element, organisation element, etc.), the income obtained will naturally be included in the scope of commercial income. Second, how the gain obtained during the sale phase of the immovable property will be evaluated in terms of tax laws is the stage in which the gain here can be evaluated in a dual structure as value increase gain or commercial gain.

Within the framework of these explanations, if any taxpayer, whether domestic/foreign, real, or legal person, builds an immovable property without commercial purposes, only for the purpose of changing hands of wealth or for the purpose of evaluating a land and residing (using it themselves) or perhaps renting out a part of it, such construction works will not be evaluated within the framework of commercial income. In other words, these construction works will not be considered as commercial income in terms of Income Tax Law and no tax liability will arise during the construction phase. In such construction works, a tax liability arises during the sale phase of the immovable property. The income obtained at this stage is taxed as "Appreciation Gains" under the heading of "Other Earnings and Incomes" within the scope of the Income Tax Law, provided that it is not continuous and not made within a commercial organization. However, if there is a situation that exceeds the scope and limits of the taxpayer's personal needs during the construction phase of this immovable property and there are also elements of a commercial organization, the construction work will be evaluated within the framework of commercial income (Tekkoyun, 2010:81).

As can be understood from all these explanations, since there is no profit arising from the constructions to be made by individuals on the lands they own within the scope of their own needs, there is no need for these persons to establish a tax liability and fulfil their related duties (notifying the start and cessation of work, having and keeping books certified, complying with the document order, etc.) within the framework of the provisions of the financial legislation. However, these persons are obliged to pay certain fees (building construction fees, etc.) that arise during the construction phase of the construction and are generally collected by local governments. In terms of tax laws, the obligation in the disposal of these constructions after completion is within the framework of the provisions of either appreciation income or commercial gain (Şenlik, 2011:202).

3.2 Taxation in Construction Works Performed with the Intention to Build and Sell Buildings on Your Own Behalf and Account (Build/Sell Works)

Construction works carried out by those who build buildings on their own land and sell the buildings they have built as independent sections (such as residential/workplace) are called construction works for the purpose of building and selling buildings on their own behalf and account or build/sell type construction works. These types of construction work are carried out by local/foreign real and legal persons.

Construction work carried out for the purpose of building and selling buildings on its own behalf and account is within the scope of income tax if it is carried out by a real person, and corporate tax if it is carried out by legal entities. However, the income obtained from such construction works will be considered as commercial income, whether it is obtained by income tax or by corporate taxpayers, and taxation will be made accordingly.

Since the income obtained from such construction works is taxed according to the provisions of commercial income, the taxation period, provisional tax, value added tax, etc. obligations of income/corporate taxpayer enterprises engaged in such construction activities are not different from those of a production enterprise that is an income or corporate taxpayer.

According to Article 37/4 of the Income Tax Law, "the earnings of those who are continuously engaged in the purchase, sale, and construction of real estates are considered as commercial earnings". Therefore, those engaged in such construction activities are not subject to a special taxation system (Şenlik, 2011:200). The important factor in terms of taxation in this type of construction work is the realisation of the sale (Kızılot, 2008:200). Because, whenever real and legal persons engaged in such construction activities realise the sale of the independent sections they produce, the positive difference between the cost and the sale price is taxed as commercial income in the period when the sale is realised and declared as the income of that year (Şenlik, 2011:203).

3.3 Taxation in Construction Works in Return for Land (Floor)

With rapid urbanisation in our country, the need for housing and workplaces is increasing day by day, and in this direction, city centres are expanding day by day. The most preferred method to evaluate land within the boundaries of growing settlement centres is construction in return for land. In this method, real and legal person landowners deliver their land shares to the contractor to obtain a certain number of independent sections in return (Aslanpınar, 2011:273).

Although construction works in return for land are very common in practice, Turkish Tax Laws do not include a direct regulation on how these works will be taxed. Taxation is mostly based on general provisions, and this situation causes various problems in such works, which contain many specific elements. Indeed, as in other production companies, there is a final production in the construction sector. However, the fact that each of the works has its own unique production, that the work is not completed in a calendar year, and that the place of production is not standardised distinguishes these works from other standard forms of production, and therefore, the need for special arrangements to be made in the taxation of such works arises. When the issues arising from the unique structure of construction works in return for land are added to this specific production structure of construction works, taxation becomes more complicated (Turut, 2007:149).

When the issue is analysed based on the problems that arise in construction works in return for land, it is important to determine both the value of the sale of the land and the value of the independent sections owned in return for the land and the tax dimension of these transactions. Therefore, taking this issue into consideration and evaluating the issue in terms of both the landowner and the contractor can help to better understand the process.

It is possible to generally classify landowners in tax terms as follows (Şen, 2011:139).

- Landowners who are not taxpayers
- Landowners who are income taxpayers
- Landowners who are corporate taxpayers

Two situations come to the forefront in the award of construction works in return for land. The first is the delivery of land by the landowner to the contractor, and the other is the delivery of independent sections by the contractor to the landowner.

3.3.1 Land Delivery to the Contractor by the Landowner

If the land is included in an economic enterprise (landowners who are corporate taxpayers) or if the landowner is engaged in the land purchase and sale business continuously, that is, within the scope of commercial activity (landowners who are income taxpayers), the land deliveries made to the contractor in exchange for housing or workplace are subject to value added tax. However, if the landowner delivers the land to the contractor in return for independent sections outside the scope of commercial activity, that is, if this transaction does not require the landowner to be a taxpayer within the scope of commercial gain (non-taxpayer landowners), the land deliveries made in this way are not subject to value-added tax (Turut, 2010:143).

In this context, it can be concluded that for the land delivered to the contractor by the landowner to be subject to the provisions of commercial gain, the landowner must be a real taxpayer, or the land purchase and sale activity must be carried out as a commercial organisation rather than a temporary activity. It can also be stated that there will be no taxation for the land owner at the stage of receiving independent sections in return for the land delivered to the contractor within the framework of a non-commercial activity (Şen, 2011:140). In this last case, it should be kept in mind that landowners will have different tax liabilities in terms of tax laws depending on whether they rent or sell the independent sections they receive in return for their land, such as real estate capital income in terms of Income Tax Law if they rent them out.

3.3.2 Delivery of the Independent Section by the Contractor to the Landowner

From the point of view of the contractor, the sum of the expenditures made by those who build on someone else's land for the construction of the independent sections they have given to the land owner and the expenditures they have made for their own independent sections gives the cost of construction. The cost of independent sections belonging to the contractor is calculated by allocating the total construction cost to these independent sections. The portion of the total construction cost corresponding to the independent sections given to the landowner is the cost of the land of the independent sections belonging to the contractor. Since the contractor is an income or corporate taxpayer due to the construction activity, the taxable event will occur upon completion of the construction and the sale of any of the independent sections (Kızılot, 2008:390).

Independent section deliveries made by the contractor to the landowners are also subject to value-added tax. If those who carry out construction work in return for land are income or corporate taxpayers, value-added tax liability will also arise. If the land is included in an economic enterprise or if the landowner continues the land purchase and sale business as a continuous activity, this land delivery to the contractor in return for housing or a workplace is subject to value-added tax. However, the tax will not be applied in the delivery of the land to the contractor in return for flats or works as a temporary activity that does not require the land owner to be taxpayer in real procedure. In this case, if the land subject to the contract is not registered to an economic enterprise and the real person is not a taxpayer, value added tax will not arise in the delivery of the land. However, if the real person is an income and corporate taxpayer, the value-added tax will be calculated in the delivery of land and housing deliveries according to the opinion of the Ministry of Treasury and Finance.

According to the current regulations determining the VAT rates applicable to goods and services, the value-added tax rates are as follows.

- 10% for land and land deliveries
- Construction contracting works %20
- Construction work pure labor 20%
- Workplace delivery 20%
- Urban transformation of workplace delivery 20%
- Housing delivery after 01.04.2022 10% up to 150 m^2, 20% over 150 m^2
- After 01.04.2022, urban transformation housing delivery 1% up to 150 m^2, 20% over 150 m^2

If the house subject to sale is sold with furniture, the delivery of the house and the delivery of the goods should be evaluated separately, and the value-added tax rate of the house should be regulated at the rate applied to the house, and the value-added tax rate of the goods should be regulated at the value-added tax rate applied to the goods.

3.4 Declaration of Earnings in Private Construction Works

One of the different aspects of special construction works from other works is the fact that the construction may last for several years since it is not completed in the year in which it started, and the issue of which year the resulting income will be considered and declared. Although private construction works usually last for more than one year, these types of construction work are not accepted as construction and repair works spread over years in Turkish Tax Laws. Therefore, no separate regulations have been made regarding the declaration and taxation of income derived from special construction works.

Earnings derived from private construction works are considered as commercial earnings within the scope of Article 37/4 of the Income Tax Law. Since there is no special regulation for the taxation of this income, the regulations for the determination and taxation of commercial income apply to private construction works. Since the sale transaction (taxable event) will be realized with the completion of the construction and delivery of the independent sections to the buyers, the income related to the independent sections sold and delivered to the buyers in the completed year is declared and taxed in the year in which they are obtained within the scope of commercial income. Independent sections that have been completed but not yet sold will not be treated as an element of income in the determination of commercial income since they are considered as stock for the enterprise. These sections are kept in stock until they are sold and are included in the commercial income of the year they are sold and declared (Çankaya, 2003:390).

4 Taxation in Contracting Construction Works

In terms of tax laws, construction work in the form of contracting is defined as the work of a construction company to perform a construction action belonging to another real or legal person for a fee determined in accordance with the terms of the contract (Güneş, 2009:600).

Earnings derived from construction and repair works in the form of contracting are taxed according to the commercial income provisions of the Income Tax Law. However, a special taxation system other than general provisions has been accepted due to the characteristics of construction works in the form of contracting if they are spread over the years. Special taxation is only applicable to construction and repair work that extends over more than one calendar year. Earnings derived from construction works in the form of contracting started and completed in the same year are taxed according to general provisions (Kızılot, 2008:59). Construction works in the form of contracting are divided into two, as nonannual construction and repair works and construction and repair works spread over numerous years according to the completion of the construction in a calendar year (Şenlik, 2011:25).

4.1 Taxation of Non-extensive Construction and Repair Works

Construction and repair work that are not spread over the years refers to construction work that construction enterprises start and finish in the same year. Therefore, the profit or loss obtained from these works is determined with certainty, since the work is completed within the same year and is taxed at the end of the year by being included in the end-of-period transactions. Such construction works, which can also be expressed as construction and repair works spread over months, are taxed in the same way as production works (Hacıköylü, 2012:34).

4.2 Taxation in Construction and Repair Works Spread Over Years

Within the scope of tax laws, earnings from construction and repair works are taxed according to the provisions of commercial earnings within the scope of income tax. However, if these works are considered within the scope of construction and repair works spread over the years, the earnings to be obtained from these works are subject to a special taxation regime other than the general provisions due to their characteristics.

The main reason that necessitates a special taxation regime for construction and repair works spread over numerous years is the difficulties encountered in determining the costs and revenues, and therefore the actual operating result, before the end of the work (Durna, 2008:31).

A commercial activity may result in profit or loss according to the positive or negative difference between the revenue generated from that activity and the expenses incurred for the activity and the total cost incurred. To make this calculation, the activity must be finalised and income and expenses must be accrued (Maç and Turut, 2011:19). In other words, in order to determine the tax base to be taxed due to the determination of earnings in construction and repair works spread over the years, the total costs and the total revenue obtained from these works must be determined (Esen, 2007:142).

Articles 42–44 of the Income Tax Law No. 193 regulate construction and repair works spread over the years separately. Article 42 of the Income Tax Law states that "In construction and repair works lasting more than one calendar year, profit or loss is determined in the year in which the work is completed, and all of it is considered as the income of that year and shown in the declaration of that year. In cases falling within the scope of this article, taxpayers are obliged to show the revenues and expenses of each construction and repair work in a separate book or on separate pages of the books they keep."

Based on this provision, for a construction and repair business to be taxable under Article 42 of the Income Tax Law, it must have the following three characteristics.

- The subject of the activity is construction and repair work
- Construction and repair work depending on the commitment
- Construction and repair works are spread over years

It is not possible to evaluate works that do not meet these three conditions together as construction and repair works spread over the years and to benefit from Article 42 of the Income Tax Law. The enterprises listed in Article 2 of the Corporate Tax Law, which regulates the title of taxpayer, determine their net corporate income in accordance with the commercial income provisions of the Income Tax Law. However, enterprises engaged in construction and repair works spread over the years are subject to a special taxation regime according to the regulations in Articles 42, 43 and 44 of the Income Tax Law explained above.

In the works carried out by the tender procedure in accordance with the provisions of the relevant legislation, the companies performing the work in the construction and repair works spread over the years are paid based on the temporary progress reports issued at certain intervals. Because progress payment reports are documents issued for the payment of the work to the contractor as the work is done, and at the same time, they also show that a certain part of the work has been done, the event giving rise to the tax in value-added tax also occurs in the construction and repair works spread over the years. On the other hand, an invoice must be issued in return for the progress payment, and the value-added tax must be shown on the invoice. The work carried out by companies engaged in construction and contracting work over the years is a service work. Therefore, the value-added tax rate to be calculated during the delivery of the works they have undertaken is 20%. (Şenlik, 2011:99)

4.2.1 Value-Added Tax on Construction and Repair Works Spread over Numerous Years

The subject, taxpayer, tax-generating event, and other issues of value-added tax are explained in the relevant articles of the law, and there is no special regulation other than the general practice within the scope of construction and repair works spread over the years (Durna, 2008:83). In other words, construction and repair works spread over the years are considered as service performance, and since the works performed by the enterprises performing the work are within the scope of commercial income, income and corporate taxpayers performing such works are liable for value-added tax in relation to their works. In addition, companies engaged in construction and repair activities over the years can deduct the value-added taxes calculated over the taxable transactions they make, unless otherwise stipulated.

4.2.2 Income Tax Withholding in Construction and Repair Works Spread over Years

From time to time, progress payments are made to those who carry out construction and repair works spread over numerous years based on the report issued for the works in question. These payments are made as an offset against the main payment after the provisional acceptance and the actual completion of the work. To compensate for the delay in taxation and to reduce the financial burden of the contractor in the payment, tax deductions are made from the progress payments paid in the construction and repair works spread over the years (Güneş, 2012:154).

Pursuant to Article 94 of the Income Tax Law and Article 15/1-a of the Corporate Tax Law, those who carry out construction and repair works spread over numerous years are obliged to withhold income tax at the time of payment from all progress payments made to the contractor in cash or on account.

The tax withholding is realised on the revenue obtained in return for the services provided. If the construction work subject to the contract is completed in the year in which it starts, no income tax withholding can be made. Pursuant to Article 94/3 of the Income Tax Law, it is stipulated that tax withholdings shall be made on progress payments paid to those who perform these works due to the works falling within the scope of Article 42. Businesses fulfilling the commitment can deduct the amounts withheld as income tax from the income declared in the tax return for the period in which the work is completed.

4.2.3 Stamp Tax on Construction and Repair Works Spread Over Years

The stamp tax is a financial obligation paid by individuals on the documents or papers they issue in legal transactions between themselves or with public institutions and organisations. In Article 1 of the Stamp Tax Law, it is stated that the subject of the tax consists of the papers written in the table numbered (1) attached to the law.

The taxpayers of stamp tax are the issuers and signatories of these papers. Individuals pay the stamp tax on the papers belonging to the transactions between official institutions and organizations and individuals (Kumrulu, Çağal and Öncel, 1999:437).

According to Stamp Tax Law No. 488, the main transactions subject to stamp tax in construction and repair works spread over the years are as follows (Durna, 2008:79).

- Contracts, undertakings, and assignments that contain a certain amount of money,
- Progress payments in the Receipts and other papers section,
- Advances (payments that have not yet been reported as progress payments),

Pursuant to Article 1 of the Stamp Tax Law No. 488, stamp tax withholding should be made at a rate of 9.48 per thousand for the year 2024 on progress payments and advance payments in the "receipts and other papers section" and at a rate of 5.69 per thousand on all kinds of tender decision of official departments and institutions with public legal personality, whether subject to the tender law.

5 Conclusion

The concept of construction, which is defined as "construction works" only in the Value Added Tax General Implementation Communiqué, is not clearly defined in some other legal regulations. For example, this concept is defined as "construction" in Article 5 of the Zoning Law and as "construction" in Article 4 of the Public Procurement Law.

Considering the size of the construction and real estate sector in Türkiye, it is important to tax this sector correctly. In fact, when there is a tax loss in the construction sector, which hosts many subsectors, this loss is reflected in the subsectors. In the Turkish tax system, regulations regarding the taxation of the income obtained by real and legal persons as a result of the sale of real estate are at the forefront. However, when the positive difference between the costs incurred during the construction phase of the immovable and the sales price is considered to be taxed, the calculation of the cost of the construction work gains importance in terms of taxation. Another important issue in construction works is the importance of the date of commencement and completion of the work in terms of taxation, whether it is a private construction work or a construction work in the form of contracting and repair. The fact that there are special provisions regarding the taxation of construction works spread over years makes the taxation of the income obtained from such construction works more complicated.

The tax laws in Türkiye mostly perform a tax audit based on whether the sale price of immovable property sold by local/foreign real and legal persons reflects the reality or not. In this audit, there are not many regulations for determining the actual sale price. For the regulation to be made, it is essential for a fair taxation to determine both the correct determination of the costs of the immovable property during the construction phase and to ensure that the sales price reflects the reality. To do this, it is important that the provisions of the tax laws contain simpler and more understandable provisions regardless of the type of real estate construction.

Bibliography

Aslanpınar, B. (2011). Miras Kalan veya Bağışlanan Arsa Karşılığında Elde Edilen Konut ve İşyeri Satışında Gelir Vergisi-I. Yaklaşım Dergisi, (223), 273.

Çankaya, İ. (2003). İnşaat Muhasebesi (2nd ed.). Meslek Yapıtları.

Durna, F. (2008). Yıllara Yaygın İnşaat ve Onarım İşlerinde Vergilendirme [Unpublished doctoral dissertation]. Retrieved from https://tez.yok.gov.tr/UlusalTezMerkezi/tezSorguSonucYeni.jsp

Esen, A. (2007). Yıllara Sair İşlerde Vergileme. Maliye Postası Dergisi, (Special Issue).

Güneş, Ş. (2009). Yıllara Yaygın İnşaat ve Onarım İşlerinin Vergileme Süreci. E-Yaklaşım Dergisi, (201), 591–599.

Güneş, Ş. (2012). Arsa Karşılığı İnşaat İşlerinde Hasılat Paylaşımı Modelinin Dayanılmaz Cazibesi. Yaklaşım Dergisi, (230), 153–155.

Hacıköylü, C. (2012). İnşaat ve Gayrimenkul Muhasebesi. In S. Şengel (Ed.), Gayrimenkul ve İnşaat İşlerinde Vergileme. Anadolu Üniversitesi Yayınları.

Kumrulu, A., Çağan, N., & Öncel, M. (1999). Vergi Hukuku. Turhan Kitabevi.

Kızılot, Ş. (2008). İnşaat Muhasebesi Vergilendirilmesi Mevzuatı ve Asgari İşçilik. Yaklaşım Yayınları.

Maç, M., & Turut, Ş. (2011). Arsa Karşılığı İnşaat İşleri ve Hasılat Payı Karşılığı Arsa Satışına İlişkin 60 Seri No.lu KDV Sirkülerindeki Açıklamalar ve Görüşlerimiz. Yaklaşım Dergisi, (226).

Pur, H. (2006). Gayrimenkullerde Vergi Uygulamaları. Suryay Yayınevi.

Özocak, H. (2007). İnşaat İşlemlerinde Vergisel Uygulamalar ve Özellik Arz Eden Konular. Retrieved from http://www.iktisadidayanisma.com

Tekkoyun, İ. (2010, January 15–16). Özel ve Taahhüt Şeklindeki İnşaat İşlerinde Vergisel Sorunlar. Paper presented at Türkiye Sektörel Muhasebe Uygulamaları Sempozyumu- I, İnşaat/Taahhüt sektöründe Muhasebe Vergi ve Denetim, Kayseri, Turkey.

Turut, Ş. (2007). Türk Vergi Sisteminde Kat Karşılığı (Arsa Karşılığı) İnşaat İşlerinin Vergilendirilmesi [Unpublished doctoral dissertation]. Retrieved from https://tez.yok.gov.tr/UlusalTezMerkezi/tezSorguSonucYeni.jsp

Turut, Ş. (2010). Vergisel ve Hukuki Boyutlarıyla Arsa Karşılığı İnşaat İşleri. Paper presented at Türkiye Sektörel Muhasebe Uygulamaları Sempozyumu- I, İnşaat/Taahhüt Sektöründe Muhasebe Vergi ve Denetim, Kayseri, Turkey.

Türüng, H. (2006). Yapı Muhasebesinde "Yıllara Yaygınlık" Kavramının Neden Olduğu Sorunlar ve Çözüm Önerileri [Unpublished doctoral dissertation]. Retrieved from https://tez.yok.gov.tr/UlusalTezMerkezi/tezSorguSonucYeni.jsp

Tokat, Y. (2010). İnşaat İşlerinin Vergilendirilmesinde Özellikli Durumlar-I, II. Yaklaşım Dergisi, (205–206), 62–71, 86–90.

Şenlik, M. (2011). İnşaat Muhasebesi. Maliye ve Hukuk Yayınları.

Şen, S. (2011). Arsa Karşılığı İnşaat İşlerinde Arsa ve Bağımsız Bölümlerin Arsa Sahibi Açısından Maliyet, KDV ve Muhasebe Uygulaması-I, II. Yaklaşım Dergisi, (220–221), 137–142, 121–129.

A Global Football Tax Proposal

M. Oğuz ARSLAN[1]

1 Introduction

Global tax proposals have been put forward for a variety of reasons, such as raising revenue to provide global public goods, eliminating negative externalities, or improving global income distribution (Uemura, 2007; Paul & Wahlberg, 2002). Undoubtedly, raising revenue is the main justification for most global tax proposals. However, some global tax proposals, such as the global carbon tax and the Tobin tax, are suitable for both limiting negative externalities and raising revenue. If these taxes are implemented, while they will succeed in limiting negative externalities, the revenue from these taxes will decline over time. Some tax proposals such as a global wealth tax will have both the function of improving global income distribution and raising revenue. Implementing such taxes would not only allow for a sustainable intervention to improve income distribution but would also generate a large and stable amount of revenue.

The Global Football Tax (the GFT) proposal we have developed is essentially a revenue generator. If implemented, the revenue generated by the GFT could be used to finance the provision of global public goods and global social policies (e.g., global income distribution). Of course, the GFT does not directly have the non-fiscal objectives of taxes such as a global carbon tax or a global wealth tax. However, this tax could indirectly achieve two goals. First, it could compensate for the environmental damage caused by international football matches. Second, given that international football matches are watched live in stadiums by relatively high-income earners due to high ticket prices, it could contribute to some extent to improving income distribution by taxing these high-income earners more.

1 Anadolu University, FEAS, Department of Public Finance, Tepebaşı 26470, Eskişehir, Türkiye moarslan@anadolu.edu.tr, ORCID ID: 0000-0001-6011-4331

2 A Very Short History of Global Tax Proposals

The emergence of global tax proposals and the idea of global taxation can be traced back to the idea of a world state. Many thinkers have argued that a world state, created by uniting humanity around a common ideal, is necessary and even obligatory for the solution of many problems, especially preventing wars. This idea, which has found supporters since ancient times, was accepted as a high thought by Dante Alighieri in the Middle Ages and Immanuel Kant in the 18th century and has continued to be defended in a way that affects many people today. However, it is not expected that a world state will emerge soon by changing or replacing the established world system. Instead, the accepted approach today is that global problems need to be solved in a coordinated way by reaching a consensus among countries. Scottish lawyer and political philosopher James Lorimer is credited as the first author to advocate a world state but to state that it should be financed by global taxation. In his study *The Ultimate Problem of International Jurisprudence (1884)*, Lorimer proposed the establishment of an international government, the expenditures of which should be covered by an international tax imposed by each state on its citizens. Lorimer argued that the proportional distribution of the tax burden among states should be based on the number of representatives each state sends to the international legislature (Frankman, 1996).

In the 20th century, first, the outbreak of World War I, then the establishment of the League of Nations, and finally World War II naturally led many writers and thinkers to focus on the prevention of war, and the issue of global taxation was not on the agenda. James Meade was the earliest author to contribute to the issue of global taxation during these years. In 1940, Meade predicted that some kind of international organization (the United Nations) would be established at the end of the war and stated that the financing of this organization could be done through direct taxation (Frankman, 1996).

After World War II, there was a significant increase in global tax proposals and global taxes were often advocated independently of the idea of a world government. During this period, authors such as James Meade, Jan Tinbergen, John Maynard Keynes, T. A. Sumberg, Wilfred Jenks, Thomas Schelling, and others proposed many global taxes and global cost-sharing schemes to finance international organizations (Frankman, 2002).

In the 1970s, the emergence of environmental problems and the concept of global commons led to a resurgence of the idea of global taxation among non-governmental organizations, academia, and some governments (Paul & Wahlberg, 2002). Since then, many global tax proposals have been put forward to provide financing for global purposes, combat global negative externalities, and improve global income distribution. The most popular of these proposals are the Tobin tax proposal and the carbon tax proposal.

On the other hand, there has been strong opposition to global tax proposals since the 1970s. This opposition, mainly coming from some developed and developing countries and the neo-liberal approach, characterizes global taxes as a harmful, unworkable, and impossible dream and develops policies in line with its approach. Today, global taxes are still seen by many as a dream. However, under the pressure of ever-increasing global problems, these taxes are again being defended as an option.

In this context, new global tax proposals are developed at short intervals. The global wealth tax proposal (Piketty, 2014, p. 515), the global e-commerce tax proposal (Azam, 2012), the tax havens utilization tax proposal (Schulzke, 2014), and the global meat tax proposal (Chloupkova et al., 2018) are among the new global tax proposals developed in recent years. The most recent global tax proposal that can be added to this basket of proposals is the GFT proposal that we have developed.

3 The Rationale for the GFT

The main justification for the GFT is its contribution to the financing the provision of global public goods and global social policies. The importance of such a revenue-generating tax can be understood when one considers that there is very limited funding available for global purposes such as the fight against infectious diseases, environmental protection, financial stability, and improving global income distribution or for some international organizations, funds, and programs under the auspices of the United Nations.

There is no doubt that continental football tournaments and Fédération Internationale de Football Association (FIFA) World Cup are festive occasions for football fans. However, the presence of tens or even hundreds of thousands of fans at these tournaments causes serious environmental damage. For example, fans are usually transported to the tournaments by air. Many fans also travel to the tournament cities by car from neighboring countries and cities near the tournament cities. This situation inevitably leads to an increase in harmful emissions from aircraft and cars. In addition, in some countries, new stadiums have to be built for the first time to host an international football championship, which causes pollution. Pollution is also caused by the (often excessive) consumption of goods and services by fans during the tournaments.

The GFT can protect the environment as a global public good by funding the elimination or reduction of pollution at the global level, even if not the pollution caused by international football matches. In this context, for example, it could be publicized that the revenue of this tax would be transferred to the United Nations Environment Program (UNEP) for environmental protection. In this way, the public would be convinced of such a tax, and the reactions against such a tax would be reduced.

The GFT could also make a slight contribution to improving global income distribution. Today, fans who want to watch international football matches live in the stadium have to pay high ticket prices. Therefore, it can be asserted that these fans are generally high-income earners. With such a tax on tickets to international football matches, high-income earners would be subjected to extra taxation. If this tax revenue is spent on activities that benefit low-income groups globally, it would be a small step towards improving the global income distribution. In this framework, again following the principle of earmarking, it could be publicly announced that the revenue of this tax would be transferred to, for example, the United Nations Children's Fund (UNICEF) to help children worldwide, the World Food Program (WFP) to fight hunger, or the Global Alliance for Vaccines and Immunization (GAVI) to fight infectious diseases globally.

The GFT could also be used to finance other global public goods or UN structures by applying the principle of earmarking. The important point here is to convince the world public opinion, and especially fans, by specifying the (higher and humanitarian) purposes for which the tax will be used.

4 The Features of the GFT

The subject of the GFT is a ticket to an international football match. At this point, first of all, it is necessary to clarify what an international football match is: An international football match is a football match between national football teams or football club teams of two countries under the supervision of international football authorities. For example, a match played under the supervision of UEFA between the Turkish National Football Team and the France National Football Team or a match between Beşiktaş FC of Türkiye and Valencia FC of Spain is an international football match.

The GFT could be levied on a fixed amount (specific) or the value (ad-valorem) of each international football match ticket purchased by fans from football clubs or authorized intermediaries. To be more practical in the first phase, it would be more appropriate to levy the tax on a fixed amount of each international match ticket purchased from football clubs. For example, a tax of $1 on each international football match ticket would be preferable for simplicity. On the other hand, the amount of tax to be applied for matches at different stages of international football tournaments can be differentiated. For example, a tax of $1 for the first-round matches, $3 for the second-round matches, $5 for the matches in the other rounds, and $10 for the final match would generate more revenue. If this tax is based on the value (price) of the ticket for an international football match, a 5% rate would generate much more tax revenue. What is meant by value or price here is the initial sale price of the ticket. In this application, it would be possible to generate more tax revenue by differentiating the tax rate to be applied for matches at different stages of international football tournaments. It may be possible to realize progressivity in this tax by further increasing the tax rate for football matches in later rounds.

On the other hand, the GFT will need to be adapted to the season ticket practices of football clubs. In this framework, some methods should be found on how this tax will be collected from fans who purchase season tickets at the beginning of the season for the international matches of their teams. For example, fans who purchase season tickets could be taxed in advance for possible international matches of their teams. At the end of the period, depending on the number of these international matches that take place, fans can be refunded for overpayments and re-taxed for underpayments.

In addition, as with national taxes, some exemptions could be introduced for the GFT. For example, tickets for international football matches that are charity or friendly matches could be exempt from this tax. This would allow more revenue to be directed to the relevant philanthropic aim.

More comprehensively, once this tax is implemented and becomes successful, over time, it may even be possible to tax international matches in many different sports, from basketball to tennis, athletics to swimming, regardless of whether they are team sports or individual sports, and thus evolve the GFT into a more comprehensive global tax called the global sports tax (GST).

5 The Collection Process of the GFT

The issue of how to collect the revenue of the GFT is significant. The institutions that can play a role in the collection of the GFT are FIFA as the global umbrella football organization, six football confederations affiliated with FIFA, and the football associations of the 211 member countries or administrations of FIFA.

The lowest administrative structures that should be used in the process of collecting the GFT are the national football associations. The national football associations will play an important role in the adaptation of national football teams and football clubs to this tax and the understanding of the technical features of the tax by the football clubs. The national football associations can also play an active role in the implementation and monitoring of the technological and financial arrangements necessary for the smooth collection of this tax by football clubs.

The collection process of the GFT can be designed similarly to the process designed for global taxes in general. In this framework, the tax revenue collected by the clubs at the bottom can be transferred to their national football association. The national association would in turn transfer this money to the confederation of which it is a member. At this stage, it may also be preferable to bypass the national association and transfer the tax revenue directly to the relevant football confederation. However, this way of collecting the tax can lead to many problems, both because the national structure is neutralized and because the confederations are faced with dozens of football clubs.

In this design, the collection of the tax from fans is in all cases carried out by football clubs. There is no direct payment of the tax by fans to the relevant national football association or confederation. The tax revenue transferred from the football clubs to the national football associations and from there to the relevant football confederation may be transferred directly to international organizations without being transferred to FIFA. Collecting this revenue at FIFA and transferring it to international organizations may be unnecessary, as it would further lengthen the tax collection process.

Fig. 1: The Collection Process of the GFT.

To shorten the process, the tax revenue collected by the football associations could be transferred directly to the international organizations without being transferred to the football confederations. In this case, however, there could be some problems, as the international organizations would have to deal with the football associations of 211 countries.

National football teams play matches both in their stadiums and in the stadiums of football clubs. When these teams play in their stadiums, the tax revenue is transferred by the management of these stadiums, and when they play in the stadiums of football clubs, it is transferred by these clubs to their national football association. In the process of collecting the GFT from fans and transferring it to a related national football association, the type of team playing a match does not matter.

To better involve football clubs in the collection of the GFT, a certain percentage of collected tax revenue may be left to the clubs. In this case, however, the tax would be diverted from its original purpose and total tax revenue would be reduced.

On the other hand, it is very important to ensure transparency in the process of collecting the GFT. In the first phase, when the tax is collected from fans, the football clubs should publicly announce the number of fans attending the match and the total amount of tax collected. At this stage, the number of fans attending the match must be accurately reported. Based on this figure, everyone can accurately calculate the tax revenue. Similarly, national football associations and continental football confederations should publish the tax revenue collected for the world to see. In this way, it can be monitored if there is any loss of tax revenue during the tax collection process.

6 The Estimated Revenue from the GFT

For the sake of simplicity, let us assume that the GFT is levied at $1 per ticket for each international football match. In this case, the number of fans at an international football match will also determine the total tax revenue from that match. In this context, the estimated revenues of the Union of European Football Associations (UEFA), the South American Football Confederation (CONMEBOL), the Asian Football Confederation (AFC), the Confederation of African Football (CAF), the Confederation of North, Central America and Caribbean Association Football (CONCACAF), FIFA, and the estimated total of these revenues are given in Figure 2.

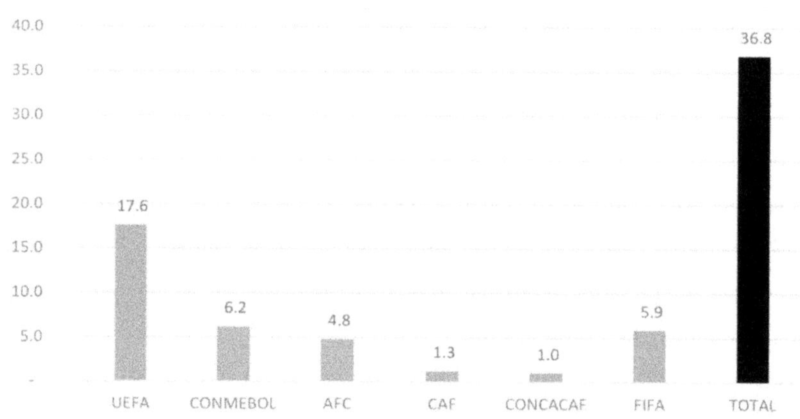

Fig. 2: The Estimated Revenue from the GFT (annual average, in M $).
Source: Author's calculation using attendance data from www.transfermarkt.com, www.worldfootball.net, www.statista.com.

As seen in the figure above, the GFT, which is proposed to be applied to tickets for international football matches at $1 for simplicity, can be expected to generate at least $36,801,339 in revenue annually. The figure also shows that the international football organization that would become the most critical if the GFT is implemented is UEFA. The second-ranked international organization, as expected, would be CONMEBOL. According to these estimates, FIFA would be third and AFC fourth. The confederations of Africa and North American continents would rank last. Therefore, the GFT may have the potential to deliver successful results as a Europe-centered global tax scheme.

Given this result, it can be easily argued that the tax revenue is underestimated due to the lack of data on tournaments. Indeed, there is no sufficient and reliable data on many international tournaments. In general, international football organizations do not pay enough attention to publish football statistics transparently. It is also not known to what extent the websites that publish the data used in this study provide accurate data. Therefore, in reality, the annual revenue amount of this tax could easily exceed $50 million.

7 A Different Version of the GFT (the GFT 2.0)

Considering that the revenue generated by the GFT will be insufficient to solve global problems, excluding fans as taxpayers and taxing FIFA, continental football confederations, football associations, and football clubs as the new taxpayers of this tax will generate more tax revenue. In this case, we can call the tax as the GFT 2.0. As shown in Figure 3, the relevant organizations, except football clubs, would pay the tax directly to the international organizations that provide global public goods. Football clubs would pay the tax to international organizations through football associations or continental football confederations.

In Figure 4, it can be seen that FIFA and the continental football confederations generated a massive total revenue of $6.747 billion in 2022. Due to data access issues, it was not possible to calculate the total revenue of football associations and football clubs. With GFT 2.0, taxing only the annual revenues of the continental football confederations and FIFA at a flat rate of 10% for simplicity would generate $674 million in tax revenues. This amount is approximately 183 times the tax revenue of the original GFT. By taxing the revenues of football associations and football clubs in the same way, the amount of revenue generated would be even higher.

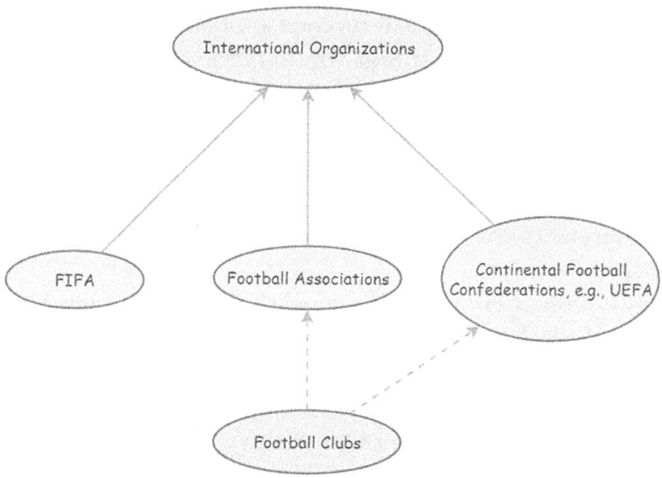

Fig. 3: The Collection Process of the GFT 2.0.

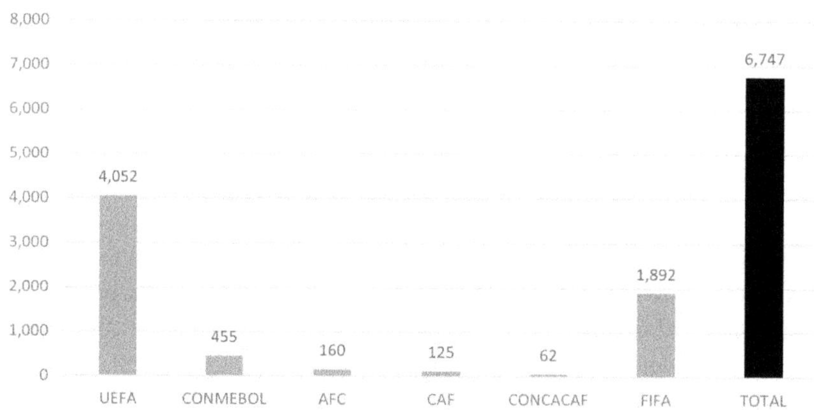

Fig. 4: Total Revenue of FIFA and Continental Football Confederations (2022, in M $).
Source: Author's compilation and calculation using data from http-1, hhtp-2, http-3, http-4, http-5, and http-6. FIFA's revenue for 2022 is calculated as the annual average of the sum of its revenues in 2018/19-2021/22.

As an option, the GFT 2.0 could be levied separately on FIFA and continental football confederations on a progressive basis, thereby ensuring tax fairness between these organizations and generating more tax revenue. For example, the GFT 2.0 using the simple progressive tax tariff shown in Table 1 would generate over $1.07 billion in tax revenue. If the same tariff were applied to the revenue of football associations and even football clubs, the amount of revenue from GFT 2.0 would be much higher.

Tab. 1: Tax Tariff of the GFT 2.0

Revenue (in million $)	Tax Rate (%)
Up to 1,000	10
1,000 to 2,500	15
Over 2,500	20

It is seen that revenue from TV broadcasting rights and commercial rights (including marketing and licensing rights) have an important place among the revenue sources of international football organizations. For example, as seen in the figure below, the revenue from TV broadcasting rights accounts for 45% of FIFA's total revenue, while revenue from commercial rights accounts for 34%.

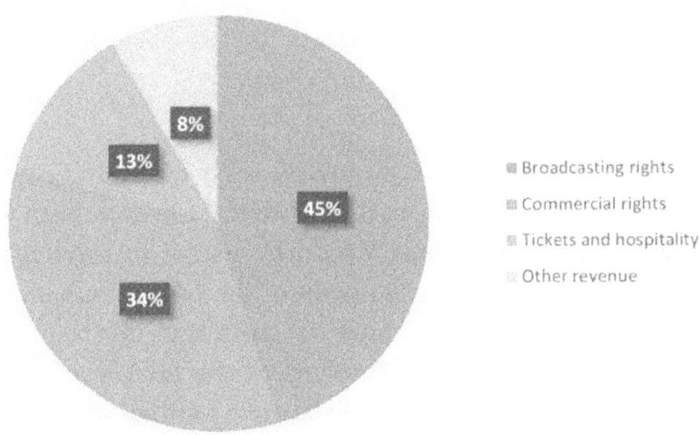

Fig. 5: The Share of Revenue Categories in FIFA's Total Revenue (2018/19-2021/22). **Source:** http-1.

As seen in Figure 6, the share of TV broadcasting rights revenue in the total revenue of UEFA, the continental football confederation with the highest revenue, is higher, while the share of revenue from commercial rights is lower. That is because UEFA organizes tournaments such as the Champions League and the Europa League every year while FIFA organizes the World Cup every four years, and, therefore, the number of matches (TV broadcasts) in the tournaments of the two organizations is different.

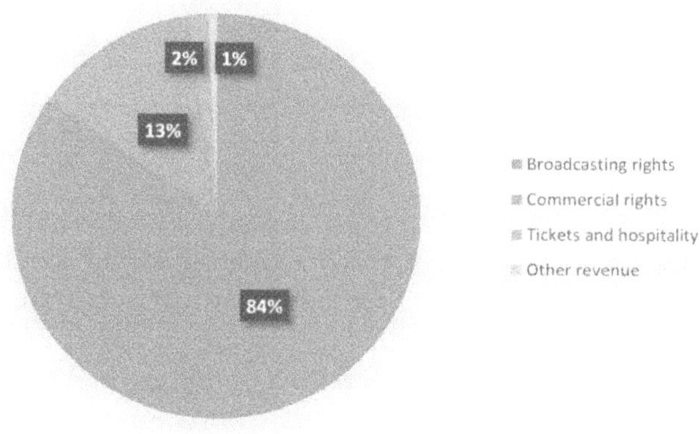

Fig. 6: The Share of Revenue Categories in UEFA's Total Revenue (2021/22).
Source: http-2.

8 General Evaluation

Compared to other global tax proposals with estimated revenues in the billions of dollars, this tax proposal is modest. However, even in its current form, the revenue from this tax would be useful in solving some global problems. One of the biggest advantages of the GFT is that it would be easy to implement. If there is a global political consensus on the implementation of this tax, it will be possible to implement the tax successfully in a short time through the already existing international football organizations. In this respect, it is likely to be more feasible than many of the global tax proposals that have already been proposed.

Moreover, the amount of revenue from the GFT could be increased by differentiating the amount of the tax. It is possible to multiply the total revenue from the tax by applying the tax in increasing amounts at the beginning, during, and at the end of tournaments. It is also possible to increase the revenue by differentiating the amount between tournaments. The amount of the tax could be differentiated between qualifying and tournament matches, or between Champions League matches and Confederations Cup matches. Alternatively, the revenue could be raised by differentiating the amount of the tax at the global level. For example, a high tax on UEFA and FIFA tournaments and a low tax on other confederations' tournaments could increase revenue.

Another way to increase the tax revenue is to impose the tax as a proportion (ad-valorem) of the initial selling price of an international football match ticket. It is possible to significantly increase tax revenue by applying higher tax rates at later rounds within the tournament. Revenue can also be raised by differentiating rates between tournaments or confederations. However, it would be more difficult to apply the tax proportionally than quantitatively.

Furthermore, the GFT is the kind of tax that could inspire other global tax schemes. Successful implementation of this tax could, over time, lead to global taxes in other sports (e.g., a global futsal tax, a global basketball tax, etc.), or it could evolve into a global match (sports) tax that would cover most sports activities at the international level.

The revenue from the GFT could be used to eliminate global pollution and serve environmental protection. Especially considering the environmental damage caused by international football tournaments, it is clear that the use of tax revenue for environmental protection would be an appropriate policy to compensate for these damages.

Given that fans of international football matches are relatively high-income earners, one could even argue that the GFT would improve global income distribution. Using tax revenue to fight global hunger and poverty could be an important step in improving global income distribution. If the tax is imposed at a higher amount instead of $1 per ticket for an international football match, the positive impact of the tax on global income distribution will increase. However, in this case, the reactions against the tax would increase, and the enforceability of the tax would be jeopardized.

A new version of the GFT, the GFT 2.0, would generate even more tax revenue. A 10% GFT 2.0 levy on the revenues of FIFA and continental football confederations would generate tens of times more tax revenue than the GFT generates. This revenue would further support the financing of the provision of some global public goods. Moreover, the GFT 2.0 would make it somewhat easier to collect tax revenues as it does not cover fans.

On the other hand, it is almost certain that there will be an opposition to the implementation of both the GFT and the GFT 2.0. The tax that the global football industry as a whole will oppose will be the GFT 2.0. The first group of structures to oppose this tax will be football clubs, which despite all their revenues, are heavily burdened with debt. It can be predicted that football associations, continental football confederations, and FIFA will also object to this tax to avoid revenue loss. In addition, TV broadcasters, multinational companies, and the like, which are in contact with all football-related organizations, will also oppose this tax, fearing that it will reduce their business volumes, and will put pressure on these organizations. As a result, the implementation of GFT 2.0 will not be possible.

Therefore, the GFT 2.0 needs to be explained to the world public with its justifications such as combating global externalities and improving global income distribution. Depending on and together with this, political structures and public organizations at the national and international levels (governments, international organizations, etc.) must make efforts to implement this tax with determination within the framework of a consensus. Unfortunately, it is not possible in the short and medium term for the political and public structures in the world, which cannot reach a consensus on the solution of most global problems, to decide on the implementation of the GFT 2.0. Nevertheless, it is critical to launch political and intellectual initiatives and mobilize world public opinion on this issue. In this regard, a quotation from Arthur Schopenhauer is entirely appropriate to the situation of the global tax proposals, in particular the GFT and the GFT 2.0: "Every good idea goes through three phases: In the first, it is declared to be idiotic; in the second, it is bitterly opposed; and in the third, it is implemented" (Wahl, 2006:8).

9 Conclusion

The idea of global taxation and global tax proposals have a history of more than a hundred years. Although they have been revisited in many periods during this time, global tax proposals have not been implemented due to opposition from some governments and neoliberal thinking. The global Tobin tax and the global carbon tax proposals are the most well-known global tax proposals.

The GFT, developed by us, is one of the latest global tax proposals. The subject of the GFT is purchasing an international football match ticket from the relevant football club. Initially, for simplicity, the tax amount is set at $1 per ticket sold. The GFT would generate approximately $37 million in revenue annually. While the estimated revenues of other global tax proposals are in the billions of dollars, this tax would generate a small amount of revenue. With the implementation of GFT 2.0, it will be possible to generate more and easier tax revenues.

If implemented, the GFT would generate an estimated revenue of approximately $37 million, while a 10% GFT 2.0 would generate an estimated revenue of $674 million. By making football associations and football clubs taxpayers, this amount could easily exceed $1 billion. The revenue generated by both versions of the tax could contribute to the financing of global public goods and international organizations, combat global negative externalities such as environmental pollution, or support the improvement of global income distribution.

On the other hand, in order to implement the GFT, and in particular the GFT 2.0, world public opinion needs to be convinced to neutralize opposition to these taxes. If such a success is achieved with the support of the media, academia, public international organizations and NGOs, and some politicians, it can be argued that these taxes will be more advantageous than many global tax proposals in terms of technical feasibility. Moreover, lessons learned and a potential success story from the implementation of any version of this tax would be an important step towards the subsequent implementation of other global taxes.

Bibliography

Azam, R. (2012). Global taxation of cross-border e-commerce income. *Virginia Tax Review*, 31(4), 639–693. https://papers.ssrn.com/sol3/Delivery.cfm/SSRN_ID3081887_code1219225.pdf?abstractid=2117022&mirid=1

Chloupkova, J., Svendsen, G. T., & Zdechovsky, T. (2018). A global meat tax: from big data to a double dividend. *Agricultural Economics – Czech*, 64(6), 256–264. https://doi.org/10.17221/270/2016-AGRICECON

Frankman, M. J. (1996). International taxation: the trajectory of an idea from Lorimer to Brandt. *World Development*, 24(5), 807–820. https://doi.org/10.1016/0305-750X(96)00002-2

Frankman, M. J. (2002). Global taxation: extending the fractal, *Gouvernance Mondiale, No.5*. Institut du développement durable et des relations internationals, https://www.iddri.org/sites/default/files/import/publications/id_0205_frankman.pdf

Paul, J. A. & Wahlberg, K. (2002). Global taxes for global priorities. Global Policy Forum. World Economy, Ecology and Development (WEED) Association. https://archive.globalpolicy.org/images/pdfs/Global_Taxes_for_Global_Priorities__Repaired_.pdf

Piketty, T. (2014). *Capital in the twenty-first century*. Cambridge, MA, Harvard University Press.

Schulzke, M. (2014). Developing a national foundation for global taxation. *Moral Philosophy and Politics*, 1(1), 105–125. https://doi.org/10.1515/mopp-2013-0014

Uemura, T. (2007). Exploring potential of global tax: as a cutting-edge measure for democratizing global governance. *The International Journal of Public Affairs*, 3, 112–129.

Wahl, P. (2006). From concept to reality: on the present state of the debate on international taxes. Friedrich Ebert Stiftung Briefing Paper, Berlin, June. https://library.fes.de/pdf-files/iez/global/50422.pdf

Internet Sources

http-1:https://publications.fifa.com/en/annual-report-2022/finances/2019-2022-cycle-in-review/2019-2022-revenue/

http-2:https://www.statista.com/statistics/279063/uefa-revenue-breakdown/

http-3:https://assets.the-afc.com/downloads/financial-assistance/AFC-Abridged-Financial-Statements-for-the-year-ended-31-December-2022.pdf

http-4:https://www.statista.com/statistics/1008640/conmebol-operating-revenue/

http-5:https://www.causeiq.com/organizations/confederation-of-north-central-american-and-caribb,133605859/

http-6:https://www.statista.com/statistics/1419839/income-of-the-football-association-caf-by-source/

AI and Tax Law: Development, Impacts, and Potentials of Natural Language Processing

Gokhan SARICIMEN[1]

1 Introduction

Artificial intelligence (AI) is a multidisciplinary concept that benefits from various scientific fields, including engineering, linguistics, and mathematics. It also encompasses various areas of expertise, such as machine learning, deep learning, natural language processing, computer vision, robotics, and speech processing. The primary objective of AI systems is to enable machines to effectively process various types of data (such as text, speech, image, and video) using capabilities similar to those of humans, including perception, learning, problem-solving, decision-making, and response.

The development of natural language processing (NLP), which is a subspecialty of AI, has begun to be used effectively in law, which presents challenging texts due to their nature. AI-based NLP models have shown remarkable examples of human-like abilities in understanding, processing, reasoning, and analysing legal documents. These technological outcomes also have brought new perspectives to tax law and legislation, a branch of law. In this context, the study aims to provide a literature review of the development of AI-based NLP models, their impact on tax law sources, and their potential use in tax law.

The study begins by examining the emergence and development of AI and NLP models. It then investigates the effects of tax-related documents on AI and NLP studies during development. Thirdly, it explores the potential applications of these models in tax law. Finally, the study also provides an overview of "corpora," which refers to comprehensive text collections used to develop NLP models.

1 Eskisehir Osmangazi University, Faculty of Economics and Administrative Sciences, Department of Public Finance, gsaricimen@ogu.edu.tr, ORCID ID: 0000-0003-2984-2992

2 Development of Natural Language Processing Models

The beginnings of AI research can be traced back to the 1930s. Alan Turing (1937), in "On Computable Numbers, with an Application to the Entscheidungsproblem", laid the foundation for the computability theory in AI. In this study, Turing introduced an abstract computational model known as the "Turing Machine". This model demonstrated which problems could be solved algorithmically. Following the computability approach, McCulloch and Pitts (1943) presented the first mathematical model of neural networks to understand their functions. Although this model was specific to neuroscience, it established the basic principles of artificial neural networks that are widely known. Donald O. Hebb (1949) proposed a theory that explains the biological underpinnings of memory and behaviour, which has significant implications for machine learning. Hebb proposed that learning occurs through the strengthening of connections between neurons, which strengthen or weaken based on the frequency of synaptic activation. This mechanism, known as "Hebbian learning" in neuroscience, is still applicable today, and it formed the basis of the functional principles of artificial neural networks. These studies, which examine the logical relationships between learning mechanisms and neural networks, laid the groundwork for developing modern machine-learning techniques based on artificial neural network models.

In 1950, Turing posed the question, "Can machines think?" in "Computing Machinery and Intelligence" and explored the intersection of computer science and philosophy. Turing proposed "the Turing Test", a thought experiment designed to assess whether a machine can think like a human. In this test, a human interrogator communicates in writing with a human and a machine without knowing their identities. If the interrogator cannot distinguish between the human and the machine based on their answers, the machine is considered to have human-like thinking capabilities. Turing also made significant contributions to the foundation of machine learning by exploring how to program machines and their ability to learn from experiences.

Following background studies, John McCarthy, Marvin Minsky, Nathaniel Rochester, and Claude Shannon announced the "Dartmouth Summer Research Project on Artificial Intelligence" in 1955. This paper was a workshop proposition to explore different aspects and potentials of AI. Its primary goal was to discover whether computers could demonstrate intelligence.

This proposal marked the first formal use of the term AI as a new research field and laid the foundation for modern studies. The Dartmouth Workshop was held in 1956 and officially initiated AI research efforts. Thus, it paved the way for studies across various disciplines and the development of sub-specialities in AI. One emerging field was NLP, situated at the intersection of human language and computer science.

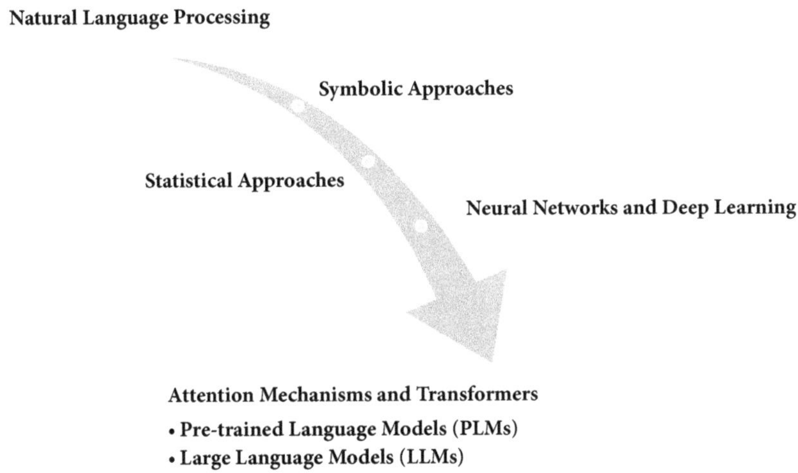

Fig. 1: Evolution of NPL Techniques.

NLP comprises a set of algorithms and models designed to enable machines to learn, understand, process, and generate outputs using human languages (Chowdhary, 2020:604). The basic approaches that have contributed to the development of NLP are symbolic approaches, statistical approaches, neural networks and deep learning, attention mechanisms, and transformer architecture (as shown in Fig. 1). All of these approaches are closely interrelated and complement each other.

The early studies in NLP focused on language modelling and machine translation, including the mathematical approach to information theory of Claude Shannon and Warren Weaver, Warren Weaver's studies on language translation, and the automatic translation experiments conducted by Georgetown University and IBM. However, due to technological limitations and insufficient collaboration between computer science and linguistics, machine translation systems yielded unsatisfactory results and failed to meet expectations (Somers, 2000b:330–331). Subsequently, the focus shifted towards understanding the structural and logical aspects of languages. Thus, the symbolic language processing approach, which sought to represent the meaning and rules of language by using symbols and logical structures, arose. Noam Chomsky's efforts in formulating language structure strengthened the connection between linguistics and AI, with his grammatical theories laying the foundation for language processing algorithms. His theories on deep structures and universal grammatical features significantly influenced the development of new methodologies in AI applications. Besides, John McCarthy, who worked on logical modelling, proposed the "Advice Taker" to automate logic-based decision-making in 1959. It was a program developed to solve problems by manipulating sentences in formal languages. With this, McCarthy aimed to make programs that learn from experience as effectively as humans in subsequent studies.

In the 1960s, Weizenbaum (1966) introduced ELIZA. This program was one of the first chatbots capable of making natural language conversations between humans and computers. Terry Winograd (1972) also developed SHRDLU, a program that could react to natural language commands. The program could interact with objects in a "block world" by performing placement, movement, and querying tasks. These programs pioneered the symbolic approach and inspired new methodologies for accurately interpreting and applying user instructions. Nevertheless, Roger Schank (1972) criticised these programs because of their limited databases and weaknesses in natural language understanding in "Conceptual Dependency: A Theory of Natural Language Understanding". Schank proposed that people learn experiences through "conceptual dependencies", which are mechanisms for interpreting new information based on past experiences. Similarly, Marvin Minsky (1974) introduced the frame system theory, in which knowledge is encoded in the human mind through structures called "frames". Minsky asserted that these frames organised clusters of interconnected information. These approaches transformed language processing and AI methods by modelling how people process and understand information.

During the 1960s and 1970s, technological improvements and the development of sophisticated algorithms led to significant progress in NLP research. In 1972, the design of the programming language Prolog enabled programmers to manipulate intricate data structures and relationships (Colmerauer & Roussel, 1996:331). Prolog, based on logical programming, was an excellent example of symbolic and logical approaches in AI and NLP and played a vital role in advancing expert systems. Afterwards, these rule-based expert systems used problem-solving and decision-making processes in specialised fields such as healthcare and law.

Until the 1980s, symbolic NLP and logical AI studies contributed to modelling human-like thinking and understanding abilities. In the 1980s, statistical approaches became more popular. During this period, statistical methods such as Hidden Markov Models, N-gram models, clustering methods, decision trees, and Bayesian classifiers came to the forefront in various NLP tasks, including language modelling, text classification, and text generation. These methods enabled NLP models to solve complex problems by using the statistical characteristics of language. Advancements in this area encouraged researchers to work with more comprehensive text data, which led to increased studies based on text collections called "corpora" (Somers, 2000a:377). Additionally, the development of convolutional neural network (CNN) and recurrent neural network (RNN) algorithms built on artificial neural networks began during this period. However, their popularity increased in the 2000s and later.

The methods of NLP had significantly advanced by the late 1990s. First, the Long Short-Term Memory (LSTM) model, based on RNN, was improved by Hochreiter and Schmidhuber (1997) to overcome the challenges faced by neural networks like CNN and RNN while learning long-range dependencies. Compared with these neural network algorithms, processing long-text data and solving complex tasks were made more effective by the LSTM model. Second, latent semantic analysis (LSA), which represents words and documents numerically, was proposed by Landauer and Dutnais (1997). LSA was a method for identifying the semantic connections between words and documents in extensive text collections, and it produced valuable results for figuring out the semantic similarities between texts.

In order to enhance word representation, Bengio et al. (2003) introduced a sophisticated word embedding algorithm based on deep learning in the 2000s. This approach served as the basis for embedding tools such as Word2Vec and GloVe. During this period, artificial neural networks and support vector machines also gained popularity. Neural networks, in particular, proved to be effective in modelling complex language structures. Collobert and Weston (2008) provided evidence that NLP models could be trained to handle multiple tasks simultaneously, such as entity recognition and tagging. This approach reinforced the idea that NLP models could multitask with deep learning. In the following years, successful results in NLP models were obtained by fusing artificial neural networks with intricate techniques and statistical methods; these developments also guided the deep learning period.

In the 2010s, advancements in deep learning methodologies led to a focus on processing large datasets. This progress triggered efforts to find new methods for representing words numerically. Mikolov et al. (2013) developed the Word2Vec model, which showed remarkable performance in capturing both syntactic and semantic word relationships in a vector space. Furthermore, Pennington et al. (2014) introduced GloVe, which offered a more comprehensive and detailed representation of word relationships by considering local contexts (sentence-level) and global usage (entirety-level) frequencies. Following these, Sutskever et al. (2014) presented the Seq2Seq model, which consists of an "encoder" for converting input into vector representations and a "decoder" for generating target language using these vectors. Bahdanau et al. (2014) used the attention mechanism technique to improve the performance of the Seq2Seq model in translation tasks because the basic encoder-decoder architecture had a bottleneck. The attention mechanism enabled the decoder to assign weights to each word generated by the encoder. Therefore, the decoder could focus on critical parts of the input text to generate output. This innovation, particularly in longer texts, maintained context and delivered more effective results in NLP tasks.

A few years later, Vaswani et al. (2017) introduced the transformer architecture based on attention mechanisms. This innovation marked a new era in NLP by offering a more effective approach to modelling long-range dependencies. Moreover, based on the transformer architecture, Devlin et al. (2018) developed BERT (Bidirectional Encoder Representations from Transformers) as a new and large language model. Unlike previous methods, BERT processes a text bi-directionally, which allows for a better understanding of long contexts within the text. Also, it allows for parameter adjustments, known as fine-tuning, to facilitate the implementation of language tasks for different purposes. Following the success of BERT, other researchers have introduced various BERT models such as RoBERTa, SBERT, and LegalBERT, as well as ELECTRA and GPT (Generative Pre-trained Transformer) models, all based on the transformer architecture. Transformer-based models like BERT are commonly used for processing extensive and lengthy text collections, and they have applications in various fields, including healthcare, finance, education, law, and media. These models are known as "pre-trained language models (PLMs)" because they require a pre-training process using large corpora.

Despite the high accuracy achieved in NLP tasks by PLMs, they had drawbacks such as the requirement for extensive data and training time, the inability to generalise without task-specific training, limited word processing capabilities, and poor performance with spelling errors. Researchers shifted their focus to Large Language Models (LLMs) to overcome these challenges and work with more extensive text data. As a result, Brown et al. released GPT-3, an LLM, in 2020. This model's generative power allowed it to learn in just a few shots, produce human-like text, and perform well on various natural language tasks. After the success of the GPT-3 model, other LLMs have been developed, such as GPT-4, PaLM, PaLM2, Megatron–Turing NLG and BLOOM. Furthermore, LLMs have allowed individuals with basic computer skills to use these technologies and process extensive datasets without coding or software knowledge.

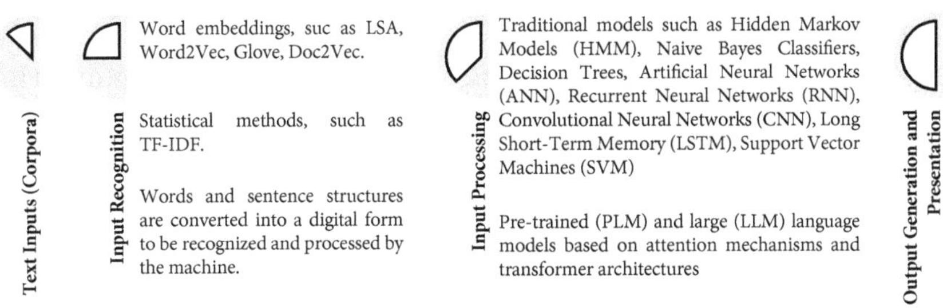

Fig. 2: Key Stages of an NLP Pipeline.

Considering all the above, Figure 2 illustrates the general workflow of NLP models.

3 Impacts of Natural Language Processing Models on Tax Law

The early stages of NLP models primarily focused on language and logical modelling, and studies were limited to linguistics and computer science until the 1970s. The emergence of PROLOG led to the development of expert systems, and through these systems, NLP studies expanded to many fields, such as law and tax law, in the literature.

The computer program "Taxman," developed by L. Thorne McCarty in 1977, was one of the innovative studies combining artificial intelligence and legal disciplines using expert systems. This program utilised symbolic logic and rule-based programming techniques to simulate tax rules, providing legal solutions for the taxation of corporate reorganisations under the 1954 Internal Revenue Code (McCarty, 1977:838–839). In 1980, Hellawell developed the CORPTAX program, which offered legal planning and analysis by conducting mathematical calculations and logical inferences based on user instructions regarding the taxation of stock redemptions. The program operated in a yes-no-number format (Hellawell, 1980:1363). Moreover, by the 1980s, studies had been undertaken to analyse cases based on legal doctrine, create legal language, automate legal documents, and develop knowledge-based legal information retrieval systems.

As stated in the previous section, statistical approaches in NLP techniques gained popularity in the 1980s, but their influence in tax law emerged later. However, expert systems in the tax law continued to increase and develop. In 1984, Robert H. Michaelsen introduced an expert system called "Taxadvisor" for individual income and transfer tax planning. This system was designed to generate outputs akin to expert decisions using various scenarios and rules. During this time, notable taxation and financial planning studies were ExperTax, Calypso, Expatax, Financial Advisor, Investor, and Paye as expert systems. Despite this progress, the need to model the law's unique language and reasoning structure continued to be a significant area of research. Addressing this need, Gardner (1987), in "An Artificial Intelligence Approach to Legal Reasoning", proposed methods for the computability of legal knowledge, language, and reasoning in AI models. He proposed ways to dissect the analysis process by identifying aspects of legal reasoning. This approach and techniques became pioneering AI works in the legal field. Generally, studies from the

1970s to the 2000s focused on modelling legal arguments and legislation using expert systems.

As technology advanced in the 2000s and beyond, firms and universities began to incorporate legal texts into AI-supported models (Surden, 2019:1326–1327). In this period, machine learning became prevalent in law with the development of applications such as Westlaw and LexisNexis. These platforms facilitated quick and accurate retrieval of various legal information from databases, including tax law. Besides these, Melz and Valente (2004) proposed the construction of a rich ontology modelling of federal tax laws in the United States. This approach laid the groundwork for developing AI models related to sources of tax law.

The widespread adoption of deep learning in NLP models has significantly impacted studies in tax law and other legal areas. Advances in word embedding techniques and the emergence of transformer models have enhanced computers' capabilities to perform complex legal reasoning and mathematical computations. Also, legal texts offered valuable resources for testing NLP models on challenging tasks. As a result, law-specific tasks, such as predicting court decisions, summarising legal texts, conducting semantic analyses, creating question-answering systems, and solving mathematical problems, have been carried out using PLM and LLM-based models. Regarding technical progress, Ilias Chalkidis introduced Law2Vec to represent legal terms in 2018. Additionally, law-specialised models have been developed, like Legal-BERT by Chalkidis et al. (2020), LexGPT by Lee (2023), and LawGPT 1.0 by Nguyen (2023). Furthermore, various models like ANGELIC continue to be developed in the legal field (Atkinson & Bench-Capon, 2023:2).

In addition to scientific studies, law and technology companies have recently developed AI applications to assist in tax and other legal issues. ROSS Intelligence introduced a legal research tool powered by IBM's Watson technology in 2016. ROSS understood legal questions using NLP techniques and provided the most relevant answers. In the same year, IBM introduced the LegalMation platform, which automates and accelerates routine legal tasks by reviewing legal documents, thus speeding up the litigation processes and increasing efficiency. In 2017, KPMG announced its intelligent audit platform, KPMG Clara, designed to make the audit process smoother and more transparent. In 2023, Blue J developed ASK BLUE J, which uses generative AI for analysing and predicting U.S. tax law. These examples have transformed the possibilities offered by language processing technologies in tax law and other legal areas into end-user products.

4 Potential Applications of NLP Models in Tax Law

In order to assess the potential of NLP models in tax law, it is essential to explore the various language tasks. Some of the critical and commonly used NLP tasks are: 1) language modelling, 2) syntax and semantic analysis, 3) named entity recognition, 4) part-of-speech tagging, 5) natural language understanding, 6) speech recognition, 7) machine translation, 8) sentiment analysis, 9) text classification, 10) summarisation, 11) question-answering systems, and 12) text generation.

Language modelling, named entity recognition, tagging, syntax and semantic analysis, and natural language understanding are pivotal in processing and analysing legal-specific textual data. Proficiency in these tasks provides more accurate results in NLP models, and this is particularly important for researchers interested in technical aspects. On the other hand, text classification, summarisation, question-answering systems, and text generation provide practical benefits to tax professionals and taxpayers by offering valuable insights and outcomes. Therefore, these tasks might be the main focus when evaluating the potential of NLP models.

4.1 Text Classifications

Text classification is training a language model to categorise text documents into different classes (Dogra et al., 2022:3). These systems operate at four levels: document, paragraph, sentence, and sub-sentence. At the document level, the algorithm determines the category of the entire document. At the paragraph level, it assigns a category to a single paragraph. At the sentence level, it classifies each sentence within a paragraph, and at the sub-sentence level, it categorises sub-phrases within a sentence. Text classification tasks aim to evaluate the model's performance and select the best classifier. Therefore, the results obtained from these tasks are significant for advancing text classification tasks in NLP (Kowsari et al., 2019:2–3).

Text classification tasks have significant potential for analysing tax-related texts. This method can help categorise numerous private letter rulings based on tax types or legal decisions according to their outcomes (e.g., approval, rejection, penalty etc.). It also helps a more systematic and efficient analysis of tax law sources at a sentence level by separating rules concerning various subjects, such as penalties, exemptions, and procedural requirements.

There are a few examples of text classification tasks at the sentence level. Khasanah and Krisnadhi (2021) analysed over 14,000 Indonesian tax appeal documents to forecast suitable tax rules against specific tax appeals. Shi et al. (2023) developed deep learning techniques to reduce audit errors, such as incorrect tax calculations and unfair penalties, by using Chinese tax audit data. At the paragraph level, Strak and Tuszynski (2022) developed a language model that analysed over 400,000 tax rulings utilising BERT-based embeddings and cosine similarity methods, aiming to identify semantically similar documents efficiently. Galli et al. (2022) analysed 226 Value Added Tax decisions issued by the Italian Regional Tax Law Commissions to foresee case outcomes based on the textual content of legal judgments. Finally, Ash et al. (2021) assessed the effectiveness of conventional NLP models in automatically tagging tax documents and identifying income sources using a dataset comprising U.S. state legal texts and sections of tax codes.

4.2 Text Summarisation

The text summarisation tasks are interested in how language models can effectively extract the key points and essential information from a given text and present them more concisely. There are two main types of summarisation methods in the field of NLP. The first is extractive summarisation, which involves identifying and selecting essential sentences from the input text to create a summary without altering the sentence structure. The second is abstractive summarisation, where the machine generates human-like expressions and sentences to provide a more coherent and fluent summary (Awasthi et al., 2021:1310). These methods, powered by language models, contribute to the rapid and efficient comprehension of information-dense documents.

Text summarisation can apply various practical applications in tax law documents. By condensing complex legal information into summaries, lawyers and taxpayers can quickly understand laws, regulations, court decisions, and other legal-related documents. It can also facilitate the quick comprehension of findings and recommendations from tax audit reports. Researchers can swiftly access desired information by scanning extensive legal documents, and students can better grasp complex tax topics.

Saravanan et al. (2008), one of the early studies in this area, conducted the text summarisation method using 200 judicial decisions related to rent control, income tax, and sales tax. Feijo and Moreira (2023) recently proposed a summarisation model called LegalSumm, designed for legal texts. In this model, they utilised a dataset containing approximately 10,000 decisions from the Brazilian Supreme Court to perform text summarisation tasks in various legal fields, including tax law.

4.3 Question-Answering Systems

Question-answering systems are advanced automated processes that are capable of understanding questions in natural language and providing the requested information. These systems can identify the information required, retrieve and extract the necessary data, and generate appropriate responses (Mollá-Aliod & Vicedo, 2010:485). Early examples of such systems include TAXMAN and other expert systems. More recent examples include providing Google's direct answers to search questions and advanced language models like ChatGPT, Gemini, and Copilot, which can answer questions on a wide range of topics in natural language.

In the tax law, question-answering systems have the potential to offer intelligent legal guidance. These systems, trained on tax-related topics, can assist taxpayers and professionals in quickly accessing answers to intricate tax law queries. Notable examples include ASK BLUE J and the recent LLM models (which allow for specialised training using tax law texts).

Additionally, some studies that evaluate the performance of NLP models in this field can be cited. For instance, Nay et al. (2024) examined GPT-4 to assess the usefulness of large language models in tax law. The findings revealed that LLMs can achieve high accuracy when trained with specific legal texts. However, their performance was still insufficient compared to expert tax attorneys. Holzenberger et al. (2020) created the Statutory Reasoning Assessment (SARA) dataset, which includes rules derived from the U.S. Internal Revenue Code and natural language questions based on these rules, to facilitate understanding legal texts and the automatic modelling of legal reasoning processes. The dataset was employed to evaluate tax law practices in Prolog and BERT models, so it has been a valuable resource for AI applications in tax law. Also, some studies tested GPT models using questions from different law schools and bar exams. For instance, Blair-Stanek et al. (2023) evaluated the performance of the GPT-4 model in answering multiple-choice exam questions in a tax law class.

4.4 Text Generation

Text generation is the process in which humans express their thoughts, and machines convert information into written or spoken language (McDonald, 2010:121). During this process, machines use language models to process the information they have learned and generate task-specific texts. Language models make numerous decisions during text generation, ranging from high-level decisions like determining content to low-level choices such as using pronouns (Reiter, 2010:574). Decisions are modelled by NLP algorithms on which the language model is developed. Along with algorithms, several data-specific factors, such as the number of words used during model training, grammatical examples, and corpus quality, also directly impact the success of text generation.

All texts generated by an NLP model are part of natural language generation. However, this passage focuses on the potential success of today's generative AI-based NLP models. These, particularly GPT models, have significant potential for use in tax law and other legal fields by using reasoning in legal texts. The potential of GPT models to generate text in tax law has been observed in various studies. For example, Barth (2023) asked ChatGPT to determine whether the electricity supplied by charging stations for electric vehicles is the supply of goods or supply of services in the European Union's value-added tax system. According to Barth, ChatGPT presented arguments that distinguished between the supply of goods and services. However, despite ChatGPT arguing for a supply of services, the European Court of Justice ultimately concluded it was a supply of goods in this dilemma. Also, Hargreaves (2023) examined prompt engineering processes that discussed a statement from the OECD's Base Erosion and Profit Shifting Action Plan using ChatGPT. Despite some responses needing more details and including irrelevant examples, ChatGPT provided well-structured answers that correctly identified the core issues.

5 The Corpora and Datasets

Corpora are collections of machine-readable texts chosen to represent a specific natural language or linguistic style. Corpora, which can be structured or unstructured, serve as a foundation and testing set for training and advancing NLP models (Xiao, 2010:147). They encompass a wide variety of text collections, including glossaries, newspapers, literary works, and legal documents. NLP models use these corpora to learn the natural intricacies and usage of language, grammatical structures, and text contexts, as well as to interpret word meanings. Models trained with corpora can effectively perform NLP tasks, whether general or domain-specific.

Datasets are critical components in the evaluation of NLP model performance. They are used by researchers to assess the accuracy and generalisation ability of language models in NLP tasks. These tasks include text classification, named entity recognition, machine translation, and others mentioned. Typically, these datasets contain texts not included in the training process and are reserved for objectively evaluating the model's performance. In academic research, the effectiveness of an NLP model is often assessed and compared based on its performance on these test datasets.

The development of corpora began before statistical language processing. The Brown Corpus, prepared by W. Nelson Francis and Henry Kucera in 1964, was the first large, balanced, and annotated corpus. It consisted of approximately 1 million words representing the written forms of modern American English and 500 texts selected from different areas (Francis & Kucera, 1979). Currently, comprehensive text corpora such as Common Crawl, Wikipedia Dump, Book Corpus, and The Pile play a significant role in helping NLP models like PLM and LLM understand language and analyse grammatical structures.

The widespread adoption of BERT and GPT models across various scientific fields has also accelerated the development of specialised corpora and test datasets for the legal domain. There are corpora and test data sets in the literature that are comprised of tax law texts. For example, the SARA, introduced by Holzenberger et al. (2020), includes a corpus containing U.S. Internal Revenue Code rules and a test dataset comprising natural language questions based on these rules. Ash et al. (2021) also compiled an extensive corpus containing legal texts and sections of tax codes from the U.S. for tasks such as text classification and document tagging based on tax types. Similarly,

Strąk and Tuszyński (2022) assembled a corpus comprising 404,796 tax rulings released by the Polish Tax Administration for use in text classification tasks. Additionally, scientific studies that adapt existing NLP models to domains such as law, healthcare, and education often include corpora designed to their specific characteristics. This means that thousands of corpora are currently available in NLP models. Consequently, any original and unique NLP study focused on tax law inherently generates its own corpus and test dataset, thereby establishing an NLP ecosystem centred on tax law language.

6 Conclusion

Although still in its early stages, the integration of NLP technologies into tax law has the potential to create new opportunities for professionals and taxpayers. These technologies help taxpayers to understand intricate tax regulations and easily access accurate information. They can also enhance tax compliance and reduce compliance costs by reducing errors in tax obligations. On the other hand, tax professionals, such as lawyers, judges, auditors, scholars, and others, can efficiently access and use resources related to tax law by utilising these technologies. Comprehensive and knowledge-intensive tax law sources are easily processed with state-of-the-art NLP models to achieve specific purposes. Thus, the excessive caseload in the legal system can be reduced by accelerating legal processes, and efficient use of resources can be ensured in academic studies.

Significant progress has been made in applying NLP models in the law-specific studies. However, tax law poses distinct challenges due to its constantly evolving nature, complex calculations, specialised terminology, and strong connection to fiscal policies. Therefore, extensive research, supported by high-quality corpora and datasets, is crucial to use NLP models in tax law. Additionally, professionals and taxpayers must embrace technological advancements and be open to integrating new systems to benefit from these technologies.

In the near future, it is expected that artificial intelligence and NLP technologies will play an increasingly significant role in shaping the field of tax law. When examining the results of a case predictor, it is important to note that relying on systems that predict legal outcomes with a success rate of around 80% is insufficient, considering that around 20% of legal cases may be resolved incorrectly (Bench-Capon, 2021:28). This argument also applies for tax-specific AI studies. It underscores the potential shortfall in success rates within a critical area such as tax law. Therefore, NLP models need to be tested with as many language tasks as possible in tax law and other legal domains, and their results need to be published to aid the development of AI technologies. Consequently, developing more precise and sophisticated systems can revolutionize tax law practices. Tax systems powered by AI-based technologies can be fairer, more accessible and more efficient.

Bibliography

Ash, E., Guillot, M., & Han, L. (2021). Machine extraction of tax laws from legislative texts. In N. Aletras, I. Androutsopoulos, L. Barrett, C. Goanta, & D. Preotiuc-Pietro (Eds.), Proceedings of the natural legal language processing workshop 2021 (pp. 76–85). Association for Computational Linguistics. https://doi.org/10.18653/v1/2021.nllp-1.7

Ash, E., & Marian, O. (2023). The making of international tax law: Empirical evidence from tax treaties text. Florida Tax Review, 24(1), 151–190. https://scholarship.law.ufl.edu/ftr/vol24/iss1/3

Atkinson, K., & Bench-Capon, T. (2023). ANGELIC II: An Improved methodology for representing legal domain knowledge. In Proceedings of the nineteenth international conference on artificial intelligence and law (pp. 12–21). Association for Computing Machinery. https://doi.org/10.1145/3594536.3595137

Awasthi, I., Gupta, K., Bhogal, P. S., Anand, S. S., & Soni, P. K. (2021). Natural language processing (NLP) based text summarization—A survey. In 6th. International conference on inventive computation technologies (pp. 1310–1317). IEEE. https://ieeexplore.ieee.org/document/9358703

Bahdanau, D., Cho, K., & Bengio, Y. (2014). Neural machine translation by jointly learning to align and translate. arXiv. https://arxiv.org/abs/1409.0473v1

Barth, F. (2023). Evolving law in AI's hands?–Preliminary experiments, thoughts and observations on the basis of Chat GPT. SSRN. http://dx.doi.org/10.2139/ssrn.4431234

Bench-Capon, T. (2021). The need for good old fashioned ai and law. Jusletter-IT, 21 December 2020, 23–35. http://dx.doi.org/10.38023/cefe7081-e6dd-49de-9592-9adbb6063fd6

Bengio, Y., Ducharme, R., Vincent, P., & Janvin, C. (2003). A neural probabilistic language model. The Journal of Machine Learning Research, 3 (Feb), 1137–1155. https://www.jmlr.org/papers/volume3/bengio03a/bengio03a.pdf

Blair-Stanek, A., Carstens, A.-M., Goldberg, D. S., Graber, M., Gray, D. C., & Stearns, M. L. (2023). GPT-4's law school grades: Con law C, crim C-, law & econ C, partnership tax B, property B-, tax B. SSRN. http://dx.doi.org/10.2139/ssrn.4443471

Brown, T. B., Mann, B., Ryder, N., Subbiah, M., Kaplan, J., Dhariwal, P., Neelakantan, A., Shyam, P., Sastry, G., Askell, A., Agarwal, S., Herbert-Voss, A., Krueger, G., Henighan, T., Child, R., Ramesh, A., Ziegler, D. M., Wu, J., Winter, C., … Amodei, D. (2020). Language models are few-shot learners. In H. Larochelle, M. Ranzato, R. Hadsell, M. F. Balcan & H. Lin (Eds). Proceedings of the 34th international conference on neural information processing systems (pp. 1877–1901). Curran Associates Inc. https://dl.acm.org/doi/abs/10.5555/3495724.3495883

Chalkidis, I., Fergadiotis, M., Malakasiotis, P., Aletras, N., & Androutsopoulos, I. (2020). LEGAL-BERT: The muppets straight out of law school. In T. Cohn, Y. He, & Y. Liu (Eds.), Findings of the association for computational linguistics: EMNLP 2020 (pp. 2898–2904). Association for Computational Linguistics. https://doi.org/10.18653/v1/2020.findings-emnlp.261

Chomsky, N. (2002). Syntactic structures (2th ed.). Mouton de Gruyter.

Chowdhary, K. R. (2020). Fundamentals of artificial intelligence. Springer India. https://doi.org/10.1007/978-81-322-3972-7_19

Collenette, J., Atkinson, K., & Bench-Capon, T. (2023). Explainable AI tools for legal reasoning about cases: A study on the European Court of Human Rights. Artificial Intelligence, 317, 1–24. https://doi.org/10.1016/j.artint.2023.103861

Collobert, R., & Weston, J. (2008). A unified architecture for natural language processing: Deep neural networks with multitask learning. In Proceedings of the 25th international conference on machine learning (pp. 160–167). Association for Computing Machinery. https://doi.org/10.1145/1390156.1390177

Colmerauer, A., & Roussel, P. (1996). The birth of Prolog. In T. J. Bergin, R. G. Gibson (Eds.), History of programming languages—II (pp. 331–367). Association for Computing Machinery. https://doi.org/10.1145/234286.1057820

Devlin, J., Chang, M.-W., Lee, K., & Toutanova, K. (2019). BERT: Pre-training of Deep Bidirectional Transformers for Language Understanding. arXiv. https://arxiv.org/abs/1810.04805

Dogra, V., Verma, S., Kavita, Chatterjee, P., Shafi, J., Choi, J., & Ijaz, M. F. (2022). A complete process of text classification system using state-of-the-art NLP models. Computational Intelligence and Neuroscience, 2022(1), 1–26. https://doi.org/10.1155/2022/1883698

Feijo, D. de V., & Moreira, V. P. (2023). Improving abstractive summarization of legal rulings through textual entailment. Artificial Intelligence and Law, 31(1), 91–113. https://doi.org/10.1007/s10506-021-09305-4

Francis, W. N., & Kucera, H. (1979). Brown corpus manual. Retrieved July 22, 2024 from http://gandalf.aksis.uib.no/icame/brown/bcm.html

Galli, F., Grundler, G., Fidelangeli, A., Galassi, A., Lagioia, F., Palmieri, E., Ruggeri, F., Sartor, G., & Torroni, P. (2022). Predicting outcomes of italian vat decisions. In Enrico Francesconi, Georg Borges, & Christoph Sorge (Eds.), Legal knowledge and information systems (pp. 188–193). IOS Press.

Gardner, A. von der L. (1987). An artificial intelligence approach to legal reasoning. MIT Press.

Hargreaves, S. (2023). Words are flowing out like endless rain into a paper cup': ChatGPT & law school assessments. Legal Education Review, 33(1), 69–105. https://doi.org/10.53300/001c.83297

Hebb, D. O. (1949). The organization of behavior; a neuropsychological theory. Wiley.

Hellawell, R. (1980). A computer program for legal planning and analysis: taxation of stock redemptions. Columbia Law Review, 80(7), 1363–1398. https://doi.org/10.2307/1122169

Hochreiter, S., & Schmidhuber, J. (1997). Long short-term memory. Neural Computation, 9(8), 1735–1780. https://doi.org/10.1162/neco.1997.9.8.1735

Holzenberger, N., Blair-Stanek, A., & Durme, B. V. (2020). A dataset for statutory reasoning in tax law entailment and question answering. arXiv. https://arxiv.org/abs/2005.05257

Khasanah, I. N., & Krisnadhi, A. A. (2021). Extreme multilabel text classification on Indonesian Tax Court Ruling using single channel CNN and IndoBERT embedding. In 6th International workshop on big data and information security (pp. 59–66). IEEE. https://ieeexplore.ieee.org/document/9631855

Kowsari, K., Jafari Meimandi, K., Heidarysafa, M., Mendu, S., Barnes, L., & Brown, D. (2019). Text classification algorithms: A survey. Information, 10(4), 1–68. https://doi.org/10.3390/info10040150

Landauer, T. K., & Dumais, S. T. (1997). A solution to Plato's problem: The latent semantic analysis theory of acquisition, induction, and representation of knowledge. Psychological Review, 104(2), 211–240. https://doi.org/10.1037/0033-295X.104.2.211

Lee, J.-S. (2023). LexGPT 0.1: Pre-trained GPT-J models with Pile of Law. arXiv. https://arxiv.org/abs/2306.05431

McCarthy, J. (1959). Programs with common sense. Retrieved July 10, 2024 from http://jmc.stanford.edu/articles/mcc59/mcc59.pdf

McCarthy, J., Minsky, M., Rochester, N., & Shannon, C. (1955). A proposal for the Dartmouth summer research project on artificial intelligence. Retrieved July 10, 2024 from http://jmc.stanford.edu/articles/dartmouth/dartmouth.pdf

McCarty, L. T. (1977). Reflections on 'Taxman': An experiment in artificial intelligence and legal reasoning. Harvard Law Review, 90(5), 837–893. https://doi.org/10.2307/1340132

McCulloch, W. S., & Pitts, W. (1943). A logical calculus of the ideas immanent in nervous activity. The Bulletin of Mathematical Biophysics, 5(4), 115–133. https://doi.org/10.1007/BF02478259

McDonald, D. D. (2010). Natural language generation. In Nitin Indurkhya & Fred J. Damerau (Eds.), Handbook of natural language processing (Second Edition, pp. 121–144). CRC Press.

Melz, E., & Valente, A. (2004). Modeling the tax code. In R. Meersman, Z. Tari, & A. Corsaro (Eds.), On the move to meaningful internet systems 2004: OTM 2004 Workshops (pp. 652–661). Springer Berlin Heidelberg.

Michaelsen, R. H. (1984). An expert system for federal tax planning. Expert Systems, 1(2), 149–167. https://doi.org/10.1111/j.1468-0394.1984.tb00440.x

Mikolov, T., Chen, K., Corrado, G., & Dean, J. (2013). Efficient estimation of word representations in vector space. arXiv. https://arxiv.org/abs/1301.3781

Minsky, M. (1974). A framework for representing knowledge. Massachusetts Institute of Technology. https://dl.acm.org/doi/10.5555/889222

Mollá-Aliod, D., & Vicedo, J.-L. (2010). Question answering. In Nitin Indurkhya & Fred J. Damerau (Eds.), Handbook of natural language processing (Second Edition, pp. 485–510). CRC Press.

Nay, J. J., Karamardian, D., Lawsky, S. B., Tao, W., Bhat, M., Jain, R., Lee, A. T., Choi, J. H., & Kasai, J. (2024). Large language models as tax attorneys: A case study in legal capabilities emergence. Philosophical Transactions of the Royal Society A: Mathematical, Physical and Engineering Sciences, 382(2270), 1–15. https://doi.org/10.1098/rsta.2023.0159

Nguyen, H.-T. (2023). A brief report on LawGPT 1.0: A virtual legal assistant based on GPT-3. arXiv. https://arxiv.org/abs/2302.05729

Pennington, J., Socher, R., & Manning, C. (2014). GloVe: Global vectors for word representation. In A. Moschitti, B. Pang, & W. Daelemans (Eds.), Proceedings of the 2014 conference on empirical methods in natural language processing (pp. 1532–1543). Association for Computational Linguistics. https://doi.org/10.3115/v1/D14-1162

Reiter, E. (2010). Natural language generation. In Alexander Clark, Chris Fox, & Shalom Lappin (Eds.), The handbook of computational linguistics and natural language processing (pp. 574–598). Wiley-Blackwell.

Saravanan, M., Ravindran, B., & Raman, S. (2008). Automatic identification of rhetorical roles using conditional random fields for legal document summarization. In Proceedings of the third international joint conference on natural language processing. IJCNLP. https://aclanthology.org/I08-1063

Schank, R. C. (1972). Conceptual dependency: A theory of natural language understanding. Cognitive Psychology, 3(4), 552–631. https://doi.org/10.1016/0010-0285(72)90022-9

Shi, Y., Wang, L., Tian, C., Wang, R., Pei, J., Hussian, A., & Bashir, A. K. (2023). A Chinese short text classification method for tax audit reports based on word importance and syntactic enhancement BERT. In I. Zitouni (Eds.), ACM Transactions on Asian and low-resource language information processing (pp. 1–15). https://doi.org/10.1145/3594635

Somers, H. (2000a). Empirical approaches to natural language processing. In Robert Dale, Hermann Moisl, & Harold Somers (Eds.), Handbook of natural language processing (pp. 377–384). Marcel Dekker.

Somers, H. (2000b). Machine translation. In Robert Dale, Hermann Moisl, & Harold Somers (Eds.), Handbook of natural language processing (pp. 329–346). Marcel Dekker.

Strąk, T., & Tuszyński, M. (2022). NLP based retrieval of semantically similar private tax rulings. Procedia Computer Science, 207, 2853–2864. https://doi.org/10.1016/j.procs.2022.09.343

Surden, H. (2019). Artificial intelligence and law: An overview. Georgia State University Law Review, 35(4), 1305–1337. https://scholar.law.colorado.edu/faculty-articles/1234/

Sutskever, I., Vinyals, O., & Le, Q. V. (2014). Sequence to sequence learning with neural networks. arXiv. https://arxiv.org/abs/1409.3215

Turing, A. M. (1937). On computable numbers, with an application to the entscheidungsproblem. Proceedings of the London Mathematical Society, 42(1), 230–265. https://doi.org/10.1112/plms/s2-42.1.230

Turing, A. M. (1950). Computing machinery and intelligence. Mind, 59(236), 433–460. http://www.jstor.org/stable/2251299

Vaswani, A., Shazeer, N., Parmar, N., Uszkoreit, J., Jones, L., Gomez, A. N., Kaiser, Ł., & Polosukhin, I. (2017). Attention is all you need. In I. Guyon, U. V. Luxburg, S. Bengio, H. Wallach, R. Fergus, S. Vishwanathan, & R. Garnett (Eds.), Advances in neural information processing systems 30 NeurIPS proceedings 2017 (pp. 1–11). Curran Associates Inc. https://proceedings.neurips.cc/paper_files/paper/2017/file/3f5ee243547dee91fbd053c1c4a845aa-Paper.pdf

Weizenbaum, J. (1966). ELIZA—a computer program for the study of natural language communication between man and machine. Communications of the ACM, 9(1), 36–45. https://doi.org/10.1145/365153.365168

Winograd, T. (1972). Understanding natural language. Cognitive Psychology, 3(1), 1–191. https://doi.org/10.1016/0010-0285(72)90002-3

Xiao, R. (2010). Corpus creation. In Nitin Indurkhya & Fred J. Damerau (Eds.), Handbook of natural language processing (Second Edition, pp. 147–165). CRC Press.

How Good is ChatGPT at Answering Public Finance Questions? Potential Impacts of Chatgpt on Public Finance Education

Hakan ÖZDEMİR[1]

1 Introduction

Artificial intelligence (AI) has become one of the most debated topics due to its capabilities and potential. Since its release in November 2022, ChatGPT has garnered significant interest. The CEO of OpenAI, Sam Altman, announced that more than a million users signed up to use GPT within a week (Tajik & Tajik, 2023:1). ChatGPT is based on a large language model (LLM) trained on vast amounts of digitized data. The latest version of LLM, GPT, has been trained on 175 billion parameters to generate text that closely resembles human-created text (Gilson et al., 2023:2). ChatGPT can understand and respond naturally to human speech. However, it sometimes provides incorrect answers and makes simple calculation errors (*LLM failure archive (ChatGPT and beyond*), 2024), raising concerns about the reliability of its responses.

ChatGPT can process large amounts of text, enhance error detection, and improve writing quality while working in multiple languages, including English, Spanish, French, and German. It can generate responses in various tones, such as formal, informal, and humorous (William et al., 2022). ChatGPT can solve exams, write poems, and generate code. It is supported by a pre-trained, comprehensive language model that allows it to understand user queries quickly and produce responses that sound original (Borji, 2023:1). This feature makes it useful for many purposes, including customer service, finance, entertainment, education, healthcare, and more (George et al., 2023:9).

ChatGPT's advanced capabilities, compared to traditional bots and voice assistants, allow it to understand context in conversations better and provide more accurate responses, improving user experience and reducing errors. This technology can be beneficial in various sectors, such as personalized teaching assistance in education, interactive experiences in entertainment,

1 Ministry of Treasury and Finance (Republic of Türkiye), hakan.ozdemir@vdk.gov.tr, ORCID-ID: 0000-0002-2740-3737

automated investment advice in finance, and smart patient care in healthcare (George et al., 2023:10).

The potential impacts of ChatGPT have been explored in various fields, including education (Arie Wahyu et al., 2023; Gilson et al., 2023; Hakiki et al., 2023; Hatmanto & Sari, 2023; Sallam, 2023; Yang, 2023), medicine (Gilson et al., 2023; Nazir et al., 2023; Sallam, 2023), social media (Som, 2023), and programming (Surameery & Shakor, 2023). The studies on ChatGPT's effects and potential are increasing daily.

In Türkiye, public finance education is typically offered within the faculties of Economics and Administrative Sciences (İİBF) or Business Faculties of universities. The Public finance departments aim to provide expertise in public finance, tax law, budgeting, and financial planning for both the public and private sectors. ChatGPT can be utilized in finance education, having numerous positive effects. Students can instantly access information about finance theories and concepts, better understand complex financial topics, and receive support in their assignments, projects, and exam preparations. Additionally, the sample problem solutions and interactive learning opportunities provided by ChatGPT can enhance students' analytical thinking skills. Educators can use ChatGPT to develop more effective and efficient teaching strategies by benefiting from its assistance in preparing course materials and lesson plans. This could improve the overall quality of finance education and positively impact students' academic success. However, for these applications to be beneficial, ChatGPT needs to demonstrate performance comparable to humans in evaluating information and reasoning to ensure the reliability of its responses.

This study aims to measure and evaluate the performance of ChatGPT in the Public Personnel Selection Examination (KPSS), which assesses the knowledge of public finance for candidates wishing to work in the public sector in Türkiye. Additionally, the study qualitatively examines the integrity of ChatGPT's responses regarding logical reasoning and the use of internal and external information to further evaluate its ability to serve as a finance educator.

2 Literature Review

ChatGPT is an AI-based chat tool that can generate human-like text. It can be used in many fields, including education, healthcare, software bug resolution, and social media. Farida Hanum et al. (2023:637) noted that using ChatGPT among students could positively affect their learning motivation. ChatGPT can enhance the accessibility and usability of educational information by providing guidance or reference materials. Students can use ChatGPT as a learning and education tool to ask questions about the course material. Interaction with ChatGPT can also help users develop language skills (Arie Wahyu et al., 2023:1034). It has the potential to be used as an interactive educational tool, especially for medical students, in medical education and information assessment (Gilson et al., 2023:7). When evaluated in terms of use scenarios, advantages, and challenges in English online courses, ChatGPT can provide a better learning experience for students (Yang, 2023:58). The integration of GPT chat into language education emerges as a versatile tool that bridges the gap between theoretical ideals and effective language teaching practices when used effectively (Hatmanto & Sari, 2023).

A study examining the attitudes of Ukrainian university students towards using AI tools in education found that students frequently used chatbots during the learning process and believed that teachers should use AI tools in their courses. However, some students reported that their assignments were rejected due to plagiarism caused by AI usage (Olena & Olga, 2023:206).

In university education departments, the impact of ChatGPT on teaching, learning, and administrative issues is being investigated. Potential uses of AI in education include supporting innovative assessment strategies, optimizing learning management systems, and identifying at-risk students (Jim & Maretta, 2023). The presence of AI-based technologies represents a significant paradigm shift in higher education infrastructure. When education systems are open to this profound change, they can utilize AI tools like ChatGPT to optimize teaching, learning, and education management.

For example, at the administrative level, ChatGPT can significantly reduce the workload of administrators by performing tasks such as responding to emails from potential applicants or organizing application data. At the teaching level, ChatGPT can perform tasks such as grading and summarizing student work, allowing teachers more time to help students gain a solid and systematic understanding of new concepts. A study by Philips et al. (2022) shows that integrating ChatGPT into an educational game can help educators gain insights into student collaboration in computer-supported collaborative learning environments (Tajik & Tajik, 2023).

In the context of using ChatGPT in learning, it is essential to remember that technology can only be a tool and cannot entirely replace the role of the teacher. Therefore, it is necessary to integrate technology into learning appropriately and effectively and to develop teachers' competencies in managing learning with technology. Teachers' roles remain crucial in having a sufficient understanding of the technology used and effectively using it in the learning process. Additionally, teachers must develop new skills and competencies to manage learning with technology (Ausat et al., 2023:16104).

3 Methodology

3.1 Data Sets

In Türkiye, those wishing to work in the public sector must take the Public Personnel Selection Examination (KPSS), conducted annually by ÖSYM (Assessment, Selection, and Placement Centre). Candidates must be university graduates to take the exam. Those wanting to work in public finance must answer 40 finance-related questions in this exam. Due to the exam's role in measuring candidates' knowledge and skills in public finance and its free availability post-exam, the KPSS public finance questions were used as the data set for this study (OSYM, 2024). The subject distribution of the public finance questions is shown in Table 1.

Tab. 1: Public Personnel Selection Examination (KPSS): Subject Distribution and Score Types (Public Finance Section)

Subject	Rate	Number of Questions
Public Finance Theory	%10	4
Public Revenues	%15	6
Public Expenses	%15	6
Public Debt	%15	6
State Budget	%15	6
Tax Law	%15	6
Fiscal Policy	%15	6
Total	**%100**	**40**

Source: (OSYM, 2013).

or this study, the public finance tests from the years 2017–2021 were used. Each year consists of 40 questions, and considering the 5-year question pool, a total of 200 questions formed the data set.

3.2 Data Entry

The latest version of ChatGPT, ChatGPT-4o, was used in this study. GPT-4o focuses on more natural human-computer interaction and can generate combinations of text, voice, and image outputs. Compared to existing models, GPT-4o offers significant improvements, especially in visual and auditory understanding and in non-English texts (OpenAI, 2024). Due to the higher accuracy of the latest ChatGPT versions, earlier versions were not used or compared.

All published questions were first transcribed into a text file along with their options. Since ChatGPT has trainability and directivity features, the questions were posed to ChatGPT exactly as they appear in the exam, without any additional information. The responses were recorded next to the questions and compared. The questioning and answering process was carried out between June 27, 2024, and July 4, 2024. The published answer keys were used as the correct answers. Questions were posed in Turkish and responses were evaluated in Turkish. An example question prompt and answer are shown in Figure 1.

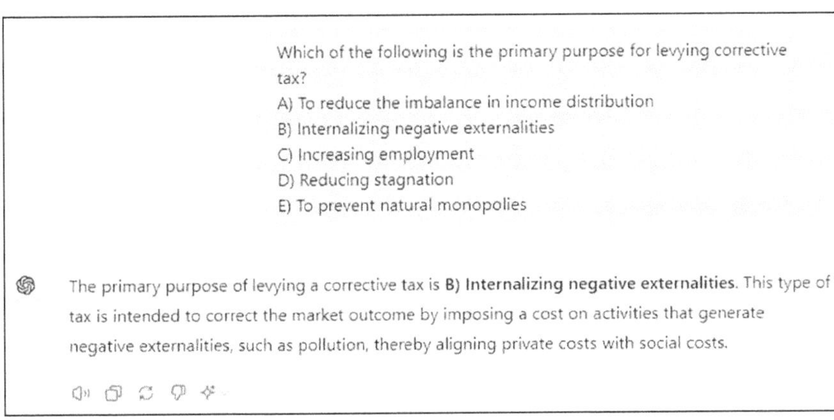

Fig. 1: Sample Question Prompt and Answer.

The data entry for the same question was done as shown below.

Tab. 2: Sample Data Entry

Question	Correct Answer	Chat GPT Response	Inquiry Date	Evaluation	Logical Reasoning	Internal Information	External Information
Which of the following is the primary purpose for levying corrective tax? A) To reduce the imbalance in income distribution B) Internalizing negative externalities C) Increasing employment D) Reducing stagnation E) To prevent natural monopolies	B	The primary purpose of levying a corrective tax is B) Internalizing negative externalities. This type of tax is intended to correct the market outcome by imposing a cost on activities that generate negative externalities, such as pollution, thereby aligning private costs with social costs.	4.07.2024	ChatGpt has answered this question correctly.	Yes	Yes	Yes

3.3 Data Analysis

After asking all questions and obtaining responses from ChatGPT, the answers were compared with the answer keys. The explanations for correct answers were examined to determine whether the correct answer was a matter of chance. Additionally, the metrics used in the study by Gilson et al. (2023) were also used in this study. The responses to the questions were examined in three categories: logical reasoning, use of internal information, and use of external information. Logical reasoning refers to whether ChatGPT explained the logic behind choosing the correct answer, internal information refers to whether ChatGPT used the information within the question, and external information refers to whether ChatGPT used external information related to the responses.

For incorrect answers, a classification was made to determine whether the incorrect answer was due to a logical reasoning error or a knowledge error. Logical error refers to ChatGPT's failure to sufficiently find and convert information into the correct answer, while knowledge error refers to ChatGPT's failure to identify a crucial piece of information expected to be known from the question stem or through external information.

3.4 Results

Table 3 presents ChatGPT-4o's performance in the KPSS exams in a comparative comparison by years.

Tab. 3: ChatGPT's Performance

ChatGPT – 4o	KPSS 2017 (n = 40), n (%)	KPSS 2018 (n = 40), n (%)	KPSS 2019 (n = 40), n (%)	KPSS 2020 (n = 40), n (%)	KPSS 2021 (n = 40), n (%)	Total
Correct	33 (82.5)	34 (85)	28 (70)	33 (82.5)	35 (87.5)	163 (81.5)
Incorrect	7 (17.5)	6 (15)	12 (30)	7 (17.5)	5 (12.5)	37 (18.5)

The overall performance of ChatGPT-4o is quite high, with an accuracy rate of 81.5%. The highest success rate was achieved in 2021 with 87.5%, while the lowest success rate was observed in 2019 with 70%. The accuracy rate of ChatGPT-4o varied between 70% and 87.5% over the years, indicating significant fluctuations in performance in some years. The incorrect answer rate varied between 12.5% and 30%, with the highest error rate observed in 2019.

These data show that ChatGPT-4o is generally successful in answering KPSS questions, but it also demonstrates variations in performance in some years. The year 2019 is particularly notable, showing a decline in performance. However, considering the overall accuracy rate, ChatGPT-4o can be considered reliable in answering KPSS questions correctly.

The questions and incorrect answers in Table 3 were qualitatively evaluated as mentioned above. The results of this evaluation are presented in Table 4.

Tab. 4: Quantitative and Qualitative Distribution of ChatGPT Responses

Metric		General (n = 200), n (%)	Correct (n = 163), n (%)	Incorrect (n = 37), n (%)
Logical Reasoning	Correct	200 (100)	163 (100)	37 (100)
	Incorrect	0 (0)	0 (0)	0 (0)
Internal Information	Correct	200 (100)	163 (100)	37 (100)
	Incorrect	0 (0)	0 (0)	0 (0)
External Information	Correct	193 (98.5)	157 (96.31)	36 (97.29)
	Incorrect	7 (1.5)	6 (3.69)	1 (2.71)
Reasons for Incorrect Answers	Logical Error	–	–	15 (40.54)
	Knowledge Error	–	–	22 (59.46)

Table 4 evaluates the quality of ChatGPT's responses to KPSS (Public Personnel Selection Examination) questions. The accuracy rates of the given responses were analysed in terms of logical reasoning, internal information, and external information. Generally, all of ChatGPT's responses were evaluated as 100% correct in terms of logical reasoning and internal information, demonstrating high consistency and accuracy in these areas. This shows that ChatGPT can provide logically sound answers and effectively utilize the information within the questions.

When examined in terms of external information, the majority of the responses were found to be correct. Overall, 98.5% of the 200 responses were correct in terms of external information, with 96.31% of the correct responses and 97.29% of the incorrect responses based on correct external information. Only a small percentage (1.5%) contained incorrect external information. This indicates that the accuracy of responses based on external information is quite high.

Looking at the reasons for incorrect responses, 40.54% were due to logical errors, and 59.46% were due to knowledge errors. This indicates that knowledge errors are the primary cause of incorrect responses. Therefore, improving the accuracy of information could further enhance ChatGPT's response quality. Overall, ChatGPT's responses to KPSS questions have a high accuracy rate, and performance can be further improved by correcting minor knowledge errors.

4 Discussion

While there are many studies on artificial intelligence, studies on what ChatGPT can do with excellent technology are increasing day by day. There are many studies based on artificial intelligence in the literature. One of the areas where Chat GPT is being researched is education.

Although there are studies in the field of education in the literature, there are very few studies on the use of ChatGPT in social sciences. There are no studies on public finance and tax education. With this regular movement in the literature, in our study we asked "How successful (reliable) is ChatGPT in the field of public finance and can we use it in public finance education?" We looked for answers to the questions. For this study, the questions presented in the Public Personnel Selection Examination implemented in Türkiye, which aims to measure the financial knowledge of candidates taking the exam, were used as a data set.

In the results of working; It was observed that without guidance, ChatGPT-4o answered 81.5% of the questions correctly in the 200-question data set. When this rate is evaluated, it can be said that ChatGPT has a high success rate in the exam. On the other hand, when the answers given by ChatGPT were evaluated qualitatively, it was seen that ChatGPT made a logical inference regarding all the answers and used all the information in the question asked. On the other hand, it has been observed from time to time that ChatGPT uses incorrect information or obtains correct information but reaches the wrong conclusion.

ChatGPT's ability to make logical inferences, its complete evaluation of the information in the question, and its 81.5 percent accuracy rate actually show that ChatGPT can be used as a tool in public finance education. For example; will correctly answer most of the questions asked by students. There is a low probability that he will answer incorrectly.

When we evaluated the wrong questions, it was seen that 40.54% of the wrong answers were caused by logical errors and 59.46% were caused by information errors. This situation shows us that the logical capabilities of ChatGPT should be improved and the information accuracy should be increased. To solve this problem, further training of ChatGPT and increasing access to up-to-date resources can be considered as options.

According to the results of the study, considering the high success rate of ChatGPT, it can be said that ChatGPT can be used as a tool in courses and trainings in the field of Public Finance. Students can use ChatGPT to ask questions and get answers to topics they are curious about, such as fiscal theory, tax law, and fiscal policy, as if they were in front of an instructor. Additionally, by using ChatGPT's guidance, they can understand complex financial issues and get support in their homework and projects. They can direct questions about finance that they are hesitant to ask instructors to ChatGPT.

From another perspective, ChatGPT can also be used as a tool to facilitate the work of those who provide education on public finance. Thanks to ChatGPT, instructors can develop more effective and efficient strategies when creating lesson plans and preparing course materials. For example, using ChatGPT in visualizing presentations or case study explanations can contribute to a better understanding of courses by students. With these features, ChatGPT can make lessons more attractive, more entertaining and more instructive. In a way, this also increases the quality of public finance education.

On the other hand, in order for students and educators to benefit from such potential benefits of ChatGPT, they need to adapt to this technology and acquire the skills to use ChatGPT effectively and efficiently. In order to develop these skills, it is necessary to provide training to both trainers and students on the effective and efficient use of ChatGPT.

5 Conclusions

Success and answers obtained in ChatGPT's questions in the field of public finance in the study. The findings of the study show that ChatGPT has a very high success rate in answering details in the field of public finance. On the other hand, ChatGPT turned out to be very successful in grounding the answers it provided. In addition, ChatGPT provides answers using all information about the questions. However, regarding ChatGPT, sometimes the incoming external information was received incorrectly and sometimes it was sent incorrectly, although it seemed correct. This shows us that although ChatGPT has a high accuracy rate, there may be low rates of wrong answers. However, this inaccuracy is negligible considering its potential uses.

The high success of ChatGPT shows that it can be a helpful tool in financial education. As a matter of fact, thanks to this tool, you can ask questions about public finance and receive appropriate answers, ChatGPT can provide more descriptive and exemplary information about financial problems, and you can even choose to visualize a topic. With such use, the information of ChatGPT's financial departments and those that can be shared are evaluated. ChatGPT may also have positive contributions for supporters in the field of public finance. ChatGPT can be used to visualize training materials, making them more descriptive.

In our study, it was observed that ChatGPT sometimes gave incorrect answers. Some of these are due to flower errors and some are due to incorrect separation and use. The low rate of error will be even lower as ChatGPT is trained more and the data is constantly updated.

The effective use of AI tools such as ChatGPT should be promoted to students. This technology enables students to access information regarding finance theories and concepts, receive assistance with their assignments and projects, and prepare for examinations. Students' academic success can be positively influenced by the interactive learning and problem-solving opportunities offered by ChatGPT, which can improve their analytical thinking and problem-solving capacity. Education institutions should incorporate AI tools such as ChatGPT into their educational programs and provide support for the effective implementation of these technologies. ChatGPT should be encouraged for its use in the preparation of course materials, the monitoring of student performance, and the development of personalized learning paths at the education management level. Future research should further investigate the function of ChatGPT in education and concentrate on the most effective methods of utilizing this technology. In particular, future research should investigate the potential for ChatGPT to be more effectively implemented across a variety of educational levels and disciplines.

6 Limitations

This study contains several important limitations. First of all, only a 5-year data set from KPSS was used in the study. This may not give you a full idea of how ChatGPT may perform in the entire field of public finance or other exams. ChatGPT may be more successful or unsuccessful in other exams or in different periods. From this perspective, the generalizability of the results may be limited.

Secondly, the answers and accuracy of ChatGPT are closely related to the ChatGPT-4o's knowledge base and training level. Public Finance is a dynamic field that is constantly evolving due to its field of science. Therefore, when the knowledge base is not updated, the number of correct answers given in this area may decrease. On the other hand, the opposite can also happen.

Finally, in the section where we evaluated the quality of the questions in the study, only the logical inference of ChatGPT and the use of internal and external information were evaluated. Evaluations such as the clarity and depth of the answers and whether users would be satisfied with this answer were not made. Even though ChatGPT provides accurate answers and is reliable, this may affect its effect in education positively or negatively.

Bibliography

Arie Wahyu, P., S, R. M., Nugroho, S., & Jean Henry, R. (2023). Transforming Education and Learning through Chat GPT: A Systematic Literature Review. Jurnal Penelitian Pendidikan IPA. https://doi.org/10.29303/jppipa.v9i11.5468

Ausat, A. M. A., Massang, B., Efendi, M., Nofirman, N., & Riady, Y. (2023). Can chat GPT replace the role of the teacher in the classroom: A fundamental analysis. Journal on Education, 5(4), 16100–16106.

Borji, A. (2023). A categorical archive of chatgpt failures. arXiv preprint arXiv:2302.03494.

Farida Hanum, S., Babby, H., & Andre Hasudungan, L. (2023). The Analysis of Chat GPT Usage Impact on Learning Motivation among Scout Students. International Journal of Research and Review. https://doi.org/10.52403/ijrr.20230774

George, A. S., George, A. H., & Martin, A. G. (2023). A review of ChatGPT AI's impact on several business sectors. Partners Universal International Innovation Journal, 1(1), 9–23.

Gilson, A., Safranek, C. W., Huang, T., Socrates, V., Chi, L., Taylor, R. A., & Chartash, D. (2023). How Does ChatGPT Perform on the United States Medical Licensing Examination (USMLE)? The Implications of Large Language Models for Medical Education and Knowledge Assessment. JMIR Med Educ, 9, e45312. https://doi.org/10.2196/45312

Hakiki, M., Radinal, F., Agariadne Dwinggo, S., Ade, F., Popi, D., Kurniati, R., & Ayu Dewi, A. (2023). Exploring the impact of using Chat-GPT on student learning outcomes in technology learning: The comprehensive experiment. Advances in Mobile Learning Educational Research. https://doi.org/10.25082/amler.2023.02.013

Hatmanto, E. D., & Sari, M. I. (2023). Aligning Theory and Practice: Leveraging Chat GPT for Effective English Language Teaching and Learning. E3S Web of Conferences.

Jim, P., & Maretta, S. (2023). Assessing the Use of Open AI Chat-GPT in a University Department of Education. 2023 14th International Conference on Information, Intelligence, Systems & Applications (IISA), 1–4. https://doi.org/10.1109/IISA59645.2023.10345910

LLM failure archive (ChatGPT and beyond). (2024). Retrieved 10/07/2024 from https://github.com/giuven95/chatgpt-failures

Nazir, F., Jawed, S., & Tariq, S. M. (2023). Chat GPT and its potential role in medicine. J Pak Med Assoc, 73(12), 2509–2510. https://doi.org/10.47391/JPMA.9558

Olena, S., & Olga, S. (2023). The Use of Gpt Chat Among Students in Ukrainian Universities. Scientific Journal of Polonia University. https://doi.org/10.23856/5828

OpenAI. (2024). Hello GPT-4o. Retrieved 22/06/2024 from https://openai.com/index/hello-gpt-4o/

OSYM. (2013). Kamu Personel Seçme Sınavı (KPSS): Konu Dağılımları ve Puan Türleri (Public Personnel Selection Examination (KPSS): Subject Distribution and Score Types). Retrieved 12/07/2024 from https://www.osym.gov.tr/Eklenti/1619,kpss-tablo-1-konularin-dagilimipdf.pdf?0

OSYM. (2024). KPSS Çıkmış Sorular (KPSS Published Questions). Retrieved 25/05/2024 from https://www.osym.gov.tr/TR,15071/kpss-cikmis-sorular.html

Phillips, T., Saleh, A., Glazewski, K. D., Hmelo-Silver, C. E., Mott, B., & Lester, J. C. (2022). Exploring the use of GPT-3 as a tool for evaluating text-based collaborative discourse. Companion Proceedings of the 12th, 54.

Sallam, M. (2023). ChatGPT utility in healthcare education, research, and practice: systematic review on the promising perspectives and valid concerns. Healthcare.

Som, S. B. (2023). The Function of chat GPT in Social Media: According to chat GPT. SSRN Electronic Journal. https://doi.org/10.2139/ssrn.4405389

Surameery, N. M. S., & Shakor, M. Y. (2023). Use Chat GPT to Solve Programming Bugs. International Journal of Information technology and Computer Engineering(31), 17–22. https://doi.org/10.55529/ijitc.31.17.22

Tajik, E., & Tajik, F. (2023). A comprehensive Examination of the potential application of Chat GPT in Higher Education Institutions. TechRxiv. Preprint, 1–10.

William, C.-G., Carlos Oscar, L., & Bonardi, M. C. (2022). Chat GPT: a promising tool for academic editing. Data & Metadata. https://doi.org/10.56294/dm202223

Yang, L. (2023). The impact of CHAT GPT on English online courses. Advances in Educational Technology and Psychology. https://doi.org/10.23977/aetp.2023.071010

Diplomacy as a Public Good: Case of Black Sea Grain Initiative

Sedef OLUKLULU[1]

1 Introduction

Diplomacy is the primary alternative to relying on force or covert methods in government execution. The degree to which a nation uses its might to peacefully resolve conflicts between states is known as diplomacy (Alier et. al. 2022). Diplomacy aims to enhance the power and influence of the state, nation, or organization it represents by promoting its interests in relation to others. In order to achieve this objective, diplomatic efforts strive to optimize the benefits of a community while avoiding the potential dangers and costs associated with the use of physical coercion, and ideally, without generating any negative feelings or animosity (Hart and Siniver, 2020). In order for other countries to consider a country's policies as legitimate, it is necessary for that country to possess alternative power potential, as well as economic and military strength. The achievement of a nation's public diplomacy is also contingent upon the integrity and efficacy of its policies (Kalın, p. 6–9, 2011).

The Russian invasion into Ukraine has resulted in significant human grief, while also inflicting harm on global commerce (Ahn, at. Al., 2023). The invasion has impacted not only commerce but also the expansion of the gross domestic product (Liadze et al., 2022), the provision of a sufficient and reliable food supply (Abay et al., 2022), and the performance of the stock market (Ahmed et al., 2022). Due to the trade commodities being essential nutrients, middle-income countries experinced price volatility while low-income countries suffered from hunger.

The primary objective of diplomacy is to sustain peace by avoiding conflicts. Based on the report (GRFC, 2024), in 2023, a total of 281.6 million individuals in 59 countries/territories experienced significant levels of acute food insecurity, necessitating immediate aid (Çolakoğlu, 2024). Figure 1 clearly demonstrates that the main cause of food insecurity is disputes between states or within a nation among different groups for the year 2022.

[1] Anadolu University, Faculty of Economics and Administrative Sciences, Public Finance Department, sedefcelik@anadolu.edu.tr, ORCID ID: 0000-0002-1335-7880.

According to UN data, the number of people impacted by hunger in 2021 was 828 million, which is 46 million higher than the previous year and 150 million higher than in 2019 (WHO Report, Accessed: 10.07.2024 https://www.who.int/news/item/06-07-2022-un-report--global-hunger-numbers-rose-to-as-many-as-828-million-in-2021). Approximately one-tenth of the global population is currently experiencing hunger, which falls significantly short of the target to eradicate hunger by the end of 2030 as outlined in the sustainable development goals.

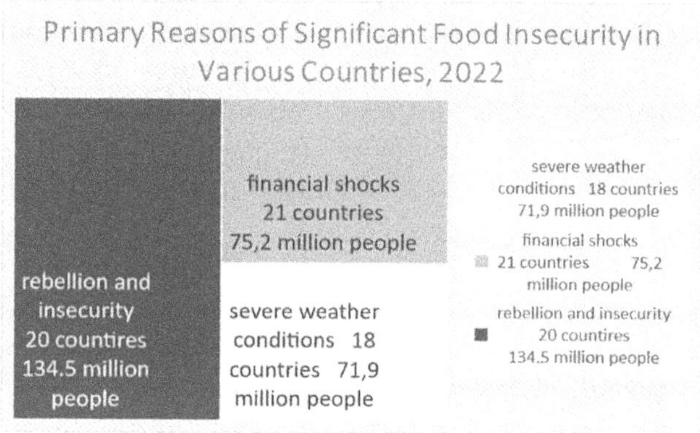

Fig. 1: Global Report on Food Crises (GRFC), 2024.

The Head of NATO stated that "Russia is using hunger as a weapon of war against Ukraine and to create division and further instability among the rest of the World". (Accessed: 01.07.2024, https://www.nato.int/cps/en/natohq/news_209450.htm?selectedLocale=en)

After a crisis is successfully handled by diplomatic processes it is impossible to prevent individuals and communities from experiencing the advantages of the resultings. The cost of an additional individual or nation benefiting from the peace and tranquility brought by diplomacy is equal to zero. Nevertheless, it is crucial to recognize that wars invariably lead to catastrophic and disastrous consequences, which include substantial costs that no nation can exclude themselves from in the contemporary era. The outcomes entail widespread destruction, forced displacement, increasing social turmoil, devastated economies, hunger poverty, huge economic setbacks, large-scale migration, and substantial loss of life. The primary goal of diplomatic efforts is supposed to be the avoidance of war. Diplomacy is a highly efficient approach to communication and conflict resolution in global affairs, free from any form of racial, sectarian, or linguistic bias within the international community. Based on the early contribution of Musgrave and Samuelson, diplomacy can be identified as a public good due to its non-excludable and non-rivalrous nature.

The goal of this study is to define the Black Sea grain initiative as a public good with unrivaled and non-excludable effects.

2 Conceptional Framework

Non-exclusion and non-rivalrous in their consumpiton are widely acknowledged as an essential feature of public goods (Yılmaz, 2010). In the context of diplomacy, public goods has two primary attributes: non-excludability, meaning it is impossible to prevent anyone from consuming them, and non-rivalry, indicating that consumption by one person does not diminish the availability for others. The Black Sea Grain Initiative is a diplomatic endeavor aimed at mitigating food scarcity and price fluctuations through international trade, with its impact extending globally. There is no competition among those who benefit from the stability of the price and availability of grain that comes with the Initiative. Given that grain is an essential dietary component, the economic status of individuals does not alter their susceptibility to fluctuations in prices resulting from the Russian-Ukrainian conflict. The marginal cost of adding an additional individual benefiting from the initiative is zero, and it cannot be excluded from the service, regardless of whether it directly contributes to the diplomatic budget.

Externalities lead to market inefficiency in resource allocation. According to most Keynesian welfare economists (such as Samuelson, Baumol, and Pigou), market failure is defined as the occurrence of inefficient outcomes in markets. The market failure theory has challenges when used as the foundation for governmental intervention. Since there is no empirical evidence to support the existence of perfect knowledge, completeness, and absence of transaction costs, these conditions have not been proven (Mazzucato, 2024, p. 6). One cause of market failure is externalities. Public goods that have positive externalities are characterized by a lack of investment due to the challenges of capturing private benefits caused by their significant spill-over effects. In situations with positive externalities, there is a lack of production or inadequate provision due to private actors not fully benefiting from the good societal outcomes of their actions. Furthermore, the private sector does not perceive diplomacy services as profitable. The free-riding problem is a result of the positive externality, which is the fact that individuals who are not engaged in the production and consumption process of diplomatic services also benefit. The private sector is unable to achieve a diplomatic success like the Black Sea grain initiative due to the inability to construct a finance mechanism to cover its costs, as exclusion is not feasible. Consequently, the expenses of diplomatic services are compensated by taxes, and they are rendered publicly.

3 Case of Black Sea Grain Deal

The invasion of Ukraine by Russia has resulted in the displacement of millions of people and has caused significant disruptions to agricultural output and trade in one of the world's vital exporting regions. In addition to the acute human misery and loss of lives and livelihoods in Ukraine, the crisis between Russia and Ukraine is severely damaging global agricultural markets and posing a threat to global food security (Abay et al, 2023).

The inclusion of both input supply and food processing companies in the agricultural sector leads to an increase in its contribution to the Ukrainian economy, accounting for around 22 percent of GDP. Ukraine ranks as the fifth largest worldwide wheat exporter, with a 10 percent market share from 2016/17 to 2020/21 (FAO, Accessed: 01.07.2024 https://www.fao.org/family-farming/detail/en/c/1476928/). Russia and Ukraine have been responsible for exporting 34 percent of the world's traded wheat, 17 percent of maize, and 73 percent of sunflower oil in recent years (FAOSTAT, Accessed: 01.07.2024 https://www.fao.org/faostat/en/#data/FBS). Türkiye emerged as the leading global importer of sunflowers in the 2020–2021 season, with 32.4 percent of total sunflower imports (Independent Türkçe, Accessed: 01.07.2024 https://www.indyturk.com/)

The Russian invasion of Ukraine led to a directly 53% rise in wheat prices. As a result of the increasing prices of essential food items, a total of 1.6 billion individuals across the globe have been declared lacking the necessary financial means to afford them (Accessed: 15.07.2024 (https://www.economist.com/leaders/2022/05/19/the-coming-food-catastrophe). Following the invasion, citizens in Istanbul rushed to the markets to mitigate the potential depletion of sunflower oil reserves and the subsequent price surge. In many marketplaces, the sale of oil was restricted to a single unit (Independent Türkçe, Accessed: 01.07.2024 https://www.indyturk.com). This was an instance of individuals experiencing Keynes' animal spirit when they acted without rational decision-making and hurriedly flocked to the marketplaces to buy as much as possible, even if they had no intention of consuming it, resulting in long queues.

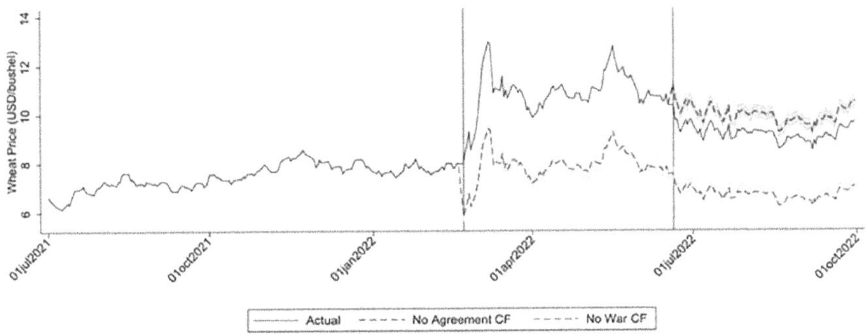

(a) Impacts on world wheat prices

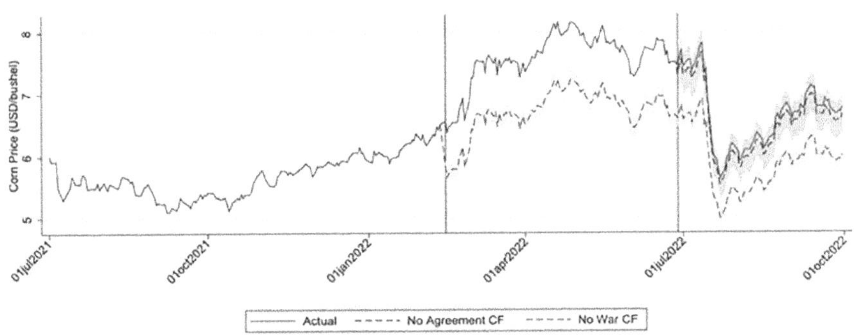

(b) Impacts on world corn prices

Fig. 2: The path that corn and wheat prices can follow under different scenarios and the current situation: (Poursina et al., 2024).

As it is shown in Figure 2 the wheat and corn prices went up until the Initiative. Between two vertical lines, the actual prices reached the highest level. It can be seen that real prices decrease after the second red line when the initiative is established.

The Black Sea Grain Initiative was a treaty concluded among Russia, Ukraine, Türkiye, and the United Nations (UN) in Istanbul on July 22, 2022, amidst Russia's military incursion into Ukraine. The objective of the agreement is to guarantee the secure transit of commercial vessels along the humanitarian maritime route (UN Black Sea Grain Initiative Coordination Centre Accessed: 15.07.2024 https://www.un.org/en/black-sea-grain-initiative/update-15-july-2023). The pact remained in effect for a duration of 120 days. The duration has been prolonged on four occasions, with the latest extension set to expire in July 2023. (UN JCC, 2022 Accessed: 15.07.2024 https://reliefweb.int/report/turkiye/joint-coordination-centre-opens-istanbul-facilitate-safe-export-commercial-foodstuffs-and-fertilizers-ukrainian-ports). The grain agreement is definitely a concrete outcome of Ankara's mediation efforts and highlights the potential of Türkiye's regional leadership in the Black Sea region (Isachenko, 2023, p25).

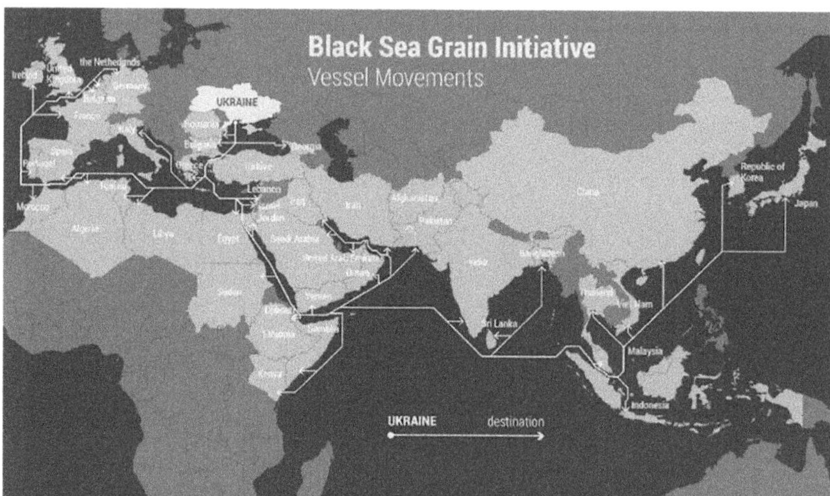

Fig. 3: Ship Route of carrying grain and foodstuff Accessed: 01.07.2024 https://www.un.org/en/black-sea-grain-initiative/vessel-movements).

Within the duration of nearly one year that the Initiative was in effect, a grand total of 32.8 million tons of grain and groceries were exported from the three designated Ukrainian ports as it is shown in Figure 3.

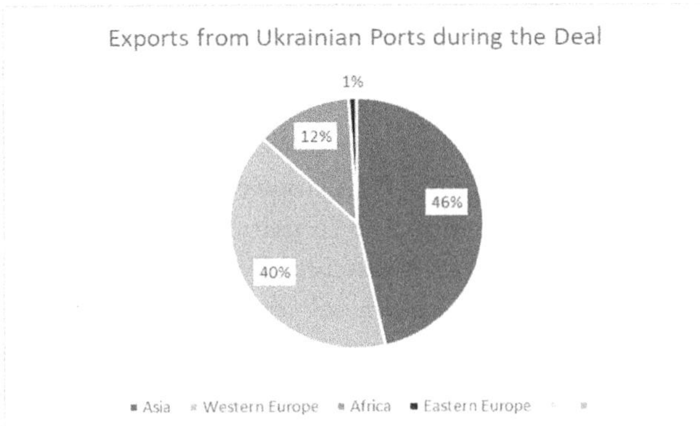

Fig. 4: The distribution of products exported from Ukrainian ports to different continents during the agreement (https://www.un.org/en/black-sea-grain-initiative/update-15-july-2023).

Grain and other agricultural products have been shipped to 45 nations over three continents, with 46% going to Asia, 40% to Western Europe, 12% to Africa, and 1% to Eastern Europe as it is shown Figure 4. Out of the two primary commodities, 90% of the corn and 60% of the wheat have been shipped to high and upper-middle-income nations as part of the deal. On the other hand, 10% of the corn and 40% of the wheat were shipped out to nations with low or lower middle incomes (United Nation BSDI Joint Coordination Centre Accessed: 15.07.2024 www.un.org/en/black-sea-grain-initiative/data).

The data clearly indicates that both low-income and high-income countries imported agricultural products from Ukraine as part of the agreement. The head of the UN, Mr. Guterres, emphasized that there is a strong need for Ukrainian and Russian food as well as fertilizers in order to stabilize markets and ensure global food security when the agreement expired without renewal (UN Black Sea Grain Initiative Joint Coordination Centre Accessed: 15.07.2024 https://www.un.org/en/black-sea-grain-initiative/achievements).

4 The key role of Türkiye in the grain initiative

The Black Sea was an Ottoman Lake for a period of three hundred years until the execution of the Küçük Kaynarca treaty in 1774, by the transfer of Crimea to Russia (Achilleos et. al., 2022, p. 70). While the Treaty of Lausanne did determine modern-day Türkiye's borders, it failed to grant Turkish authority over the straits. The accord required the establishment of an international commission to oversee ship traffic and the demilitarization of the territory surrounding the straits. Türkiye was able to reclaim control of the Bosphorus, and the Dardanelles only after the 1936 Montreux Treaty (Olszowska, 2023). Türkiye's opinion on cooperation and security in the Black Sea is that this matter pertains to the countries located in the Black Sea region. Türkiye is primarily aiming to restrict the influence of external powers in the region, even the NATO Alliance (Lancaster, p. 5 -article 22- 2023). In contrast to Türkiye's attitude, Romania and Bulgaria, both Black Sea countries and members of the European Union, have a markedly different perspective on Black Sea cooperation. They demand for stronger security relations with NATO in the Black Sea region (Hodges et. al, 2022). Undoubtedly, Türkiye's substantial military and naval power allows it to assume a leading position in the region. Following its participation in the Black Sea Grain Initiative as a primary peacekeeper, Türkiye's leadership role was further enhanced (Kakabadze, p. 1, 2023).

Ankara's unique geographic location, its membership in NATO, and President Erdoğan's proactive approach have enabled Türkiye to establish itself as a vigorous actor in the conflict in Ukraine (Isachenko, 2023, p. 24). The European Commission stated that Türkiye's positive role was crucial in enabling the development of the grain corridor, stating that "the deal… would not have been possible without the constructive role of Türkiye." (European Commissin, 2022, p. 8). The signing of the deal in Istanbul averted a potential food crisis, and our President's involvement in the process was acknowledged by numerous international stakeholders (Cumhurbaşkanlığı İletişim Başkanlığı, 2023, p. 162).

5 Conclusion

Countless individuals worldwide especially from the Horn of Africa are experiencing food insecurity, while consumers are grappling with a widespread economic problem related to the cost of living. The global risk assessment identifies the cost-of-living issues as one of the most pressing threats that will impact both low-income countries and the world as a whole in 2 years term (WEF, 2024, p. 7). Apart from the loss of thousands of lives, the effects of war spread all over the world. The conflict between Russia and Ukraine in 2022 resulted in significant increases in global food prices and remains an ongoing vulnerability to food security (Global Hunger Index, 2023, p. 9). Nations that were not involved in the conflict also experienced shortages or price increases in essential nutrients. This phenomenon is commonly referred to as a negative externality in the field of public finance theory. Negative externalities result in overproduction, when market prices fail to completely account for the detrimental costs imposed on society (Batabyal, p. 4., 2023). Countries who are not involved in the war experience the burden of rising grain prices. On the contrary, the Grain Initiative has resulted in a positive externality by ensuring price stability and increased supply of agricultural goods. Türkiye's diplomatic endeavors have had favorable outcomes for all countries through the establishment of a grain corridor.

A commodity or service must possess both the characteristics of non-excludability and non-rivalry in order to be classified as a public good. The success of Türkiye as a consequence of diplomacy benefits all countries, as the food products subject to the agreement are fundamental foodstuffs. Türkiye does not claim the expenses it has incurred for the grain corridor agreement from the countries that benefit from it. Due to Türkiye's inability to demand payment for the diplomatic services it has offered for the grain corridor from other recipient nations, the grain corridor diplomacy possesses the characteristic of being a non-excludable public benefit. Countries that derive advantages from the grain corridor agreement and evade the economic and social turmoil resulting from grain scarcity and price hikes are not rivals to one another. The grain initiative, characterized as Türkiye's diplomatic triumph, is a public good.

Bibliography

Abay, K. A., Breisinger, C., Glauber, J., Kurdi, S., Laborde, D., & Siddig, K. (2023). The Russia-Ukraine war: Implications for global and regional food security and potential policy responses. Global Food Security, 36, 100675.

Achilleos, S., Rakić, I. Č., Chen, H. H., Filipović, E. O., Frazier, A., & Stuczynski, C. (2022). Medieval and early Modern Europe and the World.

Ahmed, S., Hasan, M. M., & Kamal, M. R. (2022). Russia–Ukraine crisis: The effects on the European stock market. EuropeanFinancial Management, 1–41.

Ahn, S., Kim, D., & Steinbach, S. (2023). The impact of the Russian invasion of Ukraine on grain and oilseed trade. Agribusiness, 39(1), 291–299.

Alier, D. G., & Bill, D. B. A. (2022). The Role Of Dıplomacy In Foreıgn Polıcy Formulatıon. Ijrdo - Journal of Social Science and Humanities Research, 7(6), 150–167.

Batabyal, A. (2023). The Theory of Externalities, Munich Personal RePEc Archive, MPRA Paper No. 119233.

Cumhurbaşkanlığı İletişim Başkanlığı, (2023). Türkiye'nin istikrara katkısı: barış için çok yönlü diplomasi, Cumhurbaşkanlığı İletişim Başkanlığı Yayınları, İstanbul.

Çolakoğlu, E. (2024). Food Insecurity in the Middle East, the Black Sea Grain Initiative, and Türkiye. Güvenlik Stratejileri Dergisi, 20(47), 63–82.

European Commission (2022). Commission Staff Working Document Türkiye 2022 Report, Brussels, SWD (2022) 333 final.

FSIN and Global Network Against Food Crises. (2024). Global Report on Food Crises. Rome. https://www.fsinplatform.org/grfc2024

Hart, D., & Siniver, A. (2020). The meaning of diplomacy. International Negotiation, 26(2), 159–183.

Hodges, B., Horrell, S., & Kuz, I. (2022). Russia's militarization of the Black Sea: Implications for the United States and NATO. Center for European Policy Analysis, September, 22.

Isachenko, Daria (2023). Turkey in the Black Sea region: Ankara's reactions to the war in Ukraine against the background of regional dynamics and global confrontation, SWP Research Paper, No. 12/2023, Stiftung Wissenschaft und Politik (SWP), Berlin, https://doi.org/10.18449/2023RP12

Kakabadze, M. (2023). The Black Sea Grain Initiative: analysing the emerging, implementation and challenges.

Kalın, İ. (2011). Soft power and public diplomacy in Turkey. Perceptions: Journal of International Affairs, 16(3), 5–23.

Lancaster, M. (2023). Troubled Waters–How Russia's War in Ukraine Changes Black Sea Security. NATO Parliamentary Assembly, 2023–05.

Liadze, I., Macchiarelli, C., MortimerLee, P., & Juanino, P. S. (2022). The economic costs of the Russia–Ukraine conflict.NIESR Policy Paper 32.

Mazzucato, M. (2024). Governing the economics of the common good: from correcting market failures to shaping collective goals. Journal of Economic Policy Reform, 27(1), 1–24.

Olszowska, K. W. (2023). Turkey forever balances between East and West. Nowa Polityka Wschodnia, 37(2), 239–255.

Poursina, D., Aleks Schaefer, K., Hilburn, S., & Johnson, T. (2024). Economic impacts of the Black Sea grain initiative. Journal of Agricultural Economics, 75(1), 457–464.

von Grebmer, K., J. Bernstein, W. Geza, M. Ndlovu, M. Wiemers, L. Reiner, M. Bachmeier, A. Hanano, R. Ní Chéilleachair, T. Sheehan, C. Foley, S. Gitter, G. Larocque, and H. Fritschel (2023). 2023 Global Hunger Index: The Power of Youth in Shaping Food Systems. Bonn: Welthungerhilfe (WHH); Dublin: Concern Worldwide.

World Economic Forum (2024). The Global Risks Report 2024, 19th edition. ISBN: 978-2-940631-64-3

Yılmaz, B. E. (2010). Barış ve Güvenlik: Küresel Kamu Malı Olarak Sunumu ve Finansman Mekanizmaları. Anadolu University Journal of Social Sciences/Anadolu Üniversitesi Sosyal Bilimler Dergisi, 10(1).

Internet Sources

NATO news: https://www.nato.int/cps/en/natohq/news_209450.htm?selectedLocale=en

FAO https://www.fao.org/family-farming/detail/en/c/1476928/

IndependentTürkçe https://www.indyturk.com/node/479751/ekonomi%CC%87/sava%C5%9F-ithalat%C4%B1-durdurdu-t%C3%BCrkiye-ya%C4%9Fs%C4%B1z-kalabilir

Independent Türkçe https://www.indyturk.com/node/482791/haber/tmo-%C3%B6n%C3%BCnde-ya%C4%9F-kuyru%C4%9Fu-stoklar-t%C3%BCkendi-t%C3%BCm-%C3%BCr%C3%BCnlere-s%C4%B1n%C4%B1rlama-getirildi

UN Joint Coordination Centre, https://reliefweb.int/report/turkiye/joint-coordination-centre-opens-istanbul-facilitate-safe-export-commercial-foodstuffs-and-fertilizers-ukrainian-ports

UN Black Sea Grain Initiative Joint Coordination Centre, https://www.un.org/en/black-sea-grain-initiative

WHO, World Healt Organization https://www.who.int/news/item/06-07-2022-un-report--global-hunger-numbers-rose-to-as-many-as-828-million-in-2021

The Economist "The coming food catastrope (May 19,2022)", https://www.economist.com/leaders/2022/05/19/the-coming-food-catastrophe

How do External Shocks Affect the Share of Foreign Investors in Turkish Domestic Debt Stock?

Süleyman KASAL[1]

1 Introduction

Emerging countries are highly exposed to global conditions (Canova (2005); Uribe and Yue (2006); Ciarlone et al. (2009); Akıncı (2013)). Therefore, a country's economic and fiscal variables are highly sensitive to global conditions. Therefore, external conditions should be monitored in the implementation of fiscal and monetary policies. Because the success of these policies also depends on minimizing the effects of external shocks.

Examining and analyzing the investor base is important for both debtors and creditors. Indeed, Arslanalp and Tsuda (2014:4) argue that the investor base of sovereign debt is important for three reasons: i) it affects the cost of borrowing, ii) it affects external funding risk, iii) if domestic banks have high exposure to sovereign debt, it creates potentially harmful sovereign-bank linkages and threatens domestic financial stability[2]. According to CBRT (2018), if a debt instrument is concentrated in a single buyer, an adverse shock to this buyer will reduce the demand for that debt instrument and cause the structure of the debt stock by debt instruments to change. Moreover, sudden changes in the investor base have adverse effects on government bond

1 Anadolu University, FEAS, Department of Public Finance, skasal@anadolu.edu.tr, ORCID ID 0000-0001-8409-1090

2 In the year 2000, Turkish banks were characterized by substantial holdings of government securities within their portfolios. Notably, Demirbank exemplified this trend, sustaining its portfolio primarily through short-term borrowing (Özatay, 2009:91). In the banking sector, Demirbank was commonly referred to as a "bond bank" (Somçağ, 2006:107). However, due to an inherent maturity mismatch, the institution was unable to meet its financial obligations, resulting in its seizure by the state in December 2000. This event illustrates that a bank with a significant proportion of government securities in its assets can induce systemic risk. For a more comprehensive analysis of Demirbank, see TMSF (2009).

yields. Therefore, analyzing the investor base of government debt is critical for these reasons.

Starting with the idea that the investor base of government debt is important, our study tries to address the following questions: i) What is the importance of foreign investors' share in government debt in Türkiye? ii) How do external shocks such as geopolitical, economic and financial uncertainties affect the share of foreign investors in Türkiye's debt stock? iii) What policies should be implemented in terms of debt management to diversify the investor base and mitigate the negative impact of external shocks? The main motivation of the study is based on these three questions. The study continues with the theoretical background and literature section, followed by a description of the data and methodology. The next section presents the results of the study and this chapter concludes with a conclusion.

2 Theoretical Background and Literature

Türkiye is an emerging economy and the Turkish economy is highly sensitive to global economic, financial and geopolitical conditions (Kasal (2023a); Kasal (2023b); Kasal (2024)). This sensitivity is related to the extent to which investors' risk appetite affects the size of capital flows. The share of government bonds denominated in local currency gradually increased as a result of increased activity from foreign investors in domestic bond markets between 2007 and 2017, according to Köse et al. (2021:160). However, this made these economies more vulnerable to sudden shifts in investor confidence. In particular, when global conditions are calm, portfolio investment in the country increases, which has a positive impact on borrowing rates, and vice versa when global conditions deteriorate. As a matter of fact, while fund flows simultaneously trigger economic growth, they also increase the risks and threats that may lead to a crisis, and create negative effects on growth and income distribution (Kazgan, 2017:202).

Turkish central government debt stock share held by foreign investors and the yield on 5-year government bonds are displayed in Figure 1 (a). Figure 1 (b) shows the distribution of central government debt stock by holders. In other words, Figure 1 (b) shows the investor base within the debt stock.

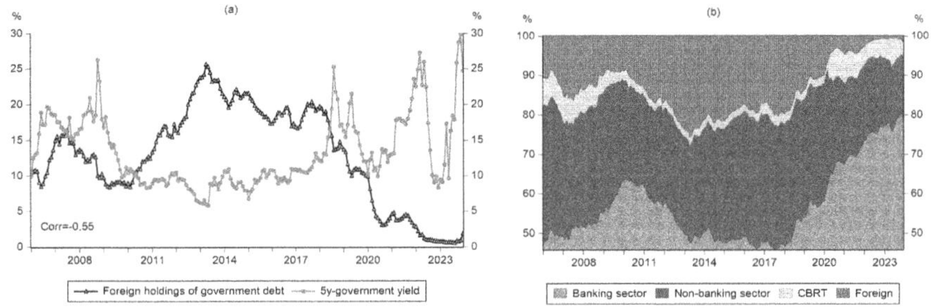

Fig. 1: Composition of Domestic Debt Stock by Holders.

Figure 1 (a) shows the negative relationship between the two variables. Especially in Türkiye, interest rates fall when the share of foreign investors in the central government debt stock increases. This is a standard relationship. This is because there is a negative relationship between bond prices and interest rates. When investor demand for bonds increases, interest rates fall. Figure 1 (b) shows the distribution of central government debt stock by holders in the 2006–2023 period. Figure 1(b) includes the banking sector, non-banking sector, central bank and foreign investors. In this period, the biggest change occurred in the banking sector and foreign investors. The share of the banking sector and foreign investors in the debt stock have high standard deviation values. This indicates that the values of the variables are spread over a wide range around the mean and thus have a high variance. The non-banking sector and the CBRT have lower standard deviation values. This indicates that the variables are spread over a narrower range around the mean and thus have a lower variance[3].

The literature includes numerous studies that investigate the impact of the investor base on the debt market from various perspectives. These studies analyze both the positive and negative effects that changes in the investor base can have on the debt market.

Andritzky (2012) analyzed the effects of investor base on returns in G-20 and Eurozone countries. The results of the study prove that an increase in the share of non-residents decreases returns. The authors point out that this effect

3 The standard deviations of the shares of the banking and non-banking sectors, foreign investors and the CBRT in the central government debt stock for the 2006–2023 period are 9.67, 4.95, 6.84 and 1.91, respectively.

is more pronounced in Eurozone countries. Arslanalp and Poghosyan (2014) investigate how changes in the investor base in advanced economies affect 10-year bond yields. The authors draw attention to the difference between core and peripheral countries. In other words, changes in the investor base affect the 10-year bond returns of peripheral countries more. Broner et al. (2014) design a simple sovereign risk model based on creditor discrimination and the crowding-out effect for the troubled countries of the Eurozone. Fundamentally, the authors conclude that creditor discrimination leads to an increase in domestic debt issuance, resulting in a crowding-out effect. This process occurs through the credit allocation mechanism, wherein increased purchases of domestic debt diminish investment and growth. During this period, sovereign spreads also increased. Yılmaz and Yücel (2016) analyze the effects of the share of foreign investors in the central government debt stock on the level and volatility of long-term interest rates in Türkiye. The results indicate that an increase in the share of foreign investors decreases long-term interest rates and increases interest rate volatility. Duyvesteyn et al. (2016) examined the relationship between political risk and bond prices in advanced and emerging economies. The results of the study indicate that countries with poor political risk ratings have lower credit ratings and spreads. Broner et al. (2022) investigated how the share of public debt held by foreigners affects the size of fiscal multipliers for the postwar period in the US and for 17 advanced economies. The study indicates that fiscal multipliers grow when the share of foreigners in public debt increases (access to foreign savings increases). Therefore, fiscal expansions are more effective when access to foreign savings increases. As can be seen from the literature, changes in the share of holders of public debt have various effects. Our study distinguishes itself from previous research by analyzing the impact of uncertainty on foreign holders of the debt stock and examining how this influence affects inflation expectations and exchange rates.

3 Data and Methods

In the study, we utilize indicators of geopolitical uncertainty, economic uncertainty, and financial uncertainty, as well as the USD/₺ exchange rate, 12-month inflation expectations, the proportion of foreign investors holding government domestic debt securities, and the 5-year government bond yield.

The economic uncertainty index is obtained from Ahir et al. (2022) and the geopolitical uncertainty index is obtained from Caldara and Iacovielli (2022). The volatility index (VIX for short) is used as an indicator of financial uncertainty. VIX data is obtained from the Federal Reserve Economic Data. USD/₺ and inflation expectations for the next 12 months are obtained from the CBRT-EVDS database, while the foreign investor ratio is obtained from the Ministry of Treasury and Finance. 5-year government bond yield data is obtained from Thomson Reuters DataStream. Descriptive statistics of the level values of the variables are given in the table below.

Tab. 1: Descriptive Statistics

	Geopolitical Uncertainty	Economic Uncertainty	Financial Uncertainty	Inflation Expectations	USD/₺	Foreign Holders	Government Yield
Mean	96.718	167.302	19.689	11.346	5.042	12.900	13.296
Med.	90.591	149.102	17.517	7.575	2.312	13.521	11.195
Max.	318.954	431.564	62.668	45.280	29.074	25.673	29.840
Min.	58.420	49.224	10.125	5.480	1.176	0.544	5.780
Std. Dev.	27.674	77.110	8.600	8.987	5.989	6.840	4.970
Ske.	3.394	0.733	2.271	2.389	2.305	-0.300	0.945
Kurt.	23.258	2.939	10.035	7.677	7.855	2.051	3.349
Jarque-Bera	4108.435	19.380	631.118	402.533	403.599	11.354	33.278

Upon analyzing the means and standard deviations, it is observed that economic uncertainty exhibits the highest mean and standard deviation among the variables. Conversely, the USD/₺ exchange rate has the lowest mean, while the government bond yield displays the lowest standard deviation. The table further reveals that the distributions of all variables deviate from normality, with several showing abnormal distributions characterized by high skewness and kurtosis values.

The correlation relations between the variables used in the study are also shown in the figure. There is a statistically significant negative correlation between the share of foreign investors in central government debt stock and uncertainty variables. There is also a statistically significant negative correlation between foreign investors' share in central government debt stock and government bond yield, exchange rate and inflation expectations. The correlation coefficient results show that there is a statistically significant negative correlation between the share of foreign investors and other variables.

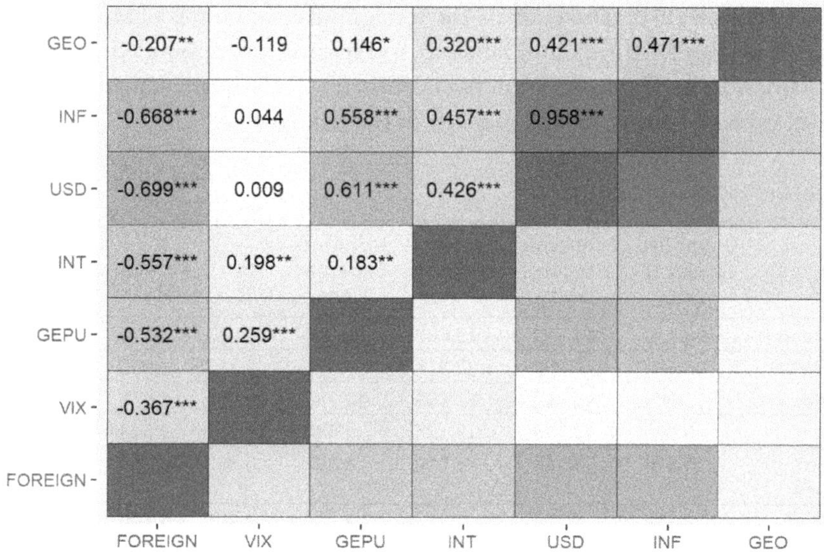

Fig. 2: Correlations.
Note: ***, **, and * denote significance levels at 1%, 5% and 10%.

In this study, all variables, except for inflation expectations and the interest rate variable, are transformed to their logarithmic levels. A seven-variable, four-lag level-VAR model is estimated for Türkiye, covering the monthly period from 2006 to 2023. The basic model is as follows:

$$y_t = \alpha + \sum^{p} A_j y_{t-j} + \varepsilon_t \tag{1}$$

$$y_t = [U_t^G, U_t^E, U_t^F, INFEXP_t, USDTRY_t, F_t, GY_t] \tag{2}$$

$$\epsilon_t = [\epsilon_t^{U^G}, \epsilon_t^{U^E}, \epsilon_t^{U^F}, \epsilon_t^{INFEXP}, \epsilon_t^{USDTRY}, \epsilon_t^{F}, \epsilon_t^{GY}] \tag{3}$$

y_t is the vector of variables consisting of observations at time t. α is the vector of constant terms. A_j is the coefficient matrix for the *jth* lag period. ε_t is the vector of error terms. In a standard VAR model, all variables are endogenous and all variables are assumed to affect each other. However, the variables we use in our study are of two different types: endogenous and exogenous. Therefore, we need to add some restrictions to our model.

In this model, uncertainties are assumed to be exogenous, meaning they are not simultaneously influenced by other variables in the Turkish economy. Consequently, uncertainties operate independently of other variables, necessitating the addition of constraints to the VAR model. Specifically, uncertainty variables are treated as exogenous; they impact other variables but are not themselves affected by them. As a result, zero restrictions are applied to matrix A in this model:

$$A_j = \begin{bmatrix} A_{11}^{(j)} & 0 & 0 & 0 & 0 & 0 & 0 \\ A_{21}^{(j)} & A_{22}^{(j)} & A_{23}^{(j)} & 0 & 0 & 0 & 0 \\ A_{31}^{(j)} & A_{32}^{(j)} & A_{33}^{(j)} & 0 & 0 & 0 & 0 \\ A_{41}^{(j)} & A_{42}^{(j)} & A_{43}^{(j)} & A_{44}^{(j)} & A_{45}^{(j)} & A_{46}^{(j)} & A_{47}^{(j)} \\ A_{51}^{(j)} & A_{52}^{(j)} & A_{53}^{(j)} & A_{54}^{(j)} & A_{55}^{(j)} & A_{56}^{(j)} & A_{57}^{(j)} \\ A_{61}^{(j)} & A_{62}^{(j)} & A_{63}^{(j)} & A_{64}^{(j)} & A_{65}^{(j)} & A_{66}^{(j)} & A_{67}^{(j)} \\ A_{71}^{(j)} & A_{72}^{(j)} & A_{73}^{(j)} & A_{74}^{(j)} & A_{75}^{(j)} & A_{76}^{(j)} & A_{77}^{(j)} \end{bmatrix} \tag{4}$$

In the VAR model, uncertainties are considered exogenous to the Turkish economy, meaning they immediately impact all variables while remaining unaffected by them. Another constraint pertains to the interactions among the uncertainties. Specifically, economic and financial uncertainties influence each other simultaneously, whereas geopolitical uncertainty does not follow this pattern. Geopolitical uncertainties have the potential to affect economic and financial uncertainties, but the reverse is not true. Lastly, a standard Cholesky decomposition is employed to analyze these shocks.

4 Analysis Results

4.1 Impulse-Response Results

This section presents the results of the impulse-response analysis. The effects of geopolitical, economic and financial uncertainties are shown in Figure 3,

Figure 4, and Figure 5, respectively. Figure 3 shows the effects of geopolitical uncertainties on various economic variables.

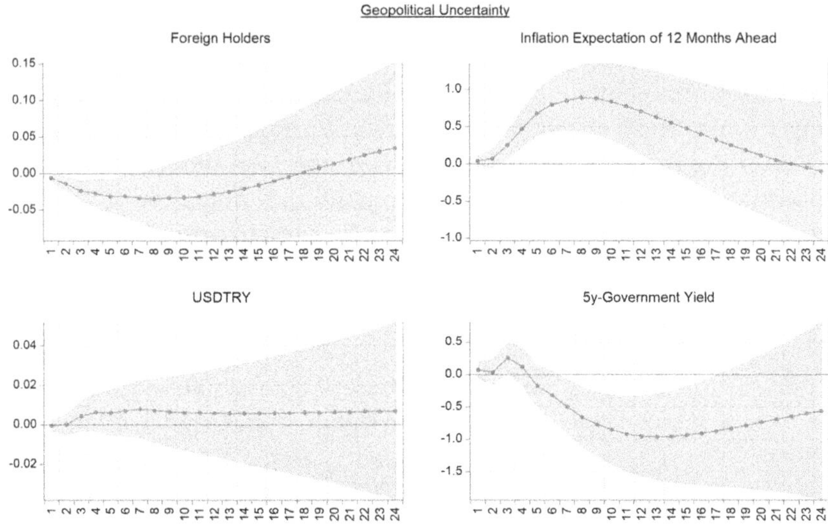

Fig. 3: Effect on variables of geopolitical uncertainty shock.

Note: The graphs showing the effects of geopolitical uncertainties on various economic variables are obtained with 1000 replications using Monte Carlo method with a 68% confidence interval.

Geopolitical uncertainties initially have significant effects on economic indicators, but these effects stabilize over time. Foreign investors' holdings of government domestic debt securities decline as uncertainty increases, but tend to increase again as uncertainty decreases. Inflation expectations for the next 12 months rise at the onset of geopolitical risks, but normalize over time. The USD/₺ exchange rate initially increases, but stabilizes over time. 5-year government bond yields, on the other hand, fall during periods of uncertainty and rise again as the uncertainty subsides. This can be interpreted as investors turning to safe havens and yields falling during periods of uncertainty, while risk appetite increases and yields rise as uncertainty decreases.

Figure 4 shows the effects of an economic uncertainty shock on various economic variables. Foreign investors react negatively to the economic

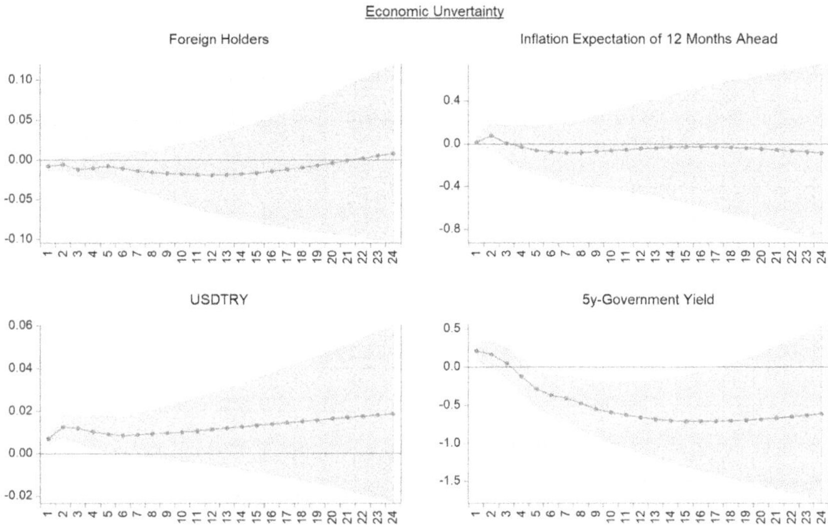

Fig. 4: Effect on variables of economic uncertainty shock.

Note: The graphs showing the effects of a shock to economic policy uncertainty on various economic variables are obtained using 1000 replications of the Monte Carlo method with a 68% confidence interval.

uncertainty shock over time and the effect of the shock disappears afterwards. 12-month-ahead inflation expectations initially increase, but soon turn negative and stabilize over time. The USD/₺ exchange rate initially increases in response to the uncertainty shock and then starts to decline. 5-year government bond yields initially increase, then decline and stabilize over time. However, due to the wide confidence intervals, there is uncertainty about the statistical significance of these effects. This suggests that economic uncertainty shocks cause market volatility in the short run, but tend to stabilize in the long run.

According to Figure 5, foreigners react significantly negatively to the financial uncertainty shock in the first few months, but this effect diminishes over time and disappears over time. The 12-month-ahead inflation expectations, on the other hand, shows a low negative response in the first few months, and then increases from month 3 onwards with a positive trend until month 12. The USD/₺ reacts to the financial uncertainty shock with a slight increase for the first 5 months and then follows a flat course. Finally, the 5-year government bond yield reacts negatively in the first few months, and then the impact of this shock begins to disappear.

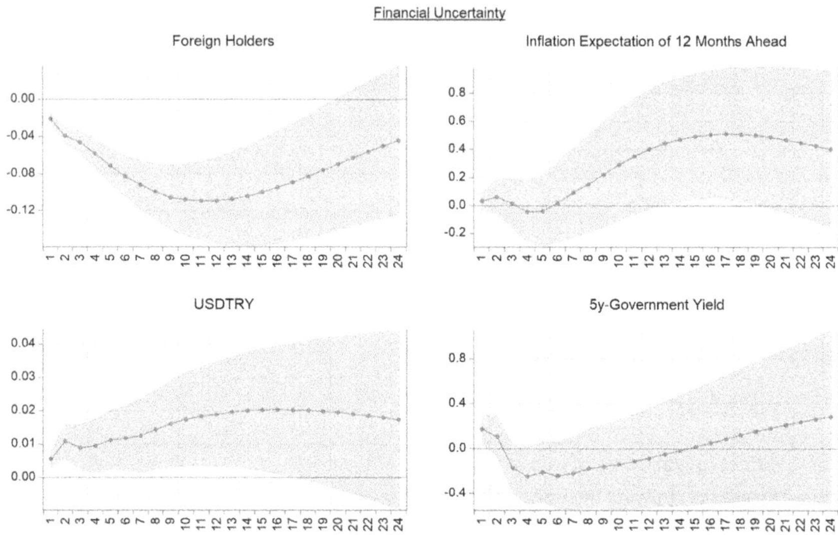

Fig. 5: Effect on variables of financial uncertainty shock.

Note: Graphs showing the effects of a shock in financial uncertainty on various economic variables are obtained with 1000 replications using the Monte Carlo method with a 68% confidence interval.

An analysis of the effects of geopolitical uncertainty, economic policy uncertainty and financial uncertainty on macroeconomic variables (Figure 6) reveals that each type of uncertainty has an initially negative impact. The 12-month-ahead inflation expectations exhibits positive initial effects across all uncertainty types but turns neutral in the long run. Although the 12-month ahead inflation expectations initially exhibits a positive response to all types of uncertainty, the impact of the shock dissipates in the long run. USD/₺ exchange rate shows a slight increase initially for all uncertainty types and then flattens out over time. The 5-year government bond yield, on the other hand, initially exhibits significant positive effects, but reverts to neutral trends in the short term. This also confirms the standard macroeconomic theory. This phenomenon occurs because outflows of funds from a country lead to an increase in the foreign exchange rate and currency substitution. The second effect is an increase in interest rates. High-interest borrowing inflates public debt, resulting in a legacy of escalating public debt (Kazgan, 2017:208).

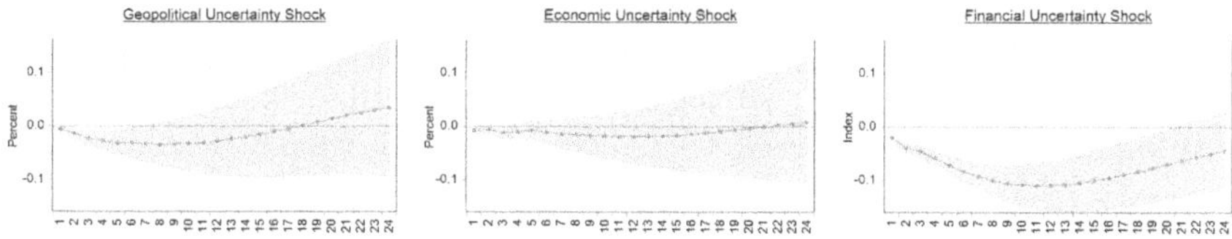

Fig. 6: Effect on foreign holders of government debt of different uncertainty shocks.
Note: Graphs showing the effects of a shock in uncertainties on various economic variables are obtained with 1000 replications using the Monte Carlo method with a 68% confidence interval.

Within the framework of the robustness analysis, the variables are detrended using the Hodrick-Prescott filter, and the VAR model is re-estimated. The results demonstrate that uncertainty shocks reduce the share of foreign investors in the debt stock. These findings offer significant insights into how investors and policymakers should respond during periods of uncertainty.

The results of the analysis provide important implications in terms of policy implications. In the context of debt management, governments can enhance their relationships with investors by thoroughly analyzing the investor base. According to the IMF (2011), understanding the nature and investment philosophy of investors, the impact of regulatory reforms on investor behavior, and the factors influencing global asset allocation decisions can help governments mitigate sudden market losses. Furthermore, broadening the investor base is crucial for effective risk management.

5 Conclusion

The structure of the debt stock is a critical factor in public debt management. It is essential for the government to effectively borrow, roll over its debt, and manage potential risks. As an emerging economy, Türkiye has been an attractive destination for foreign investors during stable periods. However, both domestic and external shocks can prompt foreign investors to seek safer assets. The 'flight to quality' phenomenon refers to sudden capital outflows, which discourage foreign investors from making long-term fixed investments. To mitigate the negative effects of uncertainties, it is necessary to develop economic and fiscal buffers, such as liquidity buffers.

In terms of public debt management, creating an optimal distribution of debt holders is an important strategy. According to Arslanalp and Poghosyan (2014), normalizing the investor base is crucial. Another policy recommendation is to implement credible policies that minimize domestic risks and strengthen economic fundamentals, thereby reducing the impact of domestic shocks. Effective and transparent communication with investors, aimed at eliminating information asymmetry, and the development of domestic financial markets are also critical policy steps.

Bibliography

Ahir, H., Bloom, N., & Furceri, D. (2022). The World Uncertainty Index (No. 29763; NBER Working Paper Series).

Akıncı, Ö. (2013). Global financial conditions, country spreads and macroeconomic fluctuations in emerging countries. Journal of International Economics, 91(2), 358–371. https://doi.org/10.1016/j.jinteco.2013.07.005

Andritzky, J. R. (2012). Government bonds and their investors: What are the facts and do they matter? (No. WP/12/158; IMF Working Paper).

Arslanalp, S., & Poghosyan, T. (2014). Foreign investor flows and sovereign bond yields in advanced economies (No. WP/14/27; IMF Working Paper).

Arslanalp, S., & Tsuda, T. (2014). Tracking global demand for emerging market sovereign debt (No. WP/14/39; IMF Working Paper).

Broner, F., Clancy, D., Erce, A., & Martin, A. (2022). Fiscal multipliers and foreign holdings of public debt. Review of Economic Studies, 89(3), 1155–1204. https://doi.org/10.1093/restud/rdab055

Broner, F., Erce, A., Martin, A., & Ventura, J. (2014). Sovereign debt markets in turbulent times: Creditor discrimination and crowding-out effects. Journal of Monetary Economics, 61(1), 114–142. https://doi.org/10.1016/j.jmoneco.2013.11.009

Caldara, D., & Iacoviello, M. (2022). Measuring geopolitical risk. American Economic Review, 112(4), 1194–1225. https://doi.org/10.1257/aer.20191823

Canova, F. (2005). The transmission of US shocks to Latin America. Journal of Applied Econometrics, 20(2), 229–251. https://doi.org/10.1002/jae.837

CBRT. (2018). İç borç stoku alıcılarının borçlanma araçlarına göre dağılımı. 2018 Enflasyon Raporu-I.

Ciarlone, A., Piselli, P., & Trebeschi, G. (2009). Emerging markets' spreads and global financial conditions. Journal of International Financial Markets, Institutions and Money, 19(2), 222–239. https://doi.org/10.1016/j.intfin.2007.11.003

Duyvesteyn, J., Martens, M., & Verwijmeren, P. (2016). Political risk and expected government bond returns. Journal of Empirical Finance, 38(Part A), 498–512. https://doi.org/10.1016/j.jempfin.2016.01.016

IMF. (2011). Managing sovereign debt and debt markets through a crisis- practical insights and policy lessons.

Kasal, S. (2023a). The role of global financial risk shocks on macroeconomic fluctuations and government debt: The case of Türkiye. Journal of Economic Policy Researches / İktisat Politikası Araştırmaları Dergisi, 10(2), 337–360. https://doi.org/10.26650/jepr1112862

Kasal, S. (2023b). What are the effects of financial stress on economic activity and government debt? An empirical examination in an emerging economy. Borsa Istanbul Review, 23(1), 254–267. https://doi.org/10.1016/j.bir.2022.10.007

Kasal, S. (2024). Unveiling the impact of geopolitical risks on Turkish economy and fiscal dynamics. Marmara Üniversitesi İktisadi ve İdari Bilimler Dergisi, 46(1), 221–232. https://doi.org/10.14780/muiibd.1411164

Kazgan, G. (2017). Türkiye ekonomisinde krizler (1929–2009) (4th ed.). İstanbul Bilgi Üniversitesi Yayınları.

Köse, M. A., Nagle, P., Ohnsorge, F., & Sugawara, N. (2021). Global waves of debt. The World Bank.

Özatay, F. (2016). Finansal krizler ve Türkiye (5th ed.). Doğan Kitap.

Somçağ, S. (2007). Türkiye'nin ekonomik krizi / oluşumu ve çıkış yolları. 2006 Yayınevi.

TMSF. (2009). Raf temizliği Demirbank. https://raftemizligi.tmsf.org.tr/E-Kitaplar/Detail/14, Date accessed: 06.15.2024.

Uribe, M., & Yue, V. Z. (2006). Country spreads and emerging countries: Who drives whom? Journal of International Economics, 69(1), 6–36. https://doi.org/10.1016/j.jinteco.2005.04.003

Yılmaz, E., & Yücel, C. (2016). Yabancı yatırımcı payının uzun dönem borçlanma faiz oranı üzerindeki etkileri (No. 2016-32; TCMB Ekonomi Notları).

Appendix

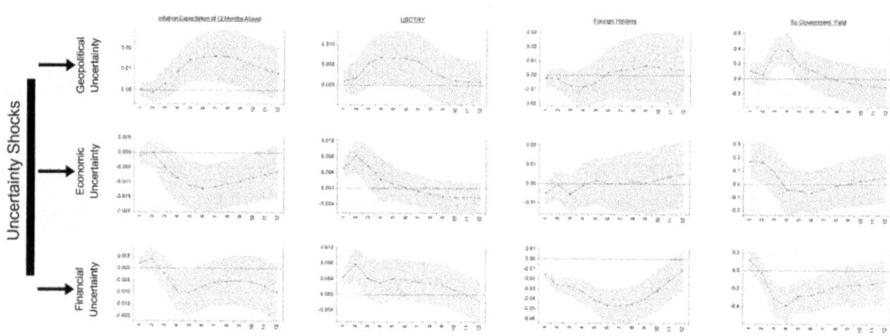

Appendix Fig. 7: Robustness Analysis Results.

Total & Government Health Expenditures and Economic Growth: Evidence from 10 SEE Countries

Hatice ALTINOK[1]

1 Introduction

Good health is not just a positive thing for human capital but is also important for economic development. Health expenditures are an important issue affecting a country's development and economic growth. As one of the expenditures that constitute human capital, health is a crucial issue in increasing both the level of employment in the economy and economic growth, as it increases personal well-being (Ifa and Guetat, 2019:19). Health expenditures increase labor productivity; this increase can lead to a significant improvement in the income and wellbeing of the population (Piabuo and Tieguhong, 2017:1). Because of this, all governments prioritize healthcare investments to sustain economic development. In addition, with the COVID-19 pandemic, which started in March 2020, governments increased health expenditures significantly. This pandemic has highlighted the critical importance of health expenditures. All countries have had to raise their health expenditures because of the virus. Besides, COVID-19 has emphasized the interconnectedness of health and the economy, reinforcing the need for adequate health expenditures to ensure sustainable economic growth.

Investments in health, which is one of the important issues of human capital, will positively affect economic growth in the short or long term. The most common example of this situation is that the developed countries put human capital first (Çetin and Cebeci; 2010; 167). According to the World Bank Report (1993), investing in health is a way to accelerate development because good health increases the labor productivity of humans and the economic growth rate of countries. Thus, health expenditure is a crucial problem for developing countries' economic policies.

The objective of this study is to identify the causal relationship between government and total health expenditure as a percentage of gross domestic

1 Anadolu University, FEAS, Department of Public Finance, haltinok@anadolu.edu.tr, ORCID ID: 0000-0002-1093-403X

product and economic growth in 10 SEE countries (Albania, Bosnia and Herzegovina, Bulgaria, Croatia, Greece, North Macedonia, Romania, Serbia, Slovenia & Türkiye) with testing Kónya (2006) bootstrap causality test. The main reason for choosing these groups of countries is their similar economic structures.

This study has four sections. The first section summarizes the literature on health expenditures and economic growth. The second section describes the methodology of this study. The third section is the empirical results. The fourth section is devoted to the conclusion.

2 Literature

From the past to the present, the literature has tested the relationship between health expenditure and economic growth using econometric methods. There is no common view that the causality between variables varies according to the socio-economic structure of countries, as the results of these studies show.

For 54 upper middle-income countries, Hayaloğlu and Bal (2015) examined the relationship between total, public and private health expenditure and economic growth. In their analysis, the authors concluded that increases in total, public and private healthcare spending have a positive impact on economic growth.

Konat (2021) used data from 1976 to 2017 to examine the relationship between healthcare spending and economic growth in 17 OECD countries. The author analyzed the latent cointegration relationship with the test suggested by Hatemi-J (2018). According to the study's results, it was determined that a positive shock in health expenditures did not affect positively on economic growth, on the contrary, a negative shock caused bidirectional causality.

Canbay ve Kırca (2021) applied the Kónya Granger causality approach to determine the relationship between health, including total, public, and private, expenditures and per capita income for Brazil, Russia, India, China, South Africa, and Türkiye using data from 2000 to 2018. They concluded that the causality relationships between all health expenditures and economic growth were observed. On the other hand, it is relevant that no causal relationship between health expenditure and per capita income.

Bedir (2016) studied the healthcare expenditure and income data of European and Middle Eastern African and Asian countries. They tried to determine the correlation between healthcare expenditure and income using data from 1995 to 2013. A bidirectional causality regarding the empirical results was observed for Czech and Russian. Also, it is important to support health expenditures in Egypt, Hungary, Korea, South Africa, and the Philippines. On the other hand, it is important to support the income side for Greece, Poland, South Africa, China, Indonesia, and Korea.

Cebeci ve Ay (2016) investigated how healthcare expenditures affect economic growth in BRICS+T using data from 2000 to 2014. The results showed that expenditures on healthcare significantly affect economic growth for all countries.

Elmi ve Sadeghi (2012) analyzed the causality and co-integration relationship between economic growth and healthcare expenditure, using data from 1990 to 2009 for developing countries. The authors used the VECM method for panel causality and co-integration. As a result, a long-term relationship was observed between economic growth and expenditures on health care.

Ak (2012) investigates the causal relationship between healthcare spending, economic growth, and life expectancy in the long run for Türkiye. The relationship between these variables except life expectancy was found in the long run. However, it concludes that they are not related in the short run.

Mehrara, Fazaeli vd. (2012) investigated the stationary and co-integration between healthcare expenditure and gross domestic product for 13 MENA countries from 1995 to 2005 using panel data. The findings showed that health expenditure and gross domestic product are non-stationary and co-integrated. Also, health expenditures as a percentage share of gross domestic product declined to gross domestic product.

Saraçoğlu ve Songur (2017) examined the relationship between health expenditure and gross domestic product per capita from 1995 to 2014 using panel data from 10 Eurasian countries, including Türkiye. The results revealed that the increase in health expenditure would have a direct positive correlation with economic growth and would also lead to an increase in health expenditure in 10 Eurasian countries.

As shown in the literature, the causal relationship between economic growth and health expenditure is a crucial issue. The results of these studies showed that there is no common opinion and the causal link between the variables varies depending on the socioeconomic structures of the countries.

3 Data and Methodology

For this study, 10 South-East European countries have been selected to provide annual data from 2006 to 2022. Total health expenditures (% gross domestic product) (TotExp), government health expenditures (% gross domestic product) (GovExp), and economic growth (EG) of the 10 SEE countries covered were taken from the World Bank database. The specified date range was determined according to the common intersection of each country's data. Due to a lack of data, Montenegro and Kosovo among the South-East European countries are not included in the analysis. Fig. 1 depicts the changes of these variables on a country-by-country basis over the period under review (2006 to 2022).

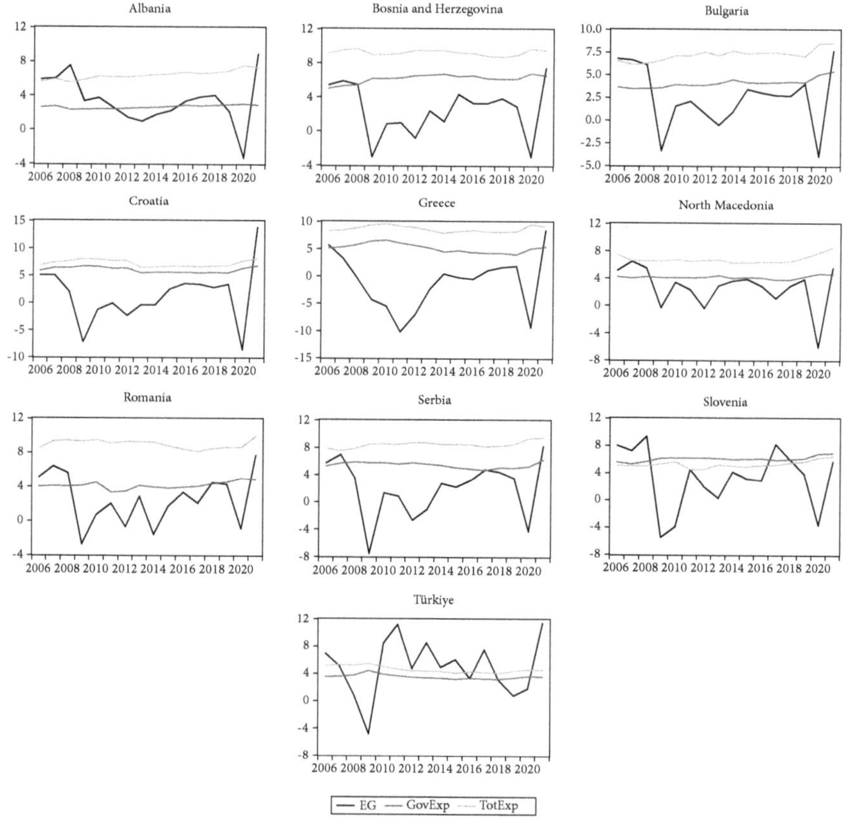

Fig. 1: Graphs by Variables.

As seen in Fig. 1, breaks of all variables were observed after the May 2020 data. With the emergence of COVID-19, when the first break occurred, the values of countries' economic growth decreased in the following months. Moreover, economic growth data also showed V-shaped growth across countries after May 2020. On the other hand, TotExp and GovExp are stable. After the COVID-19 pandemic, there is a slight increase in these two data.

Kónya (2006) developed the bootstrap causality test. It takes into account both the cross-sectional dependence between countries and the heterogeneity of the slope coefficients. Kónya bootstrap test which is derived from seemingly unrelated regression, and Wald tests with bootstrap critical values for each country. The test can show causality for each country in the panel data (Boubtane, Coulibaly, and Rault, 2013:6; Zellnerr, 1962). According to this, the relationships between these variables are determined by the models as follows:

$$EG_{1,t} = \alpha_{1,1} + \sum_{i=1}^{mlEG_1} \lambda_{1,1,i} EG_{1,t-1} + \sum_{i=1}^{mlTotExp_1} \mu_{1,1,i} TotExp_{1,t-1} + \varepsilon_{1,1,t}$$

$$EG_{2,t} = \alpha_{1,2} + \sum_{i=1}^{mlEG_1} \lambda_{1,2,i} EG_{2,t-1} + \sum_{i=1}^{mlTotExp_1} \mu_{1,2,i} TotExp_{2,t-1} + \varepsilon_{1,2,t}$$

$$\vdots \qquad \vdots \qquad \vdots$$

$$EG_{N,t} = \alpha_{1,N} + \sum_{i=1}^{mlEG_1} \lambda_{1,N,i} EG_{N,t-1} + \sum_{i=1}^{mlTotExp_1} \mu_{1,N,i} TotExp_{N,t-1} + \varepsilon_{1,N,t} \qquad \text{(Model 1)}$$

$$\vdots$$

$$TotExp_{1,t} = \alpha_{2,1} + \sum_{i=1}^{mlTotExp_2} \mu_{2,1,i} TotExp_{1,t-1} + \sum_{i=1}^{mlEG_1} \lambda_{2,1,i} EG_{1,t-1} + \varepsilon_{2,1,t}$$

$$TotExp_{2,t} = \alpha_{2,2} + \sum_{i=1}^{mlTotExp_2} \mu_{2,2,i} TotExp_{2,t-1} + \sum_{i=1}^{mlEG_1} \lambda_{2,2,i} EG_{2,t-1} + \varepsilon_{2,2,t}$$

$$\vdots \qquad \vdots \qquad \vdots$$

$$TotExp_{2,t} = \alpha_{2,N} + \sum_{i=1}^{mlTotExp_2} \mu_{2,N,i} TotExp_{N,t-1} + \sum_{i=1}^{mlEG_1} \lambda_{2,N,i} EG_{N,t-1} + \varepsilon_{2,N,t} \qquad \text{(Model 2)}$$

$$\vdots$$

$$EG_{1,t} = \alpha_{3,1} + \sum_{i=1}^{mlEG_1} \lambda_{3,1,i} EG_{1,t-1} + \sum_{i=1}^{mlGovExp_1} \mu_{3,1,i} GovExp_{1,t-1} + \varepsilon_{3,1,t}$$

$$EG_{2,t} = \alpha_{3,2} + \sum_{i=1}^{mlEG_1} \lambda_{3,2,i} EG_{2,t-1} + \sum_{i=1}^{mlGovExp_1} \mu_{3,2,i} GovExp_{2,t-1} + \varepsilon_{3,2,t}$$

$$\vdots \qquad \vdots \qquad \vdots$$

$$EG_{N,t} = \alpha_{3,N} + \sum_{i=1}^{mlEG_1} \lambda_{3,N,i} EG_{N,t-1} + \sum_{i=1}^{mlGovExp_1} \mu_{3,N,i} GovExp_{N,t-1} + \varepsilon_{3,N,t} \quad \text{(Model 3)}$$

$$\vdots$$

$$GovExp_{1,t} = \alpha_{4,1} + \sum_{i=1}^{mlGovExp_2} \mu_{4,1,i} GovExp_{1,t-1} + \sum_{i=1}^{mlEG_1} \lambda_{4,1,i} EG_{4,t-1} + \varepsilon_{4,1,t}$$

$$GovExp_{2,t} = \alpha_{4,2} + \sum_{i=1}^{mlGovExp_2} \mu_{4,2,i} GovExp_{2,t-1} + \sum_{i=1}^{mlEG_1} \lambda_{4,2,i} EG_{4,t-1} + \varepsilon_{4,2,t}$$

$$\vdots \qquad \vdots \qquad \vdots$$

$$GovExp_{2,t} = \alpha_{4,N} + \sum_{i=1}^{mlGovExp_2} \mu_{4,N,i} GovExp_{N,t-1} + \sum_{i=1}^{mlEG_1} \lambda_{4,N,i} EG_{N,t-1} + \varepsilon_{4,N,t} \quad \text{(Model 4)}$$

Model 1 tests the causality between economic growth to TotExp. Model 2 explores the causality between from TotExp to economic growth. Model 3 analyses the causality between from economic growth to GovExp. Model 4 tests the causality between from GovExp to economic growth. N represents countries (1, 2, 3, …, 10), t shows period (2006, 2007, …, 2022), and the length of lag is showed with *l* in sets of Model 1-2-3-4.

4 Empirical Results

To test the causality relationship between TotExp, GovExp, and economic growth, sross-sectional dependence and heterogeneity need to be checked before applying the Kónya (2006) causality test.

In this study, Breusch ve Pagan (1980) LM test, Pesaran (2004) LM_{adj} ve CD tests were used to test the cross-section dependence of the panel data set, which is the first condition of Kónya (2006). Table 1 shows the cross-sectional dependence test results for Model 1-2-3-4. As the p-values in the test statistics are less than 0.05, the null hypothesis is rejected, as shown in Table 1. Thus, it is revealed that there is cross-section dependence between the 10 Southeastern European countries. In other words, a shock in one country will have an impact on the other countries in the panel.

Tab. 1: Cross-section dependence test results

Method	Test stat. (p-value)	Method	Test stat. (p-value)	p-value
Model 1			Model 3	
LM test	444.3027* (0.000)	LM test	460.8325* (0.000)	0.000
CD test	20.47421* (0.000)	CD test	20.92103* (0.000)	0.000
LM_{adj} test	42.09020* (0.000)	LM_{adj} test	43.83260* (0.000)	0.000
Model 2			Model 4	
LM test	156.1845* (0.000)	LM test	226.7140* (0.000)	0.000
CD test	8.490003* (0.000)	CD test	13.75802* (0.000)	0.000
LM_{adj} test	11.71988* (0.000)	LM_{adj} test	19.15434* (0.000)	0.000

Note: * is significant at 0.05 significance levels.

The second condition of Kónya (2006) bootstrap causality test is heterogeneity between the coefficients' slope of the panel data set. Table 2 shows the heterogeneity test results for the Southeastern European countries of Model 1-2-3-4. According to Table 2, there is heterogeneity between the slope coefficients for the countries in the panel.

Tab. 2: Heterogeneity test results

Method	Test stat. (p-value)	Method	Test stat. (p-value)
Model 1		Model 3	
$\tilde{\Delta}$ test	5.350* (0.000)	$\tilde{\Delta}$ test	2.342* (0.000)
$\tilde{\Delta}_{adj}$ test	5.896* (0.000)	$\tilde{\Delta}_{adj}$ test	2.581* (0.005)

(Continued)

Tab. 2: *(Continued)*

Method	Test stat. (p-value)	Method	Test stat. (p-value)
Model 2		Model 4	
$\tilde{\Delta}$ test	2.384* (0.000)	$\tilde{\Delta}$ test	1.666* (0.048)
$\tilde{\Delta}_{adj}$ test	2.627* (0.000)	$\tilde{\Delta}_{adj}$ test	1.836* (0.033)

Note: * is significant at 0.05 significance levels.

The conditions of both cross-sectional dependence and homogeneity exist for all models. Kónya's (2006) bootstrap causality test results for Models 1 and 2 are therefore presented in Table 3. Table 4 also presents the results of Kónya's (2006) causality test for Models 3 and 4.

As seen in Table 3, Greece, Croatia and Serbia were determined to be the only countries where there is a one-way directional relationship from economic growth to TotExp was found. For all countries, there is no statistical relationship from TotExp to economic growth.

Tab. 3: The Kónya bootstrap Granger causality test results

Model 1		H_0: EG $\nrightarrow$ TotExp ve H_1: EG $\rightarrow$ TotExp		
		Bootstrap critical values		
Countries	**Wald test**	**%1**	**%5**	**%10**
Albania	0.11096756	66.32966	19.62325	15.02087
Bosnia and Herzegovina	2.0715386	86.57310	26.81024	16.26603
Bulgaria	7.3815822	168.43550	45.35497	18.23628
Croatia	20.200775*	64.69989	27.89818	17.29626
Greece	31.168843**	55.25786	25.77202	18.61890
North Macedonia	5.8429475	53.85776	27.92622	20.11028
Romania	3.8096972	54.12095	33.31641	26.63574
Serbia	71.391163**	53.81810	30.86328	20.71120
Slovenia	0.98757058	65.82303	33.37894	16.74713
Türkiye	9.062970	16.74713	27.77139	16.17736

Model 2		H_0: TotExp↛ EG ve H_1: TotExp → EG		
		Bootstrap critical values		
Countries	Wald test	%1	%5	%10
Albania	0.79441	44.43716	26.25113	16.38295
Bosnia Herzegovina	0.21517	35.69856	17.72641	10.84633
Bulgaria	1.26523	16.19489	11.21564	8.30033
Croatia	0.14813	29.24636	19.62773	13.81906
Greece	3.9740**	60.52603	22.46487	14.07887
North Macedonia	0.171281E-01	59.14609	19.27924	15.33428
Romania	1.1598852	36.62178	19.29772	7.64893
Serbia	1.84448	25.69644	20.73791	17.32570
Slovenia	1.65895	34.11000	17.85833	10.08850
Türkiye	4.28512**	105.75327	27.88542	16.84902

Note: *and ** are at the 0.1 and 0.05 significant levels. Based on 10,000 replications for the bootstrap.

The results in Table 4 show that for Albania, Bosnia and Herzegovina, Bulgaria, Croatia, Romania, Serbia, Slovenia, and Türkiye there is no statistically significant causal relationship between GovExp and economic growth. Also as seen in Table 4, there is a causality from GoxExp to economic growth was determined in Greece and North Macedonia.

Tab. 4: The Kónya bootstrap Granger causality test results

Model 3		H_0: EG ↛ GovExp ve H_1: EG → GovExp		
		Bootstrap critical values		
Countries	Wald test	%1	%5	%10
Albania	0.37008	29.10493	24.25885	17.24401
Bosnia and Herzegovina	17.295	270.05844	61.35783	41.66730
Bulgaria	0.2046	86.72858	46.53843	25.92765
Croatia	10.495	95.11774	31.70677	22.36783
Greece	10.0821	95.72706	35.87122	20.74588

(Continued)

Tab. 4: *(Continued)*

Model 3		H_0: EG ↛ GovExp ve H_1: EG → GovExp		
		Bootstrap critical values		
Countries	**Wald test**	**%1**	**%5**	**%10**
North Macedonia	2.1058	128.34389	41.67062	23.63533
Romania	10.789	59.31419	37.35018	22.76786
Serbia	0.2984	56.19623	41.83817	28.65472
Slovenia	0.444549E-01	179.58481	41.20567	21.86452
Türkiye	0.9663	40.61673	16.99652	10.68594
Model 4		H_0: GovExp↛ EG ve H_1: GovExp→ EG		
Countries	**Wald test**	**Bootstrap critical values**		
		%1	**%5**	**%10**
Albania	0.30342	17.51565	11.92438	9.19392
Bosnia and Herzegovina	0.45807	23.82329	13.50229	8.36675
Bulgaria	3.21241	21.92822	13.04419	6.78614
Croatia	0.94839E-04	44.41710	19.44959	11.60130
Greece	19.6112**	30.51600	24.97157	15.90498
North Macedonia	17.6014**	31.39673	21.04130	12.97527
Romania	0.95069	24.72321	26.54639	16.67111
Serbia	0.47658E-01	30.53195	21.26926	12.82102
Slovenia	3.2645036	27.05263	18.58982	10.980863
Türkiye	0.32563E-02	21.48821	18.47372	13.76587

Note: ** is at the 0.1 significant level. Based on 10,000 replications for the bootstrap.

5 Conclusion

Health expenditure is crucial for economic growth, as it increases labor productivity, develops human capital, improves the quality of life, and promotes economic development. This study examines the causality between total & government health expenditures as a percentage of gross domestic product and economic growth for the countries of 10 Southeastern Europe. For the countries in the SEE region, the direction of causality between the variables stems from the budgets and economic structures of the countries allocated to their health systems. As can be seen from the results of the analysis, total health expenditures have a positive impact on economic growth in most countries. An important reason for this is that the higher the economic growth of countries, the more important the total amount they allocate to health expenditure. Government health expenditure was also found to be influenced by economic growth in most countries. Only Greece and North Macedonia were found to have a relationship between total health expenditure and public health expenditure. The economic growth data for Greece and Türkiye have a higher rate than other countries. Especially after COVID-19, the share of government health expenditure in the countries increased even more. Policy-makers should focus more on the health system in their countries to increase economic growth, economic development, improve social welfare, and develop human capital. For example, an increase in employment opportunities can be observed with investment in human capital. Therefore, as countries develop their human capital, unemployment will fall and economic development will improve.

Bibliography

Boubtane, E., Coulibaly, D., & Rault, C. (2013). Immigration, growth, and unemployment: Panel VAR evidence from OECD countries. *Labour, 27*(4), 399–420.

Bedir, S. (2016). Healthcare expenditure and economic growth in developing countries. *Advances in economics and business*, *4*(2), 76–86.

Canbay, Ş., & Kırca, M. (2022). Health expenditures (total, public and private) and per capita income in the BRICS+ T: panel bootstrap causality analysis. *Journal of Economics, Finance and Administrative Science*, *27*(53), 52–67.

Cebeci, E., & Ay, A. (2016). The effects of health expenditures on economic growth: A panel regression analysis on BRICS countries and Türkiye.

Çetın, M., & Ecevıt, E. (2010). Sağlık Harcamalarının Ekonomik Büyüme Üzerindeki Etkisi: Oecd Ülkeleri Üzerine Bir Panel Regresyon Analizi. *Dogus University Journal*, *11*(2).

Ekrame, B., Dramane, C., & Christophe, R (2013). Immigration, unemployment and Gross domestic product in the host country: Bootstrap panel Granger causality analysis on OECD countries, 31.

Elmi, Z. M., & Sadeghi, S. (2012). Health care expenditures and economic growth in developing countries: panel co-integration and causality. *Middle-East Journal of Scientific Research*, *12*(1), 88–91.

Hayaloğlu, P., & Bal, H. Ç. (2015). Üst orta gelirli ülkelerde sağlık harcamaları ve ekonomik büyüme ilişkisi. *İşletme ve İktisat Çalışmaları Dergisi*, *3*(2), 35–44.

Konat, G. (2021). Sağlık harcaması ve ekonomik büyüme ilişkisi: OECD ülkeleri için panel veri analizi. *Yaşar Üniversitesi E-Dergisi*, *16*(61), 348–360.

Kónya, L. (2006). "Exports and Growth: Granger Causality Analysis On OECD Countries With A Panel Data Approach", *Economic Modelling*, 23(6), 978–992, Doi: 10.1016/J.Econmod.2006.04.008.

Mutascu, M. (2015). "A Bootstrap Panel Granger Causality of EnergyConsumption and Economic Growth in the G7 Countries", Renewableand Sustaiable Energy Reviews, 32, 166–171.

Mehrara, M., Fazaeli, A. A., Fazaeli, A. A., & Fazaeli, A. R. (2012). The relationship between health expenditures and economic growth in Middle East & North Africa (MENA) countries. *International Journal of Business Management and Economic Research*, *3*(1), 425–428.

Ifa, A., & Guetat, I. (2019). The Short And Long Run Causality Relationship Between Public Health Spending And Economic Growth: Evidence From Tunisia And Morocco. *Journal of Economic Development*, *44*(3).

Piabuo, S. M., & Tieguhong, J. C. (2017). Health expenditure and economic growth-a review of the literature and an analysis between the economic community for central African states (CEMAC) and selected African countries. *Health economics review*, *7*(1), 23.

Rengin, A. K. (2012). The relationship between health expenditures and economic growth: Turkish case. *International Journal of Business Management & Economic Research*, *3*(1), 404–409.

Saraçoğlu, S., & Songur, M. (2017). Sağlik Harcamalari ve Ekonomik Büyüme İlişkisi: Avrasya Ülkeleri Örneği. *Kafkas Üniversitesi İktisadi ve İdari Bilimler Fakültesi Dergisi*, *8*(16), 353–372.

Zellner, A. (1962). "An Efficient Method Of Estimating Seemingly Unrelated Regressions And Tests For Aggregation Bias", *Journal of the American Statistical Association*, *57*(298), 348–368.

Zhang, X., Chang, T., & Su, C. W. ve Wolde-Rufael, Y. (2016). "RevisitCausal Nexus between Military Spending and Debt: A Panel CausalityTest", Economic Modelling, 52, 939–944. https://data.worldbank.org/ (Date Accessed: 21.05.2024).

World Bank (1993). *World development report: investing in health.* New York: Oxford University Press.

Financing the Transition to a Green Economy: An Evaluation of the Relationship Between Public Debt and Renewable Energy Consumption through Panel Causality Analysis

Şebnem TOSUNOĞLU[1]

1 Introduction

Environmental degradation has emerged as one of the most pressing issues in the contemporary world, given its adverse effects on human life and biological systems. Consequently, environmental protection has become a focal point of the global policy agenda. The United Nations has designated "clean energy" as the 17th Sustainable Development Goal (SDG) to address global environmental challenges (Jianhua, 2022:1). Tackling environmental issues necessitates the transition from non-renewable to renewable energy sources. The production and utilization of renewable energy are recognized as effective strategies for reducing carbon emissions. In this regard, environmental advocates promote adopting renewable energy over fossil fuels to achieve sustainable development goals (Onuoha et al., 2023:1).

Beyond its environmental benefits, renewable energy consumption also boosts employment, enhances overall development outcomes, and reduces economies' reliance on foreign resources. The factors influencing renewable energy consumption have been extensively studied. However, the multifaceted role of energy in the environment and the economy remains a critical global policy discussion. Moreover, energy is considered vital in achieving sustainable development for nations. The demand for renewable energy has surged in recent years, which is expected to continue (Hashhemizadeh et al., 2021:1).

The transition to green energy faces significant financial challenges. Shifting from traditional energy sources to renewable energy is costly, requiring investment in new technologies and infrastructure development, with initial operational costs potentially exceeding those of conventional

[1] Anadolu University, FEAS, Department of Public Finance, ssel@anadolu.edu.tr, ORCID: 0000-0002-5591-4403

energy sources. Consequently, this transition imposes an additional financial burden on the energy industry (Auteri et al., 2024:2). This burden typically arises from various factors, including high upfront costs, extended payback periods, uncertainty in financing, regulatory ambiguities, and credit risk. The substantial investments needed for renewable energy projects can deter investors and hinder project implementation. Additionally, fluctuations in energy markets and regulatory changes can further complicate the financing of green energy projects. Overcoming these challenges necessitates the development of more effective financing models and regulatory frameworks to facilitate the transition to sustainable energy.

Borrowing is a key financing strategy in funding the green economy, aimed at supporting sustainable projects and reducing environmental impacts. This strategy is commonly used to finance large-scale green economy projects and promote sustainability advancements. Initiatives focused on sustainable energy, eco-friendly technologies, and energy efficiency projects are typically supported by either the private or public sector. Borrowing plays a crucial role in providing the necessary capital for initiating, expanding, or upgrading these projects. Financial constraints are particularly critical for the renewable energy sector, which is still in its developmental stage and heavily reliant on external financing. The high costs associated with financing can adversely impact the sector. Therefore, sources of funding such as public debt are pivotal in encouraging the implementation of renewable energy projects. Public sector involvement in financing can be an option for executing renewable energy or environmental programs. However, the potential adverse effects of the associated costs on national economies must be considered. Increased government spending can elevate public debt, which may subsequently impede investments. In other words, public debt can be seen as a source of funding for environmental protection programs, but high levels of public debt can also act as a barrier to investment in the renewable energy sector (Hashemizadeh et al., 2021:1).

The propensity to promote the use of renewable energy has led a considerable body of literature to focus on its determinants. However, the empirical analysis often overlooks the impact of public debt on renewable energy consumption. This study aims to contribute to the existing literature by investigating the effects of public debt on renewable energy consumption. In this context, the primary objective is to understand the implications of public borrowing policies on the renewable energy sector and to identify ways to enhance these effects. The study also seeks to contribute to the formulation of more sustainable and effective energy policies. In line with this core objective, the research aims to explore the determinants of renewable energy consumption in developing countries. The findings are expected to serve as a guide for both academic researchers and policymakers. Furthermore, the insights gained are anticipated to aid policymakers in devising more informed energy strategies and in developing comprehensive energy policies in the targeted countries.

The methodological foundation of this research is based on a panel data analysis of a dataset obtained from the period between 2000 and 2020. The analysis employs explanatory variables such as per capita GDP (gdp) as an indicator of economic growth, the share of trade in GDP (tro), CO_2 emissions per metric ton (co2), and the share of general public debt in GDP (debt) to explain renewable energy consumption (REN), defined as the ratio of renewable energy consumption to total energy consumption. Additionally, the Dumitrescu and Hurlin (2012) panel causality test is used to elucidate the causal relationship between public debt and renewable energy consumption in developing countries. Based on the findings, the study offers useful policy recommendations for developing nations.

2 Theoretical Background

Renewable energy sources encompass wind, solar, geothermal, hydroelectric, and biomass, which either produce no or minimal global warming emissions. Consequently, the utilization of renewable energy confers significant benefits to both public health and the environment. Promoting renewable energy sources is crucial for environmentally sustainable economic growth. The rapid economic development, industrialization, urbanization, and population growth in developing countries lead to a continuously increasing demand for all energy sources. Renewable energy offers two primary avenues for fostering economic development. Firstly, renewable energy technologies help diversify the energy mix and enhance energy security by providing a reliable, abundant, and sustainable energy supply. Additionally, the use of renewable energy yields social and environmental benefits by reducing CO_2 emissions. As CO_2 is a greenhouse gas contributing to the greenhouse effect, renewable energy helps mitigate the costs associated with repairing damage caused by environmental pollution. Secondly, the development of renewable energy sources bolsters national energy security and helps avoid energy shortages caused by external shocks. Given that the renewable energy industry is more labor-intensive than the fossil fuel industry, it also holds greater potential for job creation (Le et al., 2020:1).

Factors influencing renewable energy consumption have long been the subject of extensive research. However, the different roles that energy plays in the environment and the economy continue to be a significant policy debate worldwide. Energy is considered a vital parameter in ensuring sustainable development for countries. The demand for stable energy has increased sharply in recent years and continues to rise. Various factors, such as elevated living standards, population growth, economic competitiveness, and production improvements, contribute to the high demand for energy. To achieve sustainable development goals, environmental protection encourages the consumption of renewable energy over fossil fuel sources. The development of renewable energy sources plays a critical role in transitioning to a low-carbon economy at both regional and national levels, garnering intense interest in recent years. It is important to note that renewable energy is regarded as the only environmentally friendly, sustainable alternative capable of addressing climate change and global warming (Hashemizadeh et al., 2021:1). However, in developing countries, limited fiscal space and lack of access to financing make the high-cost upfront investments in renewable energy unfeasible. Moreover, macroeconomic and political uncertainties deter private sector investors from supporting renewable energy (World Bank).

To achieve sustainable development goals, developing countries require significant investments in various areas, such as infrastructure, human resources, and climate resilience. However, these countries face limitations in their ability to secure public or private financing, leading to unsustainable levels of borrowing to finance their development needs, thereby hindering economic progress. While renewable energy deployment necessitates financial resources, its higher costs compared to traditional sources pose a challenge (Onuoha et al., 2023:1). Mobilizing financing for low-carbon energy investment and innovation is a significant challenge in mitigating climate change. High upfront capital costs and lower rates of return compared to traditional energy sources constitute major barriers to implementing renewable energy projects.

Furthermore, renewable energy projects require substantial financing and have long payback periods (Le et al., 2020:1–2).

Achieving effective renewable energy consumption necessitates substantial capital investment. Although the overall costs associated with renewable energy production have significantly decreased in recent years due to technological advancements, there has not been a corresponding increase in investments. Investors are less inclined to take on investment risks due to fluctuations in policies and the requisite capital, making the financing of renewable energy investments one of the foremost challenges of the 21st century (Qadir et al., 2021:3591).

The high infrastructure, initial, and operational costs associated with renewable energy projects are considered fundamental financial obstacles to preferring renewable energy. To successfully address these challenges, substantial government investment is required, which, in turn, leads to increased public debt. Given that public borrowing significantly impacts fiscal policies, the implementation of an appropriate debt management strategy in the green transition is imperative. It should be emphasized that the transition to renewable energy is a complex process encompassing not only technical challenges but also financial and economic dimensions (Hashemizadeh et al., 2021:2). Consequently, public borrowing can play a critical role in an environment where renewable energy investments are heavily promoted.

Over the past decade, many developed and developing countries have grappled with economic issues, actively dealing with borrowing problems, and have consequently faced high debt levels. Numerous factors shape countries' borrowing needs. Among the most critical reasons are the expectations of reducing the savings-investment gap, diminishing current account deficits, making substantial investments, or aiming to enhance economic growth (Katırcıoğlu and Çelebi, 2018:8844). When domestic investment and foreign exchange earnings fall short of meeting national development goals, governments borrow to construct the infrastructure deemed necessary to accelerate economic growth.

For these reasons, public debt has increasingly been utilized as a source of funding for environmental programs, alongside its traditional role in the economic literature pertaining to the public sector. Specifically, borrowing to invest in renewable energy sources such as hydroelectric, wind, biomass, geothermal, and solar energy, or to create subsidies that encourage entrepreneurs to establish green businesses, will increase public debt levels. However, such increased borrowing will also lead to a rise in renewable energy consumption. Debt can directly pertain to the renewable energy sector or influence energy consumption through real income growth.

Firstly, in countries dependent on imported energy, a significant portion of the total debt may stem from the energy needs of domestic markets. In such countries, petroleum and natural gas are predominantly imported through borrowing from other countries. Therefore, debt used for such purposes, directed towards non-renewable energy sources, can exacerbate energy consumption and consequently environmental pollution (Katırcıoğlu and Çelebi, 2018:8844). Additionally, changes in debt stock can influence macroeconomic activities and, therefore, impact GDP changes, potentially affecting renewable energy consumption levels in various ways due to additional energy needs.

The inefficient use of public borrowing in investments can diminish resource availability and, consequently, harm a country's growth. As is well-known, developing countries primarily borrow to mitigate savings-investment gaps and current account deficits. As previously noted, only investment-driven growth can enhance renewable energy demand and thus foster a recovery effect in the energy sector. It can be posited that public borrowing plays a significant role in the energy consumption of heavily indebted countries, thereby making borrowing the most influential factor contributing to energy usage (Akam et al., 2021:65301).

Conversely, the financing of real income growth and energy consumption through external debt can lead to environmental degradation. Alternatively, countries affected by the debt burden (particularly those dependent on energy) may increase CO2 emissions due to additional energy needs driven by real income growth. Consequently, when external debt is invested in real estate, heavy industry, and the construction sector, it results in increased energy demand, which can potentially lead to adverse environmental effects. Undoubtedly, public debt plays a crucial role in economic development. However, a moderate level of public debt is necessary to promote economic growth. It is believed that an appropriate percentage of public debt can enhance capital flows, stimulate investment, and positively impact economic outcomes. Conversely, high levels of public debt can reduce private investment, decrease social spending, increase inflation, elevate country risk, and exert pressure on the economy. In addition to the impacts of public debt on growth, other studies have shown its effects on poverty, health, education, human rights, labor demand, and the workforce (Wang et al., 2021:382).

Ultimately, high levels of public debt can pose a barrier to public investment in renewable energy projects and limit governments' capacity to provide grants for renewable energy technology research. Furthermore, increasing public debt may lead to reduced government spending and investment aimed at balancing the budget deficit. Consequently, expenditures and investments in renewable energy may decline, resulting in decreased efficiency in renewable energy usage (Wang et al., 2021:382).

3 Related Literature

Renewable energy and public debt are two pivotal issues at the intersection of economic and environmental policies. As the demand for renewable energy continues to rise, an increasing number of studies are examining the impact of various factors—such as economic development, price fluctuations, and international trade—on energy usage. Conversely, the relationship between public debt and energy consumption has garnered scant attention in the literature. Only a limited number of studies have explored the effects of public debt levels on the adoption and utilization of renewable energy sources.

Ntanos et al. (2018) examined the relationship between renewable energy consumption and GDP per capita in European countries, revealing the positive impacts of the transition to renewable energy on economic development. The findings indicate that countries with higher GDPs exhibit a stronger correlation between renewable energy consumption and economic growth. Similarly, Raouf's (2022) study investigated the effects of public debt on energy consumption in 17 OECD countries from 1980 to 2020, concluding that public debt positively influences renewable energy use while negatively affecting non-renewable energy consumption.

Jabari et al. (2022) explored the relationship between financial sector development, external debt, and renewable energy consumption in Türkiye.

The study confirmed a positive connection between public debt levels and renewable energy consumption, emphasizing the importance of financial factors in driving sustainable energy practices. The ARDL test results demonstrated a positive relationship between renewable energy consumption and Türkiye's financial development, although the coefficient for external debt was found to be negative and significant.

Additionally, Hashemizadeh et al. (2021) provided new insights into the role of public debt in renewable energy consumption, particularly in developing economies. This research highlighted how public debt influences the adoption of renewable energy technologies, underlining the complexity of this relationship. Understanding these dynamics is crucial for designing effective policies that promote sustainable energy practices while carefully managing public finances.

Ziaei (2012) used the GMM model to investigate the impact of government debt on energy consumption in 15 European countries from 1995 to 2011. The study revealed that investment, inflation, and government debt have positive and significant effects on energy consumption. Additionally, Florea et al. (2021) focused on developing economies within the European Union, analyzing the impact of primary indicators of public finance, such as public debt and budget deficit, on renewable energy consumption. This study underscored the importance of consistent fiscal strategies in supporting sustainable energy initiatives and highlighted the role of fiscal performance in driving the transition to renewable energy sources.

Sun and Liu (2020) examined the effects of private and public debt on energy consumption in China from 1996 to 2016 using a decomposition model. The study found that per capita private debt has a positive impact, contributing significantly to China's energy consumption, whereas government debt was determined to harm energy use.

In light of the COVID-19 pandemic, Lazo et al. (2022) conducted an impact study on the electricity sector, emphasizing how concerns about declining tax revenues and public debt sustainability might affect renewable energy projects. The study highlighted the sensitivity of renewable energy investments to fluctuations in public finances, drawing attention to the need for resilient fiscal frameworks to support green energy transitions.

Jianhua (2022) investigated the impact of public debt on renewable energy consumption in 23 Asian economies over the period 1990–2019.

According to the ARDL model, an increase in public debt reduces renewable energy consumption. In the asymmetric ARDL model, positive shocks in public debt decrease energy consumption, while negative shocks increase it. The FMOLS model suggests that an increase in public debt increases energy consumption in some economies while decreasing it in others. Generally, negative shocks tend to have an energy consumption-enhancing effect.

Auteri et al. (2024) examined the relationship between government debt and renewable energy usage in G7 countries from 1990 to 2021. Employing cointegrated regression methods (FMOLS and DOLS), Quantile Regressions (QR), and bidirectional panel causality tests, the study found bidirectional causality between government debt and renewable energy consumption. The findings indicate that increasing government debt may hinder renewable energy investments, yet renewable energy positively influences government debt dynamics. The study emphasizes that policymakers should prioritize fiscal responsibility for renewable energy investments.

Erer (2024) explored the long-term adverse effects of public debt on renewable energy consumption and the positive contribution of financial development in BRICS-T countries for the period 1990–2019. Using the Westerlund cointegration test, the Driscoll-Kray regression model, and the Dumitrescu and Hurlin (2012) causality test, the study examined these relationships.

Overall, the synthesis of these studies reveals the complex relationship between public debt and renewable energy consumption. The varying findings across studies can be attributed to differences in analytical techniques, relevant factors, selected regions, and periods. This indicates the need for further research on the topic. As countries strive to achieve energy sustainability goals, understanding the dynamics between public debt levels, financial policies, and renewable energy adoption is crucial for promoting a green and resilient economy.

4 Data and Methodology

4.1 Data

Based on data availability, 73 developing countries were selected and included in the analysis. The World Bank Group classifies world economies into four income groups: low, lower-middle, upper-middle, and high. This study includes 35 lower-middle-income and 38 upper-middle-income countries.[2] The variables used in the research are as follows: the share of renewable energy consumption in total final energy consumption (ren), the share of general government debt in GDP (debt), gross domestic product per capita (gdp), CO2 emissions per metric ton (co2), and the share of trade in GDP (tro). Public debt data were obtained from the "IMF World Economic Outlook Database." Other data were sourced from the "World Bank-World Development Indicators" database. The analysis covers the period from 2000 to 2020. The descriptive statistics in the logarithmic form of the main variables and the correlation relationships between the variables are presented in Tables 1 and 2, respectively.

Tab. 1: Descriptive Statistics of Variables

Variable	Observations	Mean	Std. Deviation	Min	Max
lnren	1,533	2.97865	1.401145	-2.995732	4.588431
lndebt	1,533	3.623766	0.6287918	1.163151	5.56452
lngdp	1,533	7.86187	0.8942923	4.921308	9.678757
lntro	1,533	4.260448	0.4263127	3.066189	5.395475
lnco2	1,533	0.3749886	1.12977	-3.515517	2.730546

2 Albania, Algeria, Argentina, Armenia, Azerbaijan, Belarus, Belize, Benin, Bhutan, Bolivia, Bosnia and Herzegovina, Botswana, Brazil, Bulgaria, Cabo Verde, Cambodia, Cameroon, China, Colombia, Comoros, Democratic Republic of the Congo, Costa Rica, Côte d'Ivoire, Dominican Republic, Ecuador, Egypt, El Salvador, Eswatini, Fiji, Gabon, Georgia, Ghana, Guinea, Guatemala, Haiti, Honduras, India, Indonesia, Kazakhstan, Kenya, Lebanon, Malaysia, Marshall Islands, Mauritania, Mauritius, Mexico, Micronesia, Moldova, Morocco, Namibia, Nepal, Nicaragua, North Macedonia, Pakistan, Paraguay, Peru, Philippines, Russian Federation, Senegal, Serbia, Solomon Islands, South Africa, Tajikistan, Thailand, Tonga, Tunisia, Türkiye, Turkmenistan, Ukraine, Uzbekistan, Vanuatu, Vietnam, and Zambia.

Tab. 2: Correlation Between Variables

	lnren	lndebt	lngdp	lntro	lnco2
lnren	1.0000				
lndebt	0.2575	1.0000			
lngdp	-0.3506	-0.1165	1.0000		
lntro	-0.1102	-0.0995	0.0799	1.0000	
lnco2	-0.6710	-0.1369	0.7189	0.1840	1.0000

In the correlation analysis, a strong negative relationship (-0.6710) was found between renewable energy use and CO2 emissions, indicating the potential of renewable energy policies to reduce CO2 emissions. A positive relationship (0.7189) was identified between economic growth and CO2 emissions, highlighting the environmental costs associated with economic growth. There was also a negative correlation (-0.3506) between renewable energy use and economic growth, and a positive relationship (0.2575) between debt increase and renewable energy use, suggesting that borrowing is being utilized to support renewable energy projects.

4.2 Methodology

Drawing on the research gap in the existing literature, this study investigates the impact of public debt on renewable energy consumption in developing countries by utilizing the following determinants of renewable energy consumption:

$$ren_{it} = f(gdp_{it}, debt_{it}, tro_{it}, co2_{it}) \quad (1)$$

In the equation, i represents the countries and t represents the time dimension. The empirical model to be estimated is defined as follows:

$$lnren_{it} = \beta_0 + \beta_1 lngdp_{it} + \beta_2 lndebt_{it} + \beta_3 lntro_{it} + \beta_4 lnco2_{it} + \varepsilon_{it} \quad (2)$$

To linearize the relationships between variables and to enable comparison of their effects across different scales, all variables are included in the model in logarithmic (ln) form. In the model, β_1 represents the fixed coefficients, and ε_{it} denotes the error terms.

In this study, to address the issue of cross-sectional dependence in panel data, the Pesaran, Ullah, and Yamagata (2008) Cross-Sectional Dependence with

Bias Correction CDW+ and the Pesaran (2004) Cross-Sectional Dependence (CD) tests were first applied. If the null hypothesis is rejected in the CDW+ and CD test analyses, the presence of cross-sectional dependence among the variables is confirmed. After testing for cross-sectional dependence in the series, panel unit root and cointegration tests were conducted to examine the long-term relationships among the selected variables.

Given the potential non-stationarity in economic series, stationarity testing is essential. In the presence of cross-sectional dependence, first-generation unit root tests (such as Levin Lin Chu, Breitung, Hadri penal, Fisher ADF, and Fisher PP) fail, thus second-generation unit root tests that account for cross-sectional dependence—specifically the Cross-Sectionally Augmented IPS (CIPS) and Cross-Sectionally Augmented Dickey-Fuller (CADF) unit root tests—were used. Rejection of the null hypothesis in the CIPS and CADF tests indicates that the series are stationary, whereas failure to reject the null hypothesis suggests that the series are non-stationary.

Following the unit root tests, the study investigated the potential cointegration relationships among the variables. For this purpose, the Westerlund (2008) cointegration test was employed. The Westerlund (2008) cointegration test is typically calculated based on two statistics: group statistics and panel statistics. Rejection of the null hypothesis indicates the presence of a cointegration relationship among the variables.

In the study, following the cointegration analysis, long-term coefficients were estimated using Fully Modified Ordinary Least Squares (FMOLS) and Dynamic Ordinary Least Squares (DOLS) estimators. Finally, the causality relationship between renewable energy consumption and public borrowing was analyzed using the Dumitrescu and Hurlin (2012) panel causality test. The study aims to elucidate the causal relationship among the examined variables, providing a critical link for policymakers in formulating appropriate policies.

5 Empirical Results

5.1 Cross-Sectional Dependence Tests

In this study, to test for cross-sectional dependence among the variables, the Pesaran, Ullah, and Yamagata (2008) and Pesaran (2004) cross-sectional dependence tests were employed, with the empirical results presented in Table 3. According to the probability values, the results indicate the presence of cross-sectional dependence among the variables at the 1% significance level. The empirical findings demonstrate common and statistically significant relationships among the different observational units within the panel data set.

Tab. 3: Cross-Sectional Dependence Test Results

	CDW+		CD test	
Değişken	**Statistic**	**p-value**	**Statistic**	**p-value**
lnren	5824.13***	0.000	33.68***	0.000
lngdp	10858.91***	0.000	211.87***	0.000
lndebt	5457.64***	0.000	56.47***	0.006
lntro	4662.44***	0.000	29.67***	0.000
lnco2	6140.65***	0.000	74.32***	0.000

Note: *** denotes statistical significance at the 1% level.

5.2 Panel Unit Root Tests

Following the cross-sectional dependence test, the CIPS and CADF panel unit root tests were employed to check the stationarity of the series. The results of the CIPS and CADF unit root tests are presented in Table 4.

Tab. 4: Unit Root Test Results

	CIPS Statistic		CADF istatistiği		
Variable	**Level**	**First Difference**	**Level**	**First Difference**	
lnren	−1.957	−3.880***	−1.981	−2.814***	I (1)
lngdp	−2.336***	–	−2.284***	–	I (0)
lndebt	−1.941	−3.832***	−1.878	−2.822***	I (1)
lntro	−1.672	−3.736***	−1.613	−2.875***	I (1)
lnco2	−2.109	−3.908***	−1.987	−2.598***	I (1)

Note: ***, **, and * indicate statistical significance at the 1%, 5%, and 10% levels, respectively.

According to the unit root test results in Table 4, while the variable lngdp is stationary at level, the variables lnren, lndebt, lntro, and lnco2 become stationary when first differenced. This indicates that these variables are stationary at the I(1) level.

5.3 Panel Cointegration Test

If variables exhibit unit roots at different levels (i.e., some variables are I(0) while others are I(1)), traditional methods for cointegration analysis may not be appropriate. However, there are alternative methods suitable for such cases. To check whether the series integrated at different levels are cointegrated, the Durbin-Hausman Panel Cointegration Test developed by Westerlund (2008) was employed, using GAUSS 6.0 software. This test allows us to examine the cointegration relationship when the series are integrated at different levels. Another advantage of this test is its ability to account for cross-sectional correlations in the residuals (Güloğlu et al., 2012:606). The test results are presented in Table 5.

Tab. 5: Westerlund (2008) Cointegration Test Results

Cointegration Test Statistics	t-stat.	p-value
DH_g	0.208	0.418
DH_p	1.713	0.043**

Note: ***, **, and * indicate statistical significance at the 1%, 5%, and 10% levels, respectively.

According to the results of the DH_g test, there is no evidence of a cointegration relationship among the series. However, the DH_p test indicates a cointegration relationship among the variables at the 5% significance level. Based on the DH_p test, it can be concluded that there is a long-term relationship among the series. This confirms that the variables are cointegrated, meaning that in the long run, the connections between renewable energy consumption, GDP per capita, public debt, trade openness, and CO2 emissions are validated. Given the detection of a cointegration relationship, the next step involves estimating the long-term coefficients among the series.

5.4 Panel Regression Estimator Results for Long-Term Relationship

After conducting all the fundamental analyses of the panel data study, the next step is to investigate the direction and magnitude of the relationship among the key variables in the model. Following the establishment of cointegration, FMOLS and DOLS estimators were utilized to analyze the long-term relationship. The results are presented in Table 6.

Tab. 6: FMOLS and DOLS Estimation Results

	FMOLS		DOLS	
Variable	**Coefficient**	**t-Statistic (Prob)**	**Coefficient**	**t-Statistic (Prob)**
lnco2	−0.545138***	−11.454.680 (0.000)	−0.545506***	−8.283177 (0.000)
lngdp	0.081313***	3.489.834 (0.0005)	0.150003***	4.494977 (0.000)
lndebt	0.039733*	1.774.207 (0.0762)	0.092323***	3.242332 (0.0013)
lntro	0.002934	0.059223 (0.9528)	−0.116372	−1.583747 (0.114)

Note: ***, **, and * indicate statistical significance at the 1%, 5%, and 10% levels, respectively.

According to the FMOLS results, the variable lnco2 has a statistically significant negative effect on the dependent variable at the 1% significance level. This indicates that an increase in CO2 emissions decreases the dependent variable. Similarly, the variable lngdp is positive and statistically significant at the 1% significance level, suggesting that an increase in GDP per capita increases the dependent variable. The variable lndebt is positive and statistically significant at the 10% significance level, indicating that an increase in public debt raises the dependent variable. However, the variable lntro does not show a statistically significant effect.

When examining the DOLS results, the variable lnco2 is negative, while lngdp and lndebt are positive, and all are statistically significant at the 1% level. However, the variable lntro also does not exhibit a statistically significant effect in the DOLS model.

Overall, both models indicate that CO2 emissions have a diminishing effect on the dependent variable, while GDP per capita has an enhancing effect. The effect of debt is positive and significant in both models; however, in the FMOLS model, this effect is significant at the 10% level, whereas in the DOLS model, it is significant at the 1% level. On the other hand, the lntro variable does not show a statistically significant effect in either model. These results suggest that reducing CO2 emissions and increasing GDP per capita could have positive effects on the dependent variable, while the impact of debt needs to be managed carefully.

Considering the DOLS and FMOLS models, notable findings emerge regarding the relationship and direction between borrowing (lndebt) and renewable energy (lnren). In both models, the borrowing variable has a positive coefficient, and this relationship is statistically significant. According to the DOLS model, the borrowing coefficient is 0.092323, while in the FMOLS model, this coefficient is 0.039733. These results indicate that borrowing can increase investments in renewable energy. Renewable energy projects typically require high initial costs, and public borrowing plays a critical role in financing these projects. Government-supported projects, financed through public debt, allow for the expansion of renewable energy capacity. Furthermore, many countries offer favorable loan conditions and financial support programs funded by public borrowing to encourage renewable energy investments. Such policies make renewable energy investments attractive and contribute to their increase.

Governments are turning to renewable energy investments to achieve environmental sustainability goals. Public borrowing for financing these investments can be strategically utilized to contribute to sustainable development goals. Borrowing can accelerate investments in renewable energy, thereby contributing to long-term environmental and economic benefits. However, the positive impact of borrowing may not be sustainable in the long run, and excessive borrowing can be risky. High levels of debt can lead to debt sustainability issues and economic vulnerabilities. Therefore, the positive effect of debt should be managed carefully, and borrowing strategies should be planned with sustainability in mind.

Both estimation methods indicate that the economic growth variable has a positive effect on the dependent variable. Consequently, the positive impact of economic growth on the dependent variable, as demonstrated by both estimation methods, can be interpreted as economic growth enhancing overall welfare, leading to favorable outcomes in various economic and environmental domains. Supporting economic growth is a critical factor for achieving both economic development and sustainability goals.

The variable of CO2 emissions exhibits a strong and negative effect on the dependent variable (lnren). These results reveal that an increase in CO2 emissions has a significantly adverse impact on the dependent variable. Consequently, the strong and negative influence of CO2 emissions on renewable energy use suggests that the intensive use of fossil fuels in energy production, the inadequacy of political and economic incentives, low environmental awareness, and energy policies favoring fossil fuels may be contributing factors. Therefore, to increase renewable energy usage and reduce CO2 emissions, stronger environmental policies, incentives, and regulations are necessary.

5.5 Dumitrescu and Hurlin (2012) Panel Causality Test

To test the causality relationship, a heterogeneous panel causality approach was applied to investigate the directions of the relationships among the variables. The results from the Dumitrescu and Hurlin causality test are presented in Table 7.

Tab. 7: Dumitrescu and Hurlin (2012) Panel Causality Test Results

Causality Direction	Z-bar Statistic	Hypotheses	Granger Causality
lndebt → lnren	13.2476*** (0.000)	H0: lndebt does not Granger-cause lnren. H1: lndebt Granger-causes lnren for at least one panel.	Exists
lnren → lndebt	10.7577*** (0.000)	H0: lnren does not Granger-cause lndebt. H1: lnren Granger-causes lndebt for at least one panel.	Exists

Note: ***, **, and * indicate statistical significance at the 1%, 5%, and 10% levels, respectively. The values in parentheses represent p-values.

The table presents the results of the Granger causality test between the variables "lndebt" and "lnren." The first test examines whether the "lndebt" variable Granger-causes the "lnren" variable. With a Z-bar value of 13.2476 and a p-value of 0.0000, the null hypothesis (H0) is rejected, indicating that public debt Granger-causes renewable energy consumption.

The second test evaluates whether the "lnren" variable Granger-causes the "lndebt" variable. With a Z-bar value of 10.7577 and a p-value of 0.0000, the null hypothesis (H0) is again rejected, demonstrating that renewable energy consumption Granger-causes public debt. The results of the Dumitrescu and Hurlin (2012) panel causality test strongly highlight the bidirectional relationship between renewable energy consumption and public debt in this study.

6 Conclusion

This study focuses on analyzing the effects of public debt on renewable energy consumption. The findings of the research indicate that public debt has the potential to increase investments in renewable energy, which can provide both environmental and economic benefits. The FMOLS and DOLS models confirm that economic growth has a positive impact on renewable energy consumption, while CO2 emissions have a negative impact. These findings underscore the need to promote renewable energy use through the support of economic growth and the reduction of CO2 emissions.

Careful management of public debt can support investments in sustainable energy projects, contributing to both economic and environmental sustainability goals. Policymakers should prioritize fiscal responsibility for renewable energy investments and ensure that public debt is directed toward sustainable energy projects. This approach can provide long-term benefits both economically and environmentally. Developing countries should more effectively utilize international funds and credit facilities to finance renewable energy projects, which can help overcome high initial costs and financing uncertainties. Additionally, removing legal and regulatory barriers to renewable energy investments can encourage private sector investment in this area. A more stable and predictable regulatory environment can facilitate the realization of renewable energy projects and boost investor confidence. The careful management of public debt and the effective implementation of policies aimed at renewable energy are crucial for achieving sustainable development goals. Within this framework, the prudent management of public debt and the effective implementation of renewable energy policies will play a critical role in attaining sustainable development objectives.

The results of the Dumitrescu and Hurlin panel causality test indicate a bidirectional causality relationship between public debt and renewable energy consumption. This implies that while public debt affects renewable energy consumption, renewable energy consumption can also influence public debt.

Bibliography

Akam, D., Owolabi, O., & Nathaniel, S. P. (2021). Linking external debt and renewable energy to environmental sustainability in heavily indebted poor countries: New insights from advanced panel estimators. *Environmental Science and Pollution Research International, 28*(46), 65300–65312. https://doi.org/10.1007/s11356-021-15191-9

Auteri, M., Mele, M., Ruble, I., & Magazzino, C. (2024). The double sustainability: The link between government debt and renewable energy. "The Journal of Economic Asymmetries, 29", 100303. https://doi.org/10.1016/j.jeca.2024.100303

Dumitrescu, E.-I., & Hurlin, C. (2012). Testing for Granger non-causality in heterogeneous panels. *Economic Modelling, 29*(4), 1450–1460. https://doi.org/10.1016/j.econmod.2012.02.014

Erer, E. (2024). Kamu borcunun yenilenebilir enerji tüketimi üzerindeki rolü: BRICS-T ülkeleri üzerine bir uygulama. *Alanya Akademik Bakış Dergisi/Alanya Academic Review Journal, 8*(1), 208–223. https://doi.org/10.29023/alanyaakademik.1313854

Florea, N. M., Bădîrcea, R. M., Meghisan-Toma, G.-M., Puiu, S., Manta, A. G., & Berceanu, D. (2021). Linking public finances' performance to renewable-energy consumption in emerging economies of the European Union. *Sustainability, 13*(11), 1–14. https://doi.org/10.3390/su13116344

Guloglu, B., Tekin, R. B., & Saridogan, E. (2012). Economic determinants of technological progress in G7 countries: A re-examination. *Economics Letters, 116*(3), 604–608. https://doi.org/10.1016/j.econlet.2012.06.012

Hashemizadeh, A., Bui, Q., & Kongbuamai, N. (2021). Unpacking the role of public debt in renewable energy consumption: New insights from the emerging countries. "Energy, 224", 120187. https://doi.org/10.1016/j.energy.2021.120187

Jabari, M. S., Ağa, M., & Samour, A. (2022). Financial sector development, external debt, and Turkey's renewable energy consumption. Plos One, 17(5), e0265684. https://doi.org/10.1371/journal.pone.0265684

Jianhua, L. (2022). Exploring the asymmetric impact of public debt on renewable energy consumption behavior. "Frontiers in Psychology, 13", 922833. https://doi.org/10.3389/fpsyg.2022.922833

Katircioglu, S., & Celebi, A. (2018). Testing the role of external debt in environmental degradation: Empirical evidence from Turkey. *Environmental Science and Pollution Research International, 25*(9), 8843–8852. https://doi.org/10.1007/s11356-018-1194-0

Lazo, J., Aguirre, G., & Watts, D. (2022). An impact study of COVID-19 on the electricity sector: A comprehensive literature review and Ibero-American survey. *Renewable and Sustainable Energy Reviews, 158*, 112135. https://doi.org/10.1016/j.rser.2022.112135

Le, T.-H., Nguyen, C. P., & Park, D. (2020). Financing renewable energy development: Insights from 55 countries. "Energy Research & Social Science, 68", 101537. https://doi.org/10.1016/j.erss.2020.101537

Ntanos, S., Skordoulis, M., Kyriakopoulos, G., Arabatzis, G., Chalikias, M., Galatsidas, S., & Katsarou, A. (2018). Renewable energy and economic growth: Evidence from European countries. *Sustainability, 10*(8), 2626. https://doi.org/10.3390/su10082626

Onuoha, F. C., Dimnwobi, S. K., Okere, K. I., & Ekesiobi, C. (2023). Sustainability burden or boost? examining the effect of public debt on renewable energy consumption in Sub-Saharan Africa. Energy Sources, Part B: Economics, Planning, and Policy, 18(1). https://doi.org/10.1080/15567249.2023.2214917

Qadir, S. A., Al-Motairi, H., Tahir, F., & Al-Fagih, L. (2021). Incentives and strategies for financing the renewable energy transition: A review. *Energy Reports*, 7, 3590–3606. https://doi.org/10.1016/j.egyr.2021.06.041

Pesaran, M. Hashem, Aman Ullah, and Takashi Yamagata. "A bias-adjusted LM test of error cross-section independence." The Econometrics Journal 11.1 (2008):105–127.

Raouf, E. (2022). Public debt – energy consumption nexus. *International Journal of Energy Economics and Policy, 12*(5), 146–151. https://doi.org/10.32479/ijeep.13296

Sun, X., & Liu, X. (2020). Decomposition analysis of debt's impact on China's energy consumption. *Energy Policy, 146*, 111802. https://doi.org/10.1016/j.enpol.2020.111802

Wang, Z., Bui, Q., Zhang, B., Nawarathna, C. L. K., & Mombeuil, C. (2021). The nexus between renewable energy consumption and human development in BRICS countries: The moderating role of public debt. *Renewable Energy, 165*(P1), 381–390. https://doi.org/10.1016/j.renene.2020.11.075

World Bank: https://www.worldbank.org/en/topic/energy/overview.

Ziaei, S. M. (2012). Energy consumption in relation to government debt, inflation and investment in selected european countries. International Journal of Energy Environment and Economics, 20(5), 389–393.

Social Equity and Economic Efficiency: Evaluating the Impacts of Environmental Tax Policies

Abdurrahman TARAKTAŞ[1]

1 Introduction

Environmental taxes are economic instruments aimed at promoting environmental sustainability by imposing various taxes on economic activities to reduce environmental harm. These taxes seek to alter consumer and producer behaviors by increasing the cost of products and services that cause environmental pollution. Pigou's (1920) theory of internalizing negative externalities provides the theoretical foundation for environmental taxes. According to this theory, reflecting social costs in market prices is an effective method for reducing environmental pollution.

The economic effects of environmental taxes can be examined from various dimensions. Firstly, the impact of these taxes on the price mechanism is significant. Environmental taxes can increase the prices of goods and services, thereby reducing consumer demand, which in turn changes producer behavior (Baumol & Oates, 1988). Additionally, the effects of environmental taxes on competitiveness are a crucial area of research. The Porter Hypothesis (1996) suggests that environmental regulations and taxes can stimulate innovation, allowing firms to gain a competitive advantage.

From a social perspective, the effects of environmental taxes on income distribution are noteworthy. These taxes often place a disproportionate burden on low-income households, potentially exacerbating income distribution inequalities (Sterner & Coria, 2013). However, redistributing the revenue generated from environmental taxes through social policies can mitigate these adverse effects (Ekins, 1999). Furthermore, the positive impacts of environmental taxes on health and overall well-being should not be overlooked. Reduced environmental pollution can lead to improvements in public health, thereby enhancing societal well-being.

1 Anadolu University, ataraktas@anadolu.edu.tr, ORCID ID: 0000-0003-0649-3291

This study aims to examine the economic and social effects of environmental taxes in detail, based on existing research in the literature. The objective is to evaluate the impact of environmental taxes on both economic performance and social justice, and to provide recommendations for policymakers. By identifying gaps and discussion points in the literature, the study will propose potential solutions to enhance the effectiveness of environmental taxes.

2 Definition and Types of Environmental Taxes

Environmental taxes are fiscal regulations implemented to discourage activities harmful to the environment and to promote environmental sustainability. These taxes are generally defined as additional financial obligations imposed on the production, consumption, or disposal of environmentally harmful products (OECD, 2001).

According to Pigou's (1920) theory of internalizing negative externalities, the costs of negative externalities, such as environmental pollution, should be reflected in market prices to reduce environmental damage. The primary goal of environmental taxes is to reduce environmental harm. By increasing the cost of environmentally damaging activities, these taxes aim to reduce such activities and promote environmentally friendly alternatives. Secondly, environmental taxes seek to enhance economic efficiency. By encouraging the more efficient use of resources, these taxes can improve the overall efficiency of the economic system. Another significant objective of environmental taxes is to generate revenue. The revenue generated can be used for various environmental and social projects, such as environmental protection projects, the development of green technologies, and environmental education programs (Ekins & Speck, 2011).

Environmental taxes are implemented in various forms to reduce environmental damage and promote sustainable development. These taxes are typically applied across different sectors, such as energy, transportation, waste, and resource use, each aiming to achieve specific environmental goals (OECD, 2006).

- ***Carbon Taxes*:** Carbon taxes aim to reduce carbon dioxide emissions resulting from the combustion of fossil fuels. These taxes are calculated based on the amount of carbon emissions per ton and are commonly applied in the energy sector (Parry, 2019). Carbon taxes are considered a crucial tool in combating climate change.

- ***Energy Taxes*:** Energy taxes are implemented to reduce energy consumption and increase energy efficiency. These taxes are levied on energy sources such as electricity, natural gas, coal, and oil (European Environment Agency, 2016). Energy taxes aim to reduce environmental impacts by lowering energy demand.
- ***Transportation Taxes*:** Transportation taxes are applied to reduce the environmental impact of motor vehicles. These taxes are based on factors such as fuel consumption, emissions, and road usage (Sterner, 2007). Transportation taxes aim to reduce traffic congestion and air pollution.
- ***Waste Taxes*:** Waste taxes are implemented to reduce waste production and encourage recycling. These taxes are calculated based on the amount or type of waste (Kinnaman, 2006). Waste taxes aim to enhance environmental sustainability in waste management.
- ***Resource Use Taxes*:** Resource use taxes are applied to promote the sustainable use of natural resources. These taxes are levied on the extraction and use of resources such as water, forests, minerals, and other natural resources (Andersen et al., 2010). Resource use taxes aim to ensure the efficient and sustainable management of resources.

3 Potential Economic Impacts of Environmental Taxes

The economic impacts of environmental taxes can vary across different sectors and economic indicators. This section summarizes findings from empirical and theoretical studies on the potential economic effects of environmental taxes.

3.1 Effects on Competitiveness

The impact of environmental taxes on competitiveness is a significant concern, particularly for energy-intensive industries. Environmental taxes can increase production costs in these sectors, potentially harming international competitiveness (Ekins et al., 2011). However, according to the Porter Hypothesis, environmental taxes can also stimulate innovation, providing a competitive advantage in the long term (Porter & van der Linde, 1995). This perspective argues that environmental taxes can be a catalyst for technological advancements and efficiency improvements, not merely a cost burden. Ambec and Barla (2006) found that while environmental taxes initially increase costs, they also encourage investment in clean technologies, ultimately providing a competitive edge. This finding supports the Porter Hypothesis, indicating that environmental taxes can foster innovation.

3.2 Effects on Employment and the Labor Market

The impact of environmental taxes on employment can vary depending on how tax revenues are utilized. Some studies suggest that environmental taxes can negatively affect the labor market by increasing energy costs, which in turn raises production costs and reduces labor demand (Bovenberg & Goulder, 2002). Understanding the employment effects of environmental taxes is crucial for assessing their social dimension. Heine and Black (2019) found that environmental taxes generally have a positive effect on employment in Europe. Specifically, using tax revenues to reduce labor taxes can enhance job creation effects.

3.3 Effects on Economic Growth and Investments

The effects of environmental taxes on economic growth are complex and multifaceted. On one hand, these taxes can slow down economic activity and negatively impact investments in the short term (Goulder, 1995). On the other hand, environmental taxes can support sustainable economic growth in the long term by promoting more efficient resource use and increased investments in innovative technologies (Johnstone et al., 2010). Halkos and Paizanos (2013) note that the impact of environmental taxes on economic growth varies depending on how tax revenues are utilized and the structure of the national economy. Johnstone et al. (2010) found that environmental taxes in OECD countries increased investments in innovative, environmentally friendly technologies. This study indicates that environmental taxes can contribute to both improved environmental performance and economic growth.

3.4 Effects on Prices and Demand

The impact of environmental taxes on consumer prices, demand, and inflation is a significant area of research. Many empirical studies examining the effects of environmental taxes on prices and demand have found that these taxes alter consumer behavior. For example, a study on Sweden's carbon tax showed that the tax significantly reduced fossil fuel consumption and increased the use of renewable energy (Andersson, 2019). This study highlights the capacity of environmental taxes to influence demand through price signals. Energy and carbon taxes can raise overall price levels by increasing energy costs (Parry, 2019). This situation can disproportionately affect low-income households, increasing their financial burden. However, redistributing the revenue generated from environmental taxes directly or indirectly can mitigate these effects and protect social welfare (Sterner & Coria, 2013).

3.5 Effects on Public Finance

Environmental taxes can make significant contributions to public finance and create a more sustainable tax structure. The double dividend hypothesis suggests that environmental taxes can provide environmental benefits and improve economic efficiency by reducing other taxes (Goulder, 1995). However, the impact of environmental taxes on income distribution is complex and requires careful policy design. Low-income households may be disproportionately affected by increased energy and transportation costs, making the fair and effective redistribution of tax revenues essential.

4 Potential Social Impacts of Environmental Taxes

The social impacts of environmental taxes can be assessed across various dimensions, including income distribution, living standards, health, and social equity. This section summarizes findings from empirical and theoretical studies on the potential social impacts of environmental taxes.

4.1 Effects on Income Distribution

The impact of environmental taxes on income distribution is significant due to concerns that low-income households may be disproportionately affected by these taxes. Environmental taxes can negatively impact income distribution by imposing additional costs on basic needs, such as energy and transportation (Sterner & Coria, 2013). However, with appropriate policy support, the adverse effects on income distribution can be minimized.

Redistribution policies can play a crucial role in reducing income inequality and ensuring social justice.

4.2 Effects on Living Standards

The impact of environmental taxes on living standards is evaluated through the cost increases on household budgets and the resulting effects on social welfare. Bento and Jacobsen (2007) found that energy taxes in the U.S. could negatively affect the living standards of low-income households by raising consumer prices. However, redirecting revenues from environmental taxes to social welfare programs can balance these effects and protect the living standards of low-income households.

4.3 Effects on Health

The health impacts of environmental taxes are primarily indirect, arising from improvements in air quality. Carattini et al. (2018) demonstrated that the carbon tax in Switzerland improved air quality, positively affecting public health. This study highlights the significant indirect health benefits of environmental taxes. Reducing air pollution can contribute to decreasing respiratory diseases and other environmental health issues, thereby improving overall health levels.

4.4 Effects on Social Equity

The impact of environmental taxes on social equity depends on the fair implementation of these taxes. The potential for environmental taxes to disproportionately affect low-income households is a critical consideration for social equity. Dresner et al. (2006) found that environmental taxes could promote social equity if low-income households are supported through energy efficiency programs in the UK. Such measures can mitigate the adverse effects of environmental taxes on social equity and promote a fairer distribution. Studies conducted in different regions of the world show that the proper design and implementation of environmental taxes can enhance social equity.

4.5 Effects on Education and Awareness

Environmental taxes also have the potential to increase education and awareness on environmental issues. Afsah and Vincent (1997) showed that in areas of Indonesia where environmental taxes were implemented, there was an increase in environmental awareness and education, leading to positive changes in environmental behavior. This finding indicates that environmental taxes can have beneficial effects on societal education and awareness.

5 Conclusion and Policy Recommendations

Environmental taxes are powerful tools with the potential to achieve environmental goals, enhance economic efficiency, and promote social justice. These taxes aim to internalize environmental externalities, ensuring that polluters bear the costs of their actions and encouraging more sustainable behaviors. However, the economic and social impacts of environmental taxes are complex and need to be managed appropriately.

Economically, well-designed environmental taxes can enhance competitiveness and support long-term economic growth (Porter & van der Linde, 1995). However, short-term cost pressures on energy-intensive sectors and potential adverse effects on employment must be considered (Bovenberg & Goulder, 2002). The impact on income distribution is also crucial; low-income households may be disproportionately affected by environmental taxes, necessitating fair redistribution of tax revenues (Sterner & Coria, 2013).

Socially, environmental taxes have positive health effects, particularly through improved air quality (Carattini et al., 2018). Additionally, these taxes have the potential to promote social equity, but their implementation and the use of their revenues must be carefully designed (Dresner et al., 2006). Increasing education and awareness can also enhance the societal acceptance and effectiveness of environmental taxes (Afsah & Vincent, 1997).

As shown in Figure 1, Turkish households pay higher energy taxes compared to the average household in the European Union. This significant finding highlights Türkiye's adoption of higher taxation policies to reduce energy consumption and promote environmental sustainability. However, these high taxes can negatively impact disposable incomes and increase the risk of energy poverty. Therefore, when assessing the economic and social impacts of environmental taxes in Türkiye, it is essential to consider not only the environmental benefits but also the financial burden on households and its implications for social inequality.

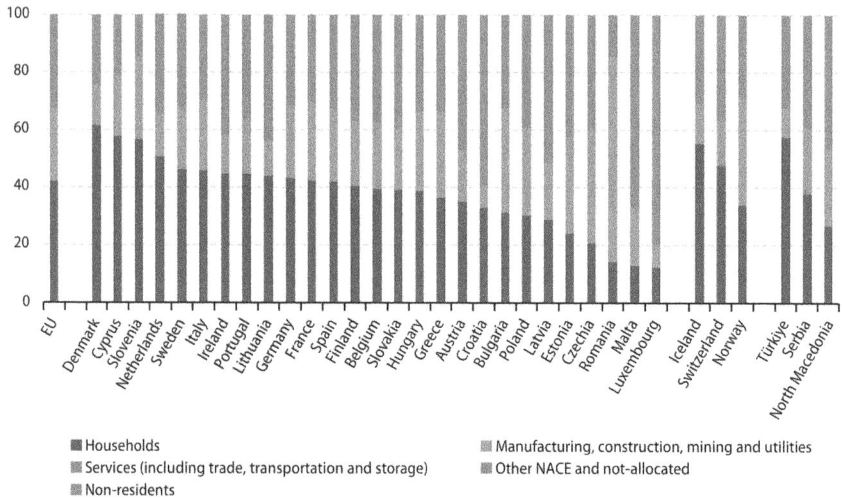

Fig. 1: Energy taxes by paying economic activity in European countries, 2021 (% of energy tax revenue).

Source: (Eurostat, 2024).

With its rapidly growing economy and increasing energy consumption, Türkiye considers environmental taxes a crucial tool for achieving environmental sustainability goals. Türkiye's current environmental policies and tax system present both opportunities and challenges for the effective implementation of environmental taxes and the promotion of social justice.

The economic impacts of environmental taxes are significant, given Türkiye's energy consumption and production structure. The country's energy-intensive sectors and reliance on fossil fuels could lead to increased cost pressures and reduced competitiveness due to environmental taxes (OECD, 2021). However, these taxes can also incentivize investments in renewable energy and energy efficiency, potentially supporting long-term economic growth.

Socially, the effects of environmental taxes on income distribution in Türkiye must be carefully considered. Low-income households could be disproportionately affected by the tax burden on essential needs such as energy and transportation, potentially exacerbating social inequalities. Nonetheless, redistributing the revenues from environmental taxes as social assistance and tax reductions for low-income households can mitigate these adverse effects.

The health impacts of environmental taxes should also not be overlooked. By reducing air pollution, environmental taxes have the potential to improve public health. Considering the air pollution issues in major Turkish cities, the implementation of environmental taxes could enhance the health levels of urban residents (TÜİK, 2020).

In this context, several recommendations for Türkiye can be proposed:

- ***Measures to Balance Income Distribution:*** To mitigate the adverse effects of environmental taxes on income distribution, tax revenues should be redistributed as social assistance and tax reductions for low-income households. Such redistribution policies are crucial for ensuring social justice and reducing the financial burden on low-income households (OECD, 2021).
- ***Promotion of Renewable Energy and Energy Efficiency Investments:*** Allocating revenues from environmental taxes to renewable energy and energy efficiency projects can reduce Türkiye's energy dependence and support long-term economic growth. These investments also have the potential to create jobs and foster economic development.
- ***Employment Support Programs:*** Employment support programs and retraining opportunities should be provided to workers in sectors affected by the implementation of environmental taxes. Such programs can facilitate workforce transitions and promote the creation of new, sustainable job opportunities (Heine and Black, 2019).
- ***Health and Air Quality Improvement Programs:*** To maximize the positive health impacts of environmental taxes, investments should be made in programs aimed at improving air quality in major cities. This can reduce healthcare costs and enhance overall public health (TÜİK, 2020).
- ***Public Education and Awareness Campaigns:*** Comprehensive public education and awareness campaigns should be organized to increase the acceptance of environmental taxes and raise environmental awareness. These campaigns can better explain the purposes and benefits of environmental taxes to the public and build societal support (Afsah and Vincent, 1997).
- ***Policy Design Adapted to Local Conditions:*** Environmental taxes should be designed and implemented flexibly, considering Türkiye's economic and social structure. Local conditions and sectoral characteristics should

be taken into account in policy design, and the impacts of environmental taxes should be continuously monitored and adjusted as needed.

- ***International Cooperation and Coordination:*** To reduce the negative impacts of environmental taxes on international competitiveness, international cooperation and coordination are essential. Türkiye can develop globally harmonized environmental policies to minimize competitive inequalities and more effectively achieve environmental goals (OECD, 2021).

Türkiye's tax system includes various environmental taxes, such as the Motor Vehicles Tax, Special Consumption Tax, Environmental Cleaning Tax, Plastic Bag Fee, and Recycling Contribution Fee. While there is no direct carbon tax in Türkiye, various regulations and incentives aim to reduce carbon emissions. For instance, incentives for renewable energy investments and support for energy efficiency projects are provided. These taxes aim to promote environmental sustainability and cover the costs of environmentally harmful activities.

To promote environmental sustainability while considering social equity, new green taxes can be proposed in the Turkish tax system. These taxes can align the goals of environmental protection and social justice.

- ***Carbon Tax:***
  - *Purpose:* To reduce carbon emissions and discourage fossil fuel use.
  - *Implementation:* A carbon tax can be levied on the production and consumption of fossil fuels. The tax rate can be determined based on the amount of carbon emitted.
  - *Social Equity:* Funds from tax revenues can be used to provide discounts on energy bills or direct financial support for low-income households.
- ***Renewable Energy Incentive Tax:***
  - *Purpose:* To encourage investments in renewable energy.
  - *Implementation:* An additional tax on energy producers using fossil fuels can be used to fund renewable energy projects.
  - *Social Equity:* Tax revenues can be used to subsidize or provide incentives for the installation of renewable energy systems for low-income households.

- ***Plastic Waste Tax:***
  - *Purpose:* To reduce plastic waste and increase recycling rates.
  - *Implementation:* A tax on the production and consumption of plastic products can be applied. The tax rate can be based on the environmental impact of the product.
  - *Social Equity:* Revenues from the plastic waste tax can be used to improve recycling infrastructure and make recycling services free for low-income households.
- ***Water Consumption Tax:***
  - *Purpose:* To promote the sustainable use of water resources.
  - *Implementation:* A tiered tax on water consumption can be applied. Higher rates can be imposed above a certain consumption threshold.
  - *Social Equity:* Basic water needs for low-income households can be exempted from the tax up to a certain level.
- ***Vehicle Emission Tax:***
  - *Purpose:* To reduce air pollution from motor vehicles.
  - *Implementation:* A tax can be applied based on the emission levels of vehicles, with higher-emission vehicles paying higher taxes.
  - *Social Equity:* Tax reductions or incentives can be provided for low-income households to purchase environmentally friendly vehicles.
- ***E-Waste Recycling Tax:***
  - *Purpose:* To encourage the recycling of electronic waste.
  - *Implementation:* A small tax on the sale of electronic devices can be used to fund e-waste recycling programs.
  - *Social Equity:* Tax revenues can be used to provide free e-waste collection and recycling services in low-income areas.
- ***Green Space Protection Tax:***
  - *Purpose:* To protect and increase green spaces.
  - *Implementation:* A tax on new developments can be used to fund the protection and creation of green spaces.
  - *Social Equity:* Tax revenues can be used to increase green spaces in low-income neighborhoods.

In conclusion, for Türkiye to effectively implement environmental taxes, it is essential to carefully evaluate the economic and social impacts and develop appropriate policy measures. Balancing the goals of economic efficiency, social justice, and environmental sustainability is critical for the success of environmental taxes, and strategies must be developed accordingly.

Bibliography

Afsah, S., & Vincent, J. R. (1997). "Putting Pressure on Polluters: Indonesia's PROPER Program". World Development.

Andersen, M. S., Speck, S., Gee, D., & Martin, J. (2010). Further environmental tax reform–illustrative potential in Ireland. EEA Staff Position Note, EEA SPN, 10(01).

Andersson, J. J. (2019). Carbon taxes and CO2 emissions: Sweden as a case study. American Economic Journal: Economic Policy, 11(4), 1–30.

Ambec, S., & Barla, P. (2006). "Can Environmental Regulations Be Good for Business? An Assessment of the Porter Hypothesis". Energy Studies Review.

Baumol, W. J., & Oates, W. E. (1988). The Theory of Environmental Policy. Cambridge University Press.

Bento, A. M., & Jacobsen, M. (2007). "Ricardian rents, environmental policy and the 'double-dividend' hypothesis". Journal of Environmental Economics and Management.

Bovenberg, A. L., & Goulder, L. H. (2002). "Environmental Taxation and Regulation". Handbook of Public Economics.

Carattini, S., Carvalho, M., & Fankhauser, S. (2018). "Overcoming public resistance to carbon taxes". Wiley Interdisciplinary Reviews: Climate Change.

Dresner, S., Dunne, L., Clinch, P., & Beuermann, C. (2006). "Social and political responses to ecological tax reform in Europe: An introduction to the special issue". Energy Policy.

Ekins, P. (1999). "European environmental taxes and charges: recent experience, issues and trends". Ecological Economics.

Ekins, P., & Speck, S. (2011). Environmental Tax Reform (ETR): A Policy for Green Growth.

Ekins, P., Pollitt, H., Barton, J., & Blobel, D. (2011). The implications for households of environmental tax reform (ETR) in Europe. Ecological Economics, 70(12), 2472–2485.

European Environment Agency (2016). Environmental taxation and EU environmental policies.

Eurostat. (2024). "Environmental taxes – A statistical guide".

Goulder, L. H. (1995). "Environmental Taxation and the 'Double Dividend': A Reader's Guide". International Tax and Public Finance.

Halkos, G. E., & Paizanos, E. A. (2013). "The Effect of Government Expenditure on the Environment: An Empirical Investigation". Ecological Economics.

Heine, D., & Black, S. (2019). "Benefits Beyond Climate: Environmental Tax Reform". International Monetary Fund.

Johnstone, N., Haščič, I., & Popp, D. (2010). "Renewable Energy Policies and Technological Innovation: Evidence Based on Patent Counts". Environmental and Resource Economics.

Kinnaman, T. C. (2006). "Policy watch: Examining the justification for residential recycling". Journal of Economic Perspectives.

Metcalf, G. E. (2009). "Designing a Carbon Tax to Reduce U.S. Greenhouse Gas Emissions". Review of Environmental Economics and Policy.

OECD (2001). Environmentally Related Taxes in OECD Countries: Issues and Strategies.

OECD (2006). The Political Economy of Environmentally Related Taxes.

OECD. (2021). "Environmental Policy Reviews: Turkey".

Parry, I. (2019). What is carbon taxation. Financ. Dev, 8, 54–55.

Pigou, A. C. (1920). The Economics of Welfare.

Porter, M. (1996). America's green strategy. Business and the environment: a reader, 33, 1072.

Porter, M. E., & van der Linde, C. (1995). "Toward a New Conception of the Environment-Competitiveness Relationship". Journal of Economic Perspectives.

Sterner, T. (2007). Fuel Taxes and the Poor: The Distributional Effects of Gasoline Taxation and Their Implications for Climate Policy.

Sterner, T., & Coria, J. (2013). Policy instruments for environmental and natural resource management. Routledge.

TÜİK. (2020). "İstatistiklerle Türkiye."

Carbon Sinks as a Global Public Good and Carbon-Based Taxation

Raşit GÜLTEKİN[1]

1 Introduction

Economically, human needs are unlimited, but generally it is accepted that the goods and services that will meet these needs are limited. However, there are such goods and services that their benefits or harms affect all individuals in the world and future generations, and it is not possible to deprive certain individuals or institutions from the consumption of these goods or services. The supply and financing of these goods and services is an issue that needs to be decided and implemented on a global scale.

Although there are many types of global public goods, the environment and its components have a dimension that concerns almost every segment of society due to their beneficial and harmful outcomes. Because carbon emissions, global warming, climate change and associated environmental problems can cause material and human losses regardless of country borders. In this respect, carbon sinks are an application and interdisciplinary field of study that requires technical and expert knowledge and has socio-economic, legal and financial aspects. Because carbon sinks, which are global public goods, reduce greenhouse gas/carbon concentration in the atmosphere and prevent it from reaching dangerous levels. However, it is important to protect carbon sinks within public discipline and ensure their sustainability.

The authority and responsibility for the supply and financing of global public goods related to the environment essentially belong to independent states. However, international regulations are decisive in terms of whether the responsibility of states is realized at the national or global level. Among these international regulations that include important and binding issues in terms of carbon sinks are the United Nations Framework Convention on Climate Change, the Kyoto Protocol and the Marrakesh Decisions. These regulations include various provisions in terms of binding environmentally

[1] Assoc. Prof., Trakya University, Faculty of Economics and Administrative Sciences, Department of Public Finance, rasitgultekin@trakya.edu.tr, ORCID: 0000-0001-8390-327X

sensitive issues to universal rules and determining the obligations of states. Some of these provisions relate to carbon taxes, a tool to ensure that governments meet their emissions commitments.

In this context, the aim of the study is to examine carbon sinks, which are global public goods, and the carbon-based taxation regime. The study used literature review and document review methods, and within this scope, national/international regulations, reports, academic studies and institutional publications were scanned. The study is structured in three main sections. In the first part of the study, global public goods will be examined theoretically, in the second part, the place of carbon sinks within the scope of global public goods will be focused on, and in the third part, carbon-based taxation issues will be evaluated. It is anticipated that the study will offer a different academic perspective on environment, taxation and sustainability approaches in the context of the subjects it covers

2 Theoretical Framework

2.1 The Concept of Global Public Goods

According to a widespread acceptance, human needs are unlimited; however, the goods and services that will meet these needs are limited. The supply of goods and services is provided by the private sector and/or the public sector. At the same time, there are two general types of goods: private goods and public goods; and in terms of public goods, there is a distinction between regional, global and international public goods.

Tab. 1: Definitions

Public Good	**A Public Good** is a commodity, measure, fact or service: - which can be consumed by one person without diminishing the amount available for consumption by another person (non-rivalry); - which is available at zero or negligible marginal cost to a large or unlimited number of consumers (non-exclusiveness); and - which does not bring about disutility to any consumer now or in the future (sustainability). The degree of non-exclusiveness determines the Public Good's degree of purity.

International Public Good	**An International Public Good (IPG)** is a Public Good which provides benefits crossing national borders of the producing country
Regional Public Good	**A Regional Public Good (RPG)** is an International Public Good which displays spill-over benefits to countries in the neighbourhood of the producing country, in a region which is smaller than the rest of the world.
Global Public Good	**A Global Public Good (GPG)** is an International Public Good which, while not necessarily to the same extent, benefits consumers all over the world.

Source: (Reisen, Soto & Weithöner, 2004:12).

In the context of the scope of the study, it cannot be said that the concept of global public goods is new. Because the concept was first mentioned in Kindleberger's article titled "International Public Goods Without International Governments" (Kindleberger, 1986; Aktaş, 2016:15). However, the concept has gained a place on the world agenda with the book titled "Global Public Goods: International Cooperation in the 21st Century" published by the United Nations Development Program (UNDP) in 1999 and its use has become widespread with the book titled "Presentation of Global Public Goods" (Kaul, 2001; Akdemir & Şahin, 2006:3; Kirmanoğlu, Yılmaz & Susam, 2006:26). It should be noted that the concept of global public goods is frequently mentioned related to the United Nations sustainable development goals in connection with problems such as environmental pollution and climate change (Bal, 2012:7).

The concept of global public goods is defined as "benefits that can be obtained by all individuals in the world (individuals currently living and future generations), that are free of competition and restrictions in their consumption, that everyone can benefit from, and that are financed globally". According to another definition, the concept refers to "goods, resources, services and political systems that are important for development and poverty reduction and whose production in sufficient quantities is only possible with the joint action of developed and developing countries, and that have large cross-border externalities". Certain characteristics of global public goods can be derived from this definition. The first of these is that the benefits of global public goods cover the entire world in terms of people and countries, and not only today but also future generations. In other words, global public goods have the quality of "globality/universality", which indicates the area of spread of their benefits. Secondly, global public goods are not subject to competition; in other words, they have the quality of "publicness", which indicates that there is no exclusion in benefiting from their benefits. Finally, the concept of global public goods can be not only a physical element but also an abstract element in the form of benefit and/or harm. Therefore, global public goods are goods that are open to the benefit of the public globally rather than individuals in a particular country, do not exclude any person, group or generation, and thus contain intergenerational externalities (Kaul & Mendoza, 2003:95; Ortaç, 2004:15; Akdemir & Şahin, 2006:4; Kirmanoğlu, Yılmaz, & Susam, 2006:27; Mutlu, 2006:55; Yalçın, 2009:290; Aktaş, 2016:24; Barış & Barlas, 2017:139).

2.2 Classification of Global Public Goods

Global public goods are divided into various types according to criteria such as "being traditional or new", "supply technique", "being human, generation or country focused", "purpose and means nature", "being production or consumption oriented", "nature of the good", "public quality and spatial dimension", "sector", "type of benefit or publicity" and "production and management dynamics", "function". In these distinctions, global public goods are divided into a type of benefit or harm; In other words, it can be an opportunity, risk, harm or threat for the world (te Velde, Morrisey & Hewitt, 2002:153–154; Kirmanoğlu, Yılmaz & Susam, 2006:47–50; Akdemir & Şahin, 2006:6–22; Mutlu, 2006:56–74; Susam, 2008:277; Yalçın, 2009:292; Bal, 2012:9; Barış & Barlas, 2017; 143–148).

Global public goods also include the environment and issues related to the environment. Because externalities related to the environment can reach dimensions that concern more than one country and can affect a wide socio-economic group. In addition, the environment as a whole has the potential to affect both today's and future generations. In this context, when global public goods are classified, "rivers, water resources, energy, forests, fisheries, waste management, biosphere, biodiversity, protected areas" are considered as global environmental public goods. Similarly, "reducing greenhouse gas emissions that cause global climate change", "protecting the ozone layer", "reducing air pollution", "preventing forest fires" and "protecting tropical forests" are considered international and global public goods. In this determination, environmental problems that have reached a global dimension require state intervention due to the inadequacy of the market economy on the one hand, and on the other hand, they require cooperation, decision-making and implementation processes on a global scale. In this respect, environmental issues constitute a type of global public good. It should be noted that the protection of forests and combating forest fires show their benefits at a regional level; Preventing global warming is a pure global public good; tropical forests are a mixed (common) global good (Mutlu, 2006:62; Yalçın, 2009:300; Bal, 2012:11; Barış & Barlas, 2017; 143–148).

2.3 Financing Global Public Goods

The supply and financing of global public goods are among the issues on which there is no consensus. The general tendency regarding the financing of global public goods is towards the internalization of externalities, that is, the reflection of benefits and costs to those who produce or consume these goods (Tekin & Vural, 2004:326). Because when the issue is evaluated in terms of authority gap, it is stated that the country that causes the externalities that are transboundary to a country should be responsible for these externalities; that the externalities in question can be internalized in this way and that if this approach is accepted as valid for international externalities (international cooperation starts "at home"), the capacity of countries to combat global interdependence will increase (Kaul, Grunberg & Stern, 1999; Aktaş, 2016:39–40). In addition, due to the increasing interest in global public goods, a significant portion of the budgets of international organizations are used in activities related to these (Akdemir & Şahin, 2006:4). However, although international organizations have an important place in the supply of global public goods, first a supply program is put on the agenda by governments, private sector, non-governmental organizations or academic circles and then official decisions are made regarding this supply and its financing. In this process, there may be countries that pay attention to global issues due to reasons such as the view of the sovereignty transfer, volunteering and free-riding, while there may be countries that focus only on national issues (Aktaş, 2016:36–37).

Since the decision-makers in national public goods are governments, authorized government bodies decide which goods will be provided in what quantity and quality, and these decisions are implemented by financing from the state budget. However, the presentation and financing of global public goods differ. Since there is no central body with taxation authority at the global level, the financing of global public goods is carried out through voluntary financing of countries and dues paid to international organizations instead of taxes. The main reason for the search for alternative ways to the state in financing is the slow, cumbersome budgeting process governed by domestic policies and priorities (Mendez, 2001:6). As a result of this search, private or joint resources provided by non-state actors, namely international official organizations, non-profit civil society organizations, multinational corporations and real persons, have also highlighted the financing of global public goods. In addition, official development assistance (ODA) provided by developed countries to developing countries can also be provided within this scope (Susam, 2008:295; Yalçın, 2009:295–298).

There are four basic methods in the presentation of global public goods: "addition", "weighted total", "best hit" and "weakest link". In the addition method, the amount of global public goods production of countries determines the total production level. In the weighted addition method, the difference in the global public goods production of countries is taken as basis. In the best hit method, the actor with the most contribution determines the amount of global public goods production; in the weakest link method, the country with the least contribution determines the amount (Sandler, 2001; Yalçın, 2009:296).

In theory, regarding the financing of global public goods or the internalization of externalities, public economy solutions based on state intervention (Pigou Approach and Plott Approach) and market economy based solutions (Kaldor-Hicks Approach, Scitovsky Approach and Coase Theory) are emphasized. However, due to the scope of the study, it is important to focus on global taxation. Because, primarily through taxes, fees and similar financial obligations, resource depletion, shortage, instability and other undesirable consequences can be intervened and financing is provided for the provision of global public goods (Binger, 2013:15; Aktaş, 2016:55). For example, taxes to be applied at the global level such as carbon taxes, fuel/flight taxes, raw material taxes, tobin tax, taxation of electronic commerce, electronic mail and internet usage taxes, world trade taxes, arms sales tax are expected to be both an effective tool in preventing negative externalities at the global level and a source for the financing of these goods. Because individual initiatives/activities carried out by a single state are insufficient in solving global problems. However, the absence of a central authority to implement global taxes poses a problem (Baumert, 1998; Tekin & Vural, 2004:334–335; Susam, 2008: 296–297; Eser & Birinci, 2013:181; Altınışık & Peker, 2014:328, Pehlivan & Aktuğ, 2019:178).

Global taxes that should be implemented simultaneously by all countries in the world have some reasons for existence and conditions for success. The first reason for existence is that global taxes are accepted as an effective policy tool to reduce the negativities related to global activities. For example, a global carbon tax will aim to reduce fuel consumption in order to combat global climate change problems caused by carbon emissions due to fossil fuel use. Secondly, global taxes are quite useful in terms of generating revenue and financing global public goods. Finally, global taxes are necessary for ensuring justice and democratizing global governance (Uemura, 2007:\114–116; Günay & Altun, 2019:85). The first condition for success is that the tax has the advantage of ease of administration and simplicity in a way that minimizes compliance costs. Secondly, it should have the basic objectives required for a defensible, sound and logical economic policy. Thirdly, the envisaged tax should provide a revenue increase that is worth the political struggle. So a global tax should involve the grouping of at least some of the world's countries (Eser & Birinci, 2013:189).

3 The Global Public Good Nature of Carbon Sinks

3.1 The Definition of Carbon Sink

The environment refers to the biological, physical, social, economic and cultural environment in which living beings maintain their relationships and interact with each other throughout their lives, and the environment, together with all its components (environment, prevention of environmental problems, forests, atmosphere, oceans) has the characteristics of a global public good. In other words, environmental issues have the basic characteristics of externality, publicity, open access and being a global public good. Because environmental problems at the national or regional level can create a global environmental problem as they accumulate (Wahl, 2006:6; Mutlu, 2006:62; Yalçın, 2009:298; Bal, 2012:2; Yavan, 2016:8).

The concept of sink is defined in the United Nations Framework Convention on Climate Change as "any process, activity or mechanism that removes a greenhouse gas, an aerosol or a precursor to a greenhouse gas from the atmosphere" (Art. 1–8). Carbon sinks refer to the sequestration rather than emission in a carbon reservoir, that is, the storage of carbon (Serengil, 2019:17); a mechanism, process or environment that draws carbon from the atmosphere and holds it (Hirsch, 2007:628; Serengil, 2019:105). In this respect, the concept refers to natural or man-made systems that absorb carbon dioxide from the atmosphere and store it (ÇŞİDB, 2024). Carbon sinks are essentially reservoirs that function to store carbon and release oxygen. The concept of reservoir in the said Convention is defined as "an element or elements of the climate system in which a greenhouse gas or a precursor to a greenhouse gas is stored" (Art. 1.7).

Within the scope of land use, land use change and forestry (LULUCF), sink areas consist of forest areas, meadows and pastures, agricultural areas, wetlands, settlements and other areas (Serengil, 2019:18). Forests and non-forest natural and semi-natural habitats such as steppes, pastures and maquis are places that sequester carbon on a local and global scale (Pamukçu Albers et al., 2023:347). However, carbon is also released from forests as a result of deforestation, forest fires or insect outbreaks, natural deaths, production activities and irregular forest management. The difference in the carbon cycle between the atmosphere and carbon sinks in forest ecosystems shows net carbon change. If this change is positive, forests are considered carbon storage pools/sinks; otherwise, they are considered carbon sources (Başkent, 2022:5).

Tab. 2: Some Ecosystems and Their Carbon Storage Capacities

Ecosystem	Carbon Storage Capacities (t C/ha)
Tropical forests	220
Temperate forests	150
Northern forests	90
Meadows and pastures	15
Agricultural fields	5

Source: (Görücü & Eker, 2009).

Carbon sinks and related activities are national, regional and global public goods. The perspective in the context of national and/or international activities related to carbon sinks is the same: to prevent and/or reduce greenhouse gas emissions into the atmosphere; to protect and/or increase greenhouse gas sinks (Pamukçu Albers et al., 2018:5).

3.2 Environmental Problems Caused by Carbon Emissions

Environmental problems are problems that arise from the effects that damage environmental components as a result of human activities. Among these, the concept of environmental degradation refers to "unwanted and dangerous changes in the environment as a result of pollution of natural resources such as water, air, soil, and the threat to animal and plant species" (Azbar & Mayaoğlu Akın, 2023:9) and the concept of environmental pollution refers to "any activity that may occur in the environment, affect the health of living beings and plants, and negatively affect the ecological system" (Özkanca Andıç & Erasa Akça, 2019:3448).

Carbon sinks are at the center of international climate regime issues that states should encourage and act in cooperation in the context of protecting and strengthening them (Røttereng, 2013:58). Because some of the environmental problems are related to gases that have a greenhouse effect in the atmosphere and emerge as environmental problems caused by carbon emissions. Carbon emissions occur as a result of fossil fuel consumption, industrialization, energy use in industrial and agricultural activities, uncontrolled activities of cement, aluminum, fertilizer, ceramics, electricity or iron and steel industry and forest fires, and global warming and related climate change occur due to carbon dioxide and other greenhouse gases accumulated in the atmosphere. Climate change causes anomalies such as drought, desertification, melting of glaciers and rise in sea/ocean levels, imbalance and deviation in precipitation, floods and inundations, typhoons, storms and tornadoes (Azbar & Mayaoğlu Akın, 2023:27).

Fig. 1: World Greenhouse Gas Emissions (1850–2022).
Source: (OWiD, 2024).

Forest, soil and ocean ecosystems are also closely related to the United Nations Sustainable Development Goals. Because global warming and the climate problems caused by greenhouse gas emissions cause damage and human loss at a global level. These damages also harm food and water security and thwart efforts towards the United Nations Sustainable Development Goals (IPCC, 2023, 4–6).

3.3 Environmentally Related Functions of Carbon Sinks

In order to understand the place and importance of carbon sinks in environmental problems related to global climate change, it would be appropriate to focus on the carbon budget approach. There are income and expenditure parts in the structure of a financial budget, and these two parts are in balance. The income part of the carbon budget includes emissions from fossil fuels, industry and land use change; the expense part includes atmospheric growth, ocean sink, land sink and cement carbonation. The carbon budget deficit reflects the amount that carbon sinks, which constitute budget expenditures, cannot absorb the carbon emissions that constitute budget revenues. This deficit increases the greenhouse gas concentration in the atmosphere, causing an increase in global warming (Çetinkaya & Akar, 2022:47).

Within the scope of LULUCF, the subcomponents where carbon accumulates and the carbon cycle takes place are defined as "carbon pools". In an ecosystem, there are carbon pools in the form of aboveground biomass (AGB), belowground biomass (BGB), dead wood (DW), dead cover (L), soil (S) and harvested wood products (HWP). The balance between carbon release from ecosystems to the atmosphere and carbon retained in ecosystems affects climate change positively/negatively and directly/indirectly (Pamukçu et al., 2018:4; Serengil, 2019:109). Therefore, carbon sinks/pools reduce the greenhouse gas concentration in the atmosphere and prevent it from reaching dangerous levels (Bettelheim & d'Origny, 2002:1834–1835).

When looked at statistically, forests, which cover approximately 30% of the world's land surface, store carbon in the air in wood material, plant matter and underground. While forests absorb 15.6 billion tons/gigatons of carbon dioxide from the atmosphere each year, they release approximately 8.1 gigatons of carbon dioxide back into the atmosphere as a result of deforestation due to fires and other causes. How well forests store carbon varies according to soil type, vegetation and climate, and the carbon retention capacity of trees varies according to their species, age and crown diameter characteristics. Whether the weather is sunny or cloudy also affects carbon retention. Although peatlands make up only 3% of the world's land area, they account for approximately one third of the carbon dioxide absorbed by the soil. Although the process takes a very long time, the seas and oceans store 80% of the world's carbon. (Görücü & Eker, 2009:5; S360Mag, 2021; Serengil, 2019:105; Hauck et al. 2020:16; Başkent, 2022:2; Gönüllü Sütçüoğlu, et al., 2022:4–6; Turgut, 2023:363–372; Karacabey, 2023:381–387).

4 Environment and Carbon Based Taxation Approach

4.1 Financing of the Global Public Good Environment

Environmental policies are based on four basic principles: "polluter pays", "precaution", "prevention" and "cooperation". The polluter pays principle, which stems from the need for a global pollution control strategy that will enable sustainable activities, states that the polluter must bear the cost of measures taken to eliminate damage to the environment. Financial and legal instruments can be used to prevent environmental problems. Financial instruments are environmental taxes, fees and incentives. Transferable emission licenses, subsidies and guarantee systems are also included in this scope. Legal instruments are prohibitions, restrictions and environmental standards that enable all kinds of limitations and ensure that non-compliant polluters are subject to sanctions (Mutlu, 2006:63–66; Özdemir, 2009:17–18; Savcı & Yıldırım, 2024:866).

Emissions trading and emissions taxation are two alternative market-based approaches to attributing the cost of pollution to emitters (Aiyegbusi, Yalamova & Essadoh-Yeddu, 2022:84). The carbon tax aims to deter emissions by placing an extra burden on them, while the ETS aims to limit emissions by setting a certain quota, thus creating a positive environmental impact. Since governments need to measure emissions in order to set carbon pricing for businesses, the carbon dioxide equivalent (CO2eq) unit of measurement is used for this purpose (Katkat Özçelik, 2024:975).

Taxes called "ecotax", "environmental taxes" or "green taxes" in the literature are included in Pigovian taxes, which are used to solve environmental problems and especially to prevent harmful externalities or to encourage environmentally friendly activities (Homam, 2015:3; Özkanca Andıç & Erasa Akça, 2019:3449). There are some issues that consider environmental taxes to be applied at a global level legitimate. First, there is a need for international resources for many environmental problems that are international in nature and cannot be solved at a national level. Second, the negative effects resulting from environmental problems can only be internalized if those who cause them are made to pay through taxes. Finally, the environment is a global public good and it is more appropriate to finance it by the public through taxes (Wahl, 2006:6–7).

Local and international experiences point to the importance of financially supporting forest-based carbon sinks. Active financial supports and the existence of a taxation regime reduce the cost of forest-based carbon sinks and support entrepreneurs who will operate in this area (Li et al, 2022:350–351). There are official development aids provided by governments as donors for the protection of forests and sustainable forest management in developing countries (Jenkins & Schaap, 2018:26). In addition, combating climate change, which has a higher potential for support on a global scale compared to similar areas due to the existence of a large number of funds, is an advantageous application area in terms of financing (Serengil, 2019:249–251).

4.2 Carbon Tax

Green taxes are taxes that stand out according to their non-fiscal purposes and fiscal purposes. Carbon taxes, energy taxes, waste and water usage taxes, environmental taxes on vehicles and plastic taxes are among the types of green taxes (Yüce, 2024:9–10). Carbon taxes, which are among the green taxes, have a widespread application area in the world. The Kyoto Protocol envisages the limitation of greenhouse gases within the scope of combating global warming and climate change and accepts the taxation of carbon emissions for this purpose (Mutlu, 2006:65). The biggest advantage of carbon taxes is that they are market-based (Hotunluoğlu & Tekeli, 2007:110–111).

Taxes applied for the purpose of financing global public goods are in the form of "direct taxation of nation states", "taxation of global trade" and "taxation of the use of global common goods". Carbon taxes are, in this respect, consumption taxes levied per unit of carbon emissions originating from fossil fuel consumption within the scope of taxation of nation states (Tekin & Vural, 2004:327; Eser & Birinci, 2013:181; Haites, 2018:956; Artun, 2024:24).

4.3 Brief Assessment About Türkiye

When the subject is evaluated in terms of an example in Türkiye, there is a Communiqué on the Procedures and Principles for the Preparation of Ecosystem-Based Functional Forest Management Plans on how to make a carbon balance sheet within the scope of sustainable forest management. The carbon inventory of forests is determined within the framework of the Communiqué (Talu et al., 2021:159).

Over the period from 1923 to 2021, Türkiye's CO2 share surged by approximately 416%, whereas the increase during the 1995–2021 period examined amounts to 56%. (Karşıyakalı et al., 2024:85). Türkiye's greenhouse gas emissions started to increase with the industrialization that occurred in the 1990s (Çetinkaya & Akar, 2022:46–47). It is seen that Türkiye's greenhouse gas emission trend is below 1% of the global total. Türkiye has undertaken to keep its emissions, which it predicted as 1,213 million tons of CO2eq for 2030, at 695 million tons of CO2eq with a 41% reduction within the scope of its international commitments and has determined 2053 for net-zero greenhouse gas emissions (REC, 2024:3).

According to the data of Turkish Statistical Institute (TÜİK), forest area is 23,245,000 hectares, meadow and pasture land is 14,617,000 and arable agricultural land is 38,563,000 hectares in 2023 (TÜİK, 2024a). Again, according to TurkStat data, total greenhouse gas emissions in 2021 were 572.0 million tons, and by types, CO2 was 455.2 million tons (79.6%), CH4 was 73.9 million tons (12.9%), N2O was 35.9 million tons (6.3%) and F gases were 6.9 million tons (1.2%) (TÜİK, 2024b). The distribution of greenhouse gas emissions by sector was as follows: energy 406.5 million tons (71.1%), agriculture 75.4 million tons (13.2%), industrial processes 74.7 million tons (13.1%) and waste 15.4 million tons (2.6%) (TÜİK, 2024c). According to the data of the Ministry of Environment, Urbanization and Climate Change (ÇŞİDB), in 2021, forests sequestered 33.94 million tons of CO2 equivalent from sink areas and processed wood products 15.72 million tons of CO2 equivalent from sink areas, totaling 49.66 million tons of carbon (ÇŞİDB, 2024). This data shows that 8.6% of the total emission is captured by carbon sinks. In Türkiye, forests can be intervened for reasons such as tourism and energy investments, opening of mining areas, new housing and agricultural areas (Talu et al., 2021:149). However, as the forest presence in Türkiye is on the rise, carbon sequestration in forests and average carbon density per hectare are increasing, making a positive contribution to the global carbon cycle (Serengil, 2019:123; Arslan, 2021:4).

In terms of taxation, although there are a number of taxes that can be associated with the environment in the Turkish tax system (motor vehicle tax, environmental cleaning tax, electricity-air gas consumption tax, special consumption tax, environmental contribution share collected on imports, recycling participation share), there is no tax called carbon tax (Artun, 2024:17; Oğuz & Yıldız, 2024:29).

5 Conclusion

Global public goods are goods and services that are accessible to all individuals, including future generations, that have no competition or restrictions in their consumption, and that are financed globally. In this respect, global public goods are physical elements, benefits or harms that are global/universal and public. The universal nature of the benefits of global public goods requires countries to act together in terms of providing and financing these goods. The environment and carbon sinks within the environmental components are also generally included in global public goods. Global warming, especially caused by greenhouse gas emissions, and the climate change and environmental problems it causes threaten all of humanity.

Carbon sinks are natural or artificial areas that function to store carbon and release oxygen. Forest areas, meadows and pastures, agricultural areas, wetlands, residential areas and other areas, as well as oceans, are places that store carbon on a local and global scale. If the carbon cycle between carbon sinks and the atmosphere is positive, carbon storage occurs, otherwise carbon release occurs. The expected function of carbon sinks depends on the protection, increase and qualification of these areas.

Countries with high carbon sequestration and oxygen emission are countries that provide oxygen to the atmosphere and contribute to the solution of global climate problems. In this respect, it would be appropriate for countries with high carbon emissions to transfer resources to countries in this position in parallel with the taxation approach based on carbon emission. Because it would not be fair within the framework of approaches to financing global public goods for only the countries where these areas are located to bear the costs of creating, preserving and developing carbon sinks. However, at this point, it is clear that there is a need for universal rules that regulate the subject in terms of tax law elements and techniques, as well as transparent, reliable and up-to-date carbon budget data.

Bibliography

360Mag. (2021). Karbon yutakları: Doğa iklim değişikliğiyle mücadeleye nasıl yardımcı olur? https://www.s360mag.com/post/karbon-yutaklari

Aiyegbusi, O., Yalamova, R., & Essadoh-Yeddu, J. (2022). Meeting CO_2 targets with carbon pricing through taxation and trading. Earth Sciences And Human Constructions, 2, 81–88. DOI: https://doi.org/10.37394/232024.2022.2.12

Akdemir, A., & Şahin, M. (2006). Küresel kamusal malların üretim ve yönetim dinamikleri bağlamında sınıflandırılması. Maliye Dergisi. 150, 1–24.

Aktaş, M. (2016). Küresel kamusal malların uluslararası işbirliklerinde kullanımı ve türkiye için öneriler-uzmanlık tezi. Ankara: T. C. Kalkınma Bakanlığı Yayınları No: 2959.

Altınışık, İ., & Peker, H. (2014). Küresel kamusal mallar ve finansmanı. Selçuk Üniversitesi Sosyal Bilimler Meslek Yüksekokulu Dergisi. 12(1–2), 323–332.

Arslan, A. (2021). İklim değişikliğinin ormanlar ve sürdürülebilir orman yönetimi üzerindeki etkileri-Türkiye raporu https://world.ormuh.org.tr/

Artun, E. (2024). Karbon vergisinin Türkiye'de yenilenebilir enerjiye yönlendirme aracı olarak kullanılması. Yaşar Hukuk Dergisi, 6(1), 15–48.

Azbar, N., & Mayaoğlu Akın, C. (2023). Yeşil çevre terimler sözlüğü: Avrupa Birliği Yeşil Mutabakat'ta geçen teknik terimlerin açıklamasını içeren kitapçık. İzmir: Batı Anadolu Sanayici ve İş İnsanları Dernekleri Federasyonu (BASİFED).

Bal, H. (2012). Çevre sorunları ve bu sorunların çözümü çerçevesinde küresel kamusal mallar, dışsallıklar ve küresel kamusal malların arzına ilişkin sorunlar. Global Journal of Economics and Business Studies. 1(2), 1–11.

Barış, A., & Barlas, E. (2017). Kamu maliyesi teorisinde küresel kamusal mallar. Sosyal Bilimler Araştırmaları Dergisi. 12(1), 129–152.

Başkent, E. (2022). Orman ekosistemlerinde karbon dinamiğinin temel bileşenleri ve planlamadaki yeri. ArtGRID-Journal of Architecture, Engineering & Fine Arts, 4(1), 1–15.

Baumert, K. (1998). Global taxes and fees: recent developments and overcoming obstacles. https://archive.globalpolicy.org/socecon/glotax/baumert.htm

Bettelheim, E. C. & d'Origny, G. (2002). Carbon sinks and emissions trading under the kyoto protocol: a legal analysis in Philosophical transactions: mathematical, physical and engineering sciences, carbon, biodiversity, conservation and income: an analysis of a free-market approach to land-use change and forestry in developing and developed countries, (360)1797, 1827–1851 DOI: http://10.1098/rsta.2002.1035

Binger, A. (2003). Global public goods and potential mechanisms for financing availability. Background paperprepared for the Fifth Session of the Committee for Development Policy meeting.

Çetinkaya, G., & Akar, S. (2022). Türkiye'nin küresel karbon bütçesindeki payı: öngörü senaryoları ile bir değerlendirme. Maliye Çalışmaları Dergisi, 68, 33–50.

Çevre ve İklim Derneği [REC]. (2024). Türkiye'nin karbon yakalama, kullanma ve depolama potansiyeli. Ankara: Kaynak, Çevre ve İklim Derneği Yayınları.

ÇŞİDB (2024). Yutak Alanlar ve Karbon Tutumları. https://cevreselgostergeler.csb.gov.tr/

Eser, L., & Birinci, N. (2013). Global vergi önerileri ve uygulanabilirlikleri. Atatürk Üniversitesi İktisadi ve İdari Bilimler Dergisi. 27(1), 177–195.

Gönüllü Sütçüoğlu. G., Karcı Demirkol, A., Zamani A., & Kalaycı Önaç, A. (2022). Kent ormanlarının karbon yakalama potansiyeli. 6th International Students Science Congress Proceedings. DOI: https://doi.org/10.52460/issc.2022.054

Görücü, Ö., & Eker, Ö. (2019). Kahramanmaraş Ayvalı baraj havzasında karbon emisyonu ve ekonomisi üzerine araştırmalar. II. Ormancılıkta Sosyo-Ekonomik Sorunlar Kongresi Bildiriler Kitabı. İsparta: Süleyma Demirel Üniversitesi.

Günay H. F., & Altun N. (2019). Küresel ölçekte önerilen vergilerin mali ve sosyal etkilerinin değerlendirilmesi. Gümüşhane Üniversitesi Sosyal Bilimler Enstitüsü Elektronik Dergisi, 10(1), 84–96.

Hauck, J., Zeising, M., Le Quéré, C., Gruber, N., Bakker DCE, Bopp, L., Chau TTT., Gürses, Ö., Ilyina, T., Landschützer, P., Lenton, A., Resplandy, L., Rödenbeck, C., Schwinger, J. & Séférian, R. (2020). Consistency and challenges in the ocean carbon sink estimate for the global carbon budget. Frontiers in Marine Science, 7, 1–22. DOI: http://10.3389/fmars.2020.571720

Hirsch, D. D. (2007). Trading in ecosystem services: carbon sinks and the clean development mechanism. Journal of Land Use & Environmental Law, (22)2, 623–639, https://ssrn.com/abstract=1071927

Homam, M. (2015). Economic efficiency of carbon tax versus carbon cap-and-trade. http://individual.utoronto.ca/homam/Carbon_tax_versus_cap__trade.pdf

Hotunluoğlu, H., & Tekeli, R. (2007). Karbon vergisinin ekonomik analizi ve etkileri: Karbon vergisinin emisyon azaltıcı etkisi var mı?. Sosyoekonomi, 6(6), 107–126 DOI: https://doi.org/10.17233/se.31848

Intergovernmental Panel on Climate Change [IPCC] (2023). Summary for Policymakers. In: Climate Change 2023: Synthesis Report. DOI: https://10.59327/IPCC/AR6-9789291691647.001

Jenkins, M. & Schaap, B. (2018). Untapped potential: forest ecosystem services for achieving SDG 15. https://www.un.org/esa/forests/wp-content/uploads/

Karacabey, B. (2023). İklim değişikliğinin Türkiye orman ekosistemlerine etkisi. in İklim değişimi çerçevesinde su kaynaklarının mevcut durumu ve geleceği, Ankara: Türkiye Bilimler Akademisi.

Karşıyakalı B, Aydın Ü. & Şanlısoy S., (2024). The causal relationship between environmental taxes for sustainable development and greenhouse gas emissions (co2): a case study of Türkiye. Trakya Üniversitesi İktisadi ve İdari Bilimler Fakültesi e-Dergi, 13(1), 82–100.

Katkat Özçelik, M. (2024). Karbon fiyatlandırması ve muhasebesi. Mali Çözüm Dergisi, 34(184), 973–999.

Kaul, I. (2001). Global public goods: taking the concept forward, New York: UNDP Office of Development Studies Discussion Paper No: 17.

Kaul, I., Grunberg, I., & Stern, M. A. (1999). Defining Global Public Goods. in Global public goods: international cooperation in the 21st century. New York: Oxford University Press.

Kaul, I., & Mendoza, R. U.(2003). Advancing the concept of public goods. in Providing Global Public Goods: Managing Globalization (Ed. I. Kaul). New York: Oxford Academic. DOI: https://doi.org/10.1093/0195157400.003.0004

Kindleberger, C. (1986). International public goods without international government. The American Economic Review. 76(1), 1–13.

Kirmanoğlu, H., Yılmaz, B., E., & Susam, N., (2006). Maliye teorisi'nin çıkmazı: küresel kamusal mallar (Kalkınma yardımları içinde küresel kamusal malların finansmanı). Maliye Dergisi. 150, 25–52.

Li, R., Wang, D., Jiang, H., Huang, Y., & Yang, S. (2022). The influencing factors and mechanisms of the willingness of enterprises to reduce the demand for carbon sequestration reduction by forestry carbon sinks under the “double carbon” goal. Highlights in Science, Engineering and Technology, 25, 348–355. DOI: https://doi.org/10.54097/hset.v25i.3536

Mendez. R. P. (2001). The case for global taxes: an overvıew. United Nations ad hoc Expert Group Meeting on Innovations in Mobilizing Global Resources for Development United Nations Headquarters, New York 25 – 26 June 2001. http://larrywillmore.net/Mendez.pdf

Mutlu, A. (2006). Küresel kamusal mallar bağlamında sağlık hizmetleri ve çevre kirlenmesi: üretim, finansman ve yönetim sorunları. Maliye Dergisi. 150, 53–78.

Oğuz, S. & Yıldız, S. (2024). Bir çevre vergisi olarak karbon vergisi. Anadolu University Journal of Faculty of Economics, 6(1), 19–35.

Ortaç, F. (2004). Global kamu malları ve finansmanı. Ankara: Gazi Kitabevi.

Our Word in Data [OWiD]. (2024). Greenhouse gas emissions. https://ourworldindata.org/greenhouse-gas-emissions

Özdemir, B. (2009). Küresel kirlenme sürdürülebilir ekonomik büyüme ve çevre vergileri. Maliye Dergisi, 156), 1–36.

Özkanca Andıç, N., & Erasa Akça, İ. (2019). Küresel kamusal bir mal olan çevrenin korunmasına yönelik vergileme yeşil vergiler ve Türkiye uygulaması. International Journal of Social and Humanities Sciences Research, 6(44), 3447–3453. DOI: https://doi:https://doi.org/10.26450/jshsr.1566

Pamukçu Albers, P. (2023). Yutak alanların artırılması ve yönetilmesi için imkan ve kısıtların değerlendirilmesi ve öneriler. in Yutak alanların Türkiye’de iklim krizi ile mücadelede orman ekosistemleri ve yutak alan yönetimi. İstanbul: TÜSİAD Yayın No. TÜSİAD-T/2023-5/632.

Pamukçu Albers, P., Lise, Y., & Özdemir, E. (2018). İklim değişikliği ile mücadelede orman karbon standardı uygulama projesi: ulusal ağaçlandırma karbonu standardı önerisi. Ankara: Doğa Koruma Merkezi ve Orman Genel Müdürlüğü.

Haites, E. (2018). Carbon taxes and greenhouse gas emissions trading systems: what have we learned? Climate Policy, 18(8), 955–966, DOI: https://doi.org/10.1080/14693062.2018.1492897

Pehlivan, O., & Aktuğ, M. (2019). Küresel kamusal malların sunumu ve finansmanına ilişkin sorunlar. in Güncel Maliye Tartışmaları: 1/ Prof.Dr. Ömer Faruk Batırel’e Armağan. Ankara: Seçkin.

Røttereng., J. S. (2018). The comparative politics of climate change mitigation measures: who promotes carbon sinks and why? Global Environmental Politics, 18(1): 52–75. DOI: https://doi.org/10.1162/GLEP_a_00444

Reisen, H., Soto., & Weithöner, T. (2004). Financing global and regional public goods through ODA: Analysis and evidence from the OECD Creditor reporting system. OECD Working Paper No. 232. DOI: https://doi.org/10.1787/030687754666

Sandler, T. (2001). On financing global and international public goods. Policy Research Working Paper No: 2638, Washington: World Bank Economic Policy and Prospects Group.

Savcı, M. & Yıldırım, K. (2024). İklim değişikliği ve çevresel maliyetler: kirleten öder ilkesi çerçevesinde bir değerlendirme. Fiscaoeconomia, 8(2): 862–886. DOI: https://doi.org/10.25295/fsecon.1438142

Serengil, Y. (2019). İklim Değişikliği ve Karbon Yönetimi. Ankara: UNDP.

Susam, N. (2008). Kamu maliyesinde sınır ötesi bir kavram: küresel kamusal mallar. Erzincan Binali Yıldırım Üniversitesi Hukuk Fakültesi Dergisi. XII(1–2), 277–303.

te Velde, D. W., Morrisey, O., & Hewitt, A. (2002). Allocating aid to international public goods. International public goods: incentives, measurement and financing. Washington DC: Kluwer Acedemic Publichers and World Bank.

Talu, N., Demir, M., Deniz, A., & Tosun, O. (2021). İklime uyum projesi-Türkiye'de iklim değişikliğine uyum çalışmaları. https://iklimeuyum.org/dokumanlar/

Tekin, A., & Vural, İ. Y (2004). Global kamusal malların finansman aracı olarak global vergi önerileri. Selçuk Üniversitesi SBE Dergisi. 12, 323–337.

Turgut, H. (2023). Karbon yutakları: turbalıklar. in İklim değişikliği: Orman ekosistemlerinde etkileri ve yönetimi, Ankara: Palme Yayınevi.

TÜİK. (2024a). Tarım ve Orman Alanları. https://data.tuik.gov.tr/

TÜİK. (2024b). Sera Gazı Emisyonları (Milyon Ton CO_2 Eşdeğeri) (Milyon Ton CO_2 Eşdeğeri). https://data.tuik.gov.tr/

TÜİK. (2024c). Sektörlere Göre Toplam Sera Gazı Emisyonları (Milyon Ton CO_2 Eşdeğeri). https://data.tuik.gov.tr/

Uemura, T. (2007). Exploring potential of global tax: as a cutting edge-measure for democratizing global governance. International Journal of Public Affairs, 3, 112–129.

Wahl, P. (2006). From concept to reality-on the present state of the debate on international taxes. Debate on International Taxes/FES Briefing Paper. https://library.fes.de/pdf-files/iez/global/50422.pdf

Yalçın, A. (2009). Küresel çevre politikalarının küresel kamusal mallar perspektifinden değerlendirilmesi. Balıkesir Üniversitesi Sosyal Bilimler Enstitüsü Dergisi. 12(21), 288–309.

Yavan, S. (2016). Çevre küresel kamusal malının finansmanına alternatif bir yöntem: uluslararası sosyal regülasyonlar. Dumlupınar Üniversitesi Sosyal Bilimler Dergisi, 50, 1–25.

Yüce, M. (2024). Yeşil ekonomi için bir araç: Yeşil vergiler. İklim Değişikliği, Sürdürülebilirlik ve Uluslararası İş Birlikleri Kongresi Bildiriler Kitabı. Düzce: T.C. Düzce Üniversitesi.

Tax Incentives for Smart Homes Based on Renewable Energy Sources in the Provision of Sustainable Energy

Müslüm GÜMÜŞ[1]

1 Introduction

Today, most of the world's energy needs are met by fossil fuels such as coal, oil and natural gas, which are non-renewable and cause serious environmental damage when used. The intensive use of fossil-based energy sources brings with it many problems ranging from global warming, pollution, economic crises, foreign dependency, and even wars. However, unlike fossil-based energy sources, renewable energy sources are readily available in nature, do not deplete and do not harm the environment. Although many countries have recently implemented incentive policies to promote renewable energy sources, a significant portion of the energy consumed still comes from fossil-based energy sources.

Türkiye, which imports a large share of its energy resources from fossil fuels, has made significant progress in expanding the use of renewable energy in power generation thanks to renewable energy-oriented policies and investments. The share of renewable energy in Türkiye's electricity generation has increased to 42% in 2023. However, the share of renewable energy in total final energy demand is around 16%. Globally, this ratio is around 20%. In Türkiye, the share of the residential and services sector in final energy consumption is 31% according to 2021 data (T.C. Çevre, Şehircilik ve İklim Değişikliği Bakanlığı, 2024). In 2022, 48.3% of the energy consumed in households was natural gas, 17.1% was electricity, and 14.3% was coal (TÜİK, 2024).

In Türkiye, feed-in tariffs, land grants, insurance premium exemptions, and various tax benefits are provided to promote renewable energy sources. However, there is no direct tax incentive for smart home systems that use renewable energy sources and can help reduce global warming by reducing greenhouse gas emissions while ensuring energy efficiency.

1 Hakkari University, Faculty of Economics and Administrative Sciences, Department of Finance, muslumgumus@hakkari.edu.tr, ORCID ID: 0000-0001-9790-7028

In our study, we first examine the concepts and sources of energy and renewable energy, and we highlight the development of renewable energy sources in the world and in Türkiye and the tax incentives for them. Then, we discuss the tax incentives offered for energy- efficient and comfort-oriented smart buildings as a solution to ensure energy sustainability.

2 Energy Sources

Energy is a basic resource that is needed in every moment of our life in order to perform all the works that facilitate our daily life (Demir & Baş, 2020:809). The introduction and use of energy in human life started especially with the transition to sedentary life. Thus, the need for energy resources emerged, people began to develop the use of energy over time and used energy in almost every walk of life, especially with the industrial revolution. As a result, energy resources began to be considered as an indispensable source of life, from heating homes to meeting daily needs, from the fuels of vehicles to the machinery used in industry (Sarıtunalı, 2021:410).

Energy needs for humans are mainly met by fossil resources such as coal, oil, and natural gas. However, these resources are alarming due to the millions of years it takes to replace them when they are consumed and the damage they cause to nature (Demir & Baş, 2020:809). In recent years, energy consumption has increased with the rapid growth of population, industrialization, urbanization and improvement of quality of life; this situation has caused rapid depletion of fossil resources and environmental pollution. The most important environmental problems in energy activities are generally caused by the use of fossil fuels in industry, heating, transportation and electricity generation (Oskay, 2014:79). Many negative effects such as air, environmental and marine pollution, climate change, global warming, industrial waste, energy shortages and economic stagnation, continuous increase in electrical energy and fuel prices, unemployment, foreign dependence and wars occur during the applications from the production stage of using fossil resources to preparation for use, transportation, distribution and consumption (Sarıtunalı, 2021:410). Therefore, it is necessary to use existing resources efficiently, recover energy and prioritize renewable energy sources. Although the trend towards the production and consumption of renewable energy sources has increased recently, a significant portion of the energy consumed is still made up of non-renewable energy sources (Sarıtunalı, 2021:410).

Tab. 1: Total Energy Supply by Source (2021)

Energy Resources	World	World (%)	Türkiye	Türkiye (%)
Coal	168.145.390	27,2	1.721.196	25,7
Natural gas	145.989.141	23,6	2.056.454	30,7
Nuclear	30.660.087	5	–	–
Hydro	15.456.239	2,5	201.336	3
Wind, solar, etc.	16.825.797	2,7	695.869	10,3
Biofuels and waste	58.488.832	9,5	188.505	2,8
Petrol	182.226.123	29,5	1.818.227	27,2
Total	617.791.609	100	6.681.587	100

Source: Prepared by using data from International Energy Agency (2024a) and International Energy Agency (2024b).

As shown in Table 1, the share of renewable energy sources in the total energy supply is around 20% worldwide. In Türkiye, the share of renewable energy sources in the total energy supply is about 16%. While the share of biofuels and energy from waste in total energy supply is 9.5% worldwide, it is 2.8% in Türkiye. However, Türkiye, which has significant potential in terms of energy resources such as wind and solar energy, has made significant progress in exploiting this potential. While the energy obtained from wind, solar, etc. sources corresponds to 2.7% of the total energy supply in the world, this ratio is 10.3% in Türkiye.

3 Renewable Energy Sources

In its simplest definition, renewable energy resources are energy resources whose sources are found in nature, are sustainable and, unlike fossil fuels, do not emit greenhouse gases or emit negligible amounts of greenhouse gases into the environment and are therefore "clean" (Uluatam, 2010:34). In other words, renewable energy is an energy resource whose sources are readily available in nature and are not depleted/renewed/sustained by human use (Çelikkaya, 2017:54). Renewable energy consists of energy sources such as wind, solar, geothermal, biomass, hydro (ocean, tidal, wave) and hydrogen (Bayraç & Çıldır, 2017:202). Renewable energy sources have unlimited reserves, are obtained from domestic and natural resources, and are considered to be completely environmentally friendly resources that do not directly increase the level of carbon dioxide in the atmosphere (Çelikkaya, 2017:55).

Solar energy is one of the leading renewable energy sources. Solar energy is the radiant energy released by the fusion process (the transformation of hydrogen gas into helium) in the core of the sun. The sun is a clean and inexhaustible source of renewable energy. Studies on the use of solar energy have accelerated especially after the 1970s, solar energy systems have shown technological progress and cost reduction, and have established themselves as an environmentally clean energy source (T.C. Enerji ve Tabii Kaynaklar Bakanlığı, 2024a). Wind can be defined as the pressure-induced air movement resulting from the different air temperature, humidity and pressure caused by the different heating of the earth's surface by solar radiation (T.C. Enerji ve Tabii Kaynaklar Bakanlığı, 2024b). Wind energy is obtained by converting the kinetic energy of the air into mechanical energy and then into electrical energy through wind turbines, which are the main structural elements of wind power plants (T.C. Enerji ve Tabii Kaynaklar Bakanlığı, 2024b). Biomass, another renewable energy source, refers to the resources obtained from vegetable oil wastes, agricultural wastes without food and feed value, forest products other than industrial wood, and by-products from the processing of used tires (Law No. 5346, Art. 3/9). Geothermal energy is the heat energy carried to the surface by hot water, steam and gases, which may contain more dissolved minerals, various salts and gases than the surrounding groundwater and surface water, and which is above the regional atmospheric average temperature, and which may contain more dissolved minerals, various salts and gases than the surrounding groundwater and surface water (T.C. Enerji ve Tabii Kaynaklar Bakanlığı, 2024c). Türkiye is the 1st country in Europe in terms of geothermal potential and the 4th country in the world in terms of installed capacity (T.C. Enerji ve Tabii Kaynaklar Bakanlığı, 2024c). Finally, hydraulic energy is the energy obtained from rivers. Electricity generation is realized with this energy obtained from rivers (Bağcı, 2019:107).

While the domestic nature of renewable energy resources reduces the external dependence of countries on energy resources, they are also particularly important in terms of sustainability as they are uninterrupted and clean energy resources. For reasons such as the contribution of renewable energy resources to economic growth and as an effective source in the fight against global warming, it can be seen that the use of renewable energy resources is encouraged in many countries and alternative energy investments are promoted in energy policies (Bayraç & Çıldır, 2017:210). For this reason, thanks to the incentives for the diffusion of renewable energy in most countries of the world, the contribution of renewable energy to the global final energy production, which was 8.5% in 2013, gradually increased to 19.1% in 2014, to 23.7% in 2015 (Bayraç & Çildir, 2017:202) and to about 20% in 2021.

4 Energy Sustainability

The accumulation of gases caused by human activities and defined as greenhouse gases in the atmosphere in a way that disrupts the natural balance causes an increase in the average temperature of the atmosphere and global warming, resulting in climate change (Tüzüner, 2007:6). Population growth and population density in the world also cause environmental pollution by increasing CO2 emissions in the short and long term; therefore, natural resources are rapidly consumed (Pata & Yurtkuran, 2018:312). Climate change, which is emerging as a global environmental problem, causes an increase in drought with a decrease in precipitation in arid and semi-arid areas and an increase in flood events in places with abundant rainfall. In addition, as a result of climate change that causes glaciers to melt, the water level in oceans and seas rises due to melting, causing problems such as flooding of low-lying coastlines, reduction of forests and plant diversity (Tüzüner, 2007:6).

The linear economic model based on fossil fuels, which feeds the understanding of population growth and increased consumption, first warmed the earth and brought it to the climate crisis; then the deepening problems of the crisis caused the destruction of nature, such as heat and cold waves, storms, floods, droughts, forest fires, loss of biodiversity (Ecer et al., 2021:126). The increasing use of energy, especially since the industrial revolution, has led to a significant increase in greenhouse gas emissions due to the carbon dioxide content of fossil resources as the most widely used energy source on a global scale. The energy sector, the largest contributor to global warming, is responsible for 75.6% of global greenhouse gas emissions. Coal has the largest share of energy-related GHG emissions with 44%, followed by oil, natural gas and biofuels (Pak & Özdemir, 2023:33). In Türkiye, energy consumption is responsible for 72% of GHG emissions. Of this consumption, 33% is realized in housing and services, 31% in industry, and 25% in transportation (KPMG, 2022:14).

In order to efficiently increase the production and consumption of alternative energy sources and maintain a sustainable economy, long-term structural changes need to be implemented, in addition to supporting more energy-related research activities, promoting the production of alternative energy sources that contribute to reducing CO2 emissions, and increasing the share of consumption of these sources in total energy (Pata & Yurtkuran, 2018:312). The transition to renewable energy involves many changes, including the adoption of sustainable energy sources and energy efficient technologies, investments in measures to ensure energy efficiency in buildings, and changes in direct and indirect energy use behavior (Kılınç Pala, 2024:600). Therefore, sustainable energy requires the active participation of many actors, including individual consumers, households, businesses, and organizations (Steg et al., 2021:2).

5 Energy Outlook for Türkiye

According to 2020 data, energy consumption by sector is 33% in construction, 33% in industry, and 31% in transportation. The share of renewable energy in the building sector is 15.5%, in industry 16.8% and in transport 4.1% (REN21, 2023). Today, coal is the most used resource in global electricity generation with a share of 36%, while the share of total clean energy in global electricity generation is 38%. In Türkiye, natural gas has the largest share in electricity generation with 33.2%, followed by coal with 30.9%. In terms of installed capacity, hydropower has the largest share with 30.9% (Özbektaş et al., 2023:347). In June 2022, the share of installed solar power in the total installed capacity in Türkiye is 8.35%. In 2021, the share of solar electricity in the country's total electricity generation is 3.8%. In June 2022, the share of installed capacity based on biomass and waste heat energy in the total installed capacity in Türkiye is 2.14% (Özbektaş et al., 2023:347). Türkiye ranks 5th in Europe and 12th in the world in terms of installed renewable energy capacity. By the end of 2022, 54% of Türkiye's installed capacity will consist of renewable energy sources (T.C. Dışişleri Bakanlığı, 2024).

In the world and in Türkiye, fossil resources are mostly used in the energy sector. In developing countries like Türkiye, which cannot produce the energy they need and have to import it, energy imports disrupt the current account balance of countries. Türkiye is not a rich country in terms of these non-renewable fossil resources. Therefore, it imports a large part of the energy it needs from foreign countries, which puts a huge burden on Türkiye's current account balance (Bağcı, 2019:115).

In Türkiye, which has recently made significant progress in the expansion of renewable energy in electricity generation with the contribution of renewable energy-focused policies and investments on the axis of energy security and clean energy transformation, the share of renewable energy in electricity generation exceeded 40% in 2021, while the total contribution of wind and solar approached 20%. In 2023, both wind and solar break records, reaching 10.5% and 5.8% of electricity generation, respectively. 86% of solar generation comes from unlicensed power plants (KPMG, 2022:16).

Tab. 2: Share of Türkiye's Energy Resources in Electricity Generation (2023)

Energy Resources	Share in Electricity Generation (%)
Imported coal	22,4
Locally-mined coal	14,2
Natural gas	20,9
Fuel Oil	0,4
Hydro	19,4
Solar	5,8
Wind	10,5
Geothermal	3,4
Biomass	2,6
Other	0,4

Source: Prepared by using the data from EÜAŞ 2023 Annual Report p. 19–20.

As shown in Table 2, according to the data for 2023, the share of electricity generated from renewable energy sources, namely hydro, solar, wind, geothermal and biomass, in the total electricity generated in Türkiye is around 42%. The share of non-renewable energy sources such as coal, oil and natural gas is around 58%. Among these, coal has the highest share with about 37%.

Türkiye has a very advantageous potential in terms of renewable energy resources, especially solar, wind and geothermal, but the rate of economic utilization has not yet reached the desired level (Sabancı University Istanbul International Energy and Climate Center, 2022). Therefore, Türkiye needs to accelerate its transition to a green economy by converting its high static energy potential, especially solar and wind energy, into kinetic energy and significantly reduce its dependence on foreign energy (Özen et al. 2015:92).

5.1 Action plans for renewable energy sources in Türkiye

The first global negotiation on climate change was the United Nations Framework Convention on Climate Change, which was opened for signature at the 1992 Earth Summit in Rio de Janeiro and entered into force in 1994. This was followed by the Kyoto Protocol, which was opened for signature in 1997 but did not enter into force until 2005, and finally the Paris Climate Summit in 2015, which was the first global step on climate (Güner & Turan, 2017:48). In 2019, the European Green Deal was proposed by the European Commission. This "consensus", which is the long-awaited final climate action plan of the European Union (EU), aims to decarbonize Europe by 2050; for this purpose, it envisages a radical transformation of the economy and the achievement of climate neutrality (harmlessness) on the European continent (Ecer et al., 2021:127).

In Türkiye, the environmental problem was first mentioned in the Fourth Five-Year Development Plan (1979–1983). The need for environmental sustainability was emphasized for the first time in the Fifth Five-Year Development Plan (1985–1989). Following this plan, the Sixth Five-Year Development Plan (1990–1994) emphasized the importance of using renewable energy resources in the production phase in order to prevent the destruction of natural life (Özen et al., 2015:86). Despite being located in a region rich in renewable energy resources, one of Türkiye's most important problems is its dependence on foreign energy sources. This problem should be solved with renewable energy investments that are low cost and compatible with sustainable environmental goals (Kılınç Pala, 2024:603).

As a UN member state, Türkiye participated in the Paris Climate Summit in 2015 and signed the Paris Agreement on April 22, 2016. As a party to the Paris Agreement, Türkiye demonstrated its determination to transition to a low-carbon economy with the "Net Zero Emissions Target by 2053".

In addition, as part of its harmonization efforts with the European Union, it declared the "2021 Green Deal Action Plan" in line with the "European Green Deal" (Cumhurbaşkanlığı Genelgesi, 2021/15). The Green Deal Action Plan 2021 includes 32 goals and 81 actions under the headings of carbon regulation at the border, green and circular economy, green financing, clean, economical and secure energy supply, sustainable agriculture, sustainable and intelligent transportation, climate change mitigation, diplomacy, and information and awareness activities on the European Green Deal (T.C. Ticaret Bakanlığı, 2021:9). In addition, the Green Deal Action Plan was announced in the Medium-Term Program 2024–2026, which was published in the Official Gazette in 2023. During the program period, in line with the 2053 net-zero emission target and national development priorities, it is stated that the green transformation process will be accelerated with an approach that supports greenhouse gas emission reduction, enhances adaptation capacity to climate change, prioritizes competitiveness and efficiency, considers fair transition, and improves national incentive mechanisms by making maximum use of global financial resources (2024–2026 Medium-Term Program, 2023).

5.2 Legal regulations for renewable energy sources in Türkiye

The "Law on the Use of Renewable Energy Resources for Electricity Generation" No. 5346, which was enacted in 2005 and became the first legal regulation on renewable energy resources in Türkiye, aims to expand the use of renewable energy resources for electricity generation, to introduce these resources into the economy in a reliable, economical and high-quality manner, to increase the diversity of resources, to reduce greenhouse gas emissions, to utilize waste, to protect the environment and to develop the manufacturing sector necessary for achieving these goals. The Renewable Energy Resource Support Mechanism was established by an additional article added to Act No. 5346 of 2010 in order to determine the procedures and principles regarding the prices, terms, amounts and payments to be made to those engaged in production activities based on renewable energy resources (Act No. 5346, Art. 14). Law No. 5346, which entered into force in 2005, was supplemented with a number of additional articles and some of its articles were amended between 2007 and 2024. In 2013, the "Regulation on Certification and Support of Renewable Energy Resources" was enacted to regulate the issuance of renewable energy resource certificates to legal entities that hold generation licenses for generation facilities based on renewable energy resources, and the establishment and operation of the Renewable Energy Resources Support Mechanism, to be operated pursuant to Law No. 5346, in order to promote the generation of electricity based on renewable energy resources.

6 Incentives for Renewable Energy Sources in the World and Türkiye

If we look at the incentive instruments applied to the financing problems of energy projects, we can see that renewable energy resources are generally supported within the framework of two different incentive mechanisms: regulatory and fiscal. While fixed price guarantees, premium guarantees, quota obligations and tendering methods are included in the group of regulatory policies, public subsidies and grants, tax exemptions and reductions are included in the group of fiscal incentives (Yurdadoğ & Tosunoğlu, 2017: 7). While subsidies and rebates are one pillar of cost-reducing investment policies to encourage the use of renewable energy sources, tax incentives are the other. These include investment tax credits, accelerated depreciation, production tax credits, property tax credits, income tax incentives, Value-added tax (VAT) exemptions, environmental tax exemptions, import tax reductions, grants, equipment loans, and similar practices. These incentives apply to large investments as well as small individual installations. Therefore, such policies are directed not only to investors, who represent the supply in the energy market, but also to consumers, who represent the demand (Uluatam, 2010:37).

Among the practices implemented in the world to encourage renewable energy investments are financial incentives (feed-in tariffs), especially through tariffs that support electricity generation, regulations that ensure that companies include a mandatory share of renewable energy sources in their electricity generation portfolio (renewable portfolio standards), direct financial support (subsidy) for renewable energy investments made for investors' personal heating/cooling needs, and incentives such as tax incentives or financing for companies investing in this field, as well as incentives such as tax deductions for homes and workplaces that meet energy efficiency regulations (KPMG, 2016:95).

Tax incentives for renewable energy sources can be summarized as follows (Çelikkaya, 2017:70–74):

- Investment allowances for capital expenditures (such as machinery, equipment, land and fixtures), usually in the form of reduced VAT or VAT refunds (still attractive in many countries, notably the US, Belgium and France),
- Income tax exemption,
- Accelerated depreciation option,
- Deduction of R&D expenditures from income tax base,
- Three types of property tax incentives: exemption, rebate and refund (European countries prefer temporary exemptions or reductions in property tax rates by region and building type, while Asian countries prefer tax refunds). The US uses all three mechanisms: exemption, rebate and refund),
- Special Consumption Tax exemption for the sale of generated electricity (applied in many countries in Europe and the USA).

Although there are different practices on a state basis in the USA, generally there are tax incentives in the form of sales tax exemption, property tax exemption and tax reduction for renewable energy sources (Çelikkaya, 2018:365). In EU countries, corporate tax reduction, accelerated depreciation, reduced VAT rate on residences, reduced VAT rate on machinery and equipment, property tax exemption, energy tax exemption, income tax exemption, SCT exemption, and some exemptions in local taxes are applied (Çelikkaya, 2018:368). There are various incentives for renewable energy sources in China. Super discount on R&D expenditures, reduced corporate tax on the gross income of new technology companies, reduced VAT on electricity sales from renewable energy sources, VAT refund on biodiesel, 50%-100% discounted motor vehicle tax on electric vehicles are some of these incentives. In addition, corporate tax exemption is applied for a certain period and rate for income obtained from renewable energy sources. (Çelikkaya, 2018:369).

Tax incentives for renewable energy resources in Türkiye can be summarized as follows (KPMG, 2023; Akdoğan & Kovancılar, 2022:85; Samancı, 2020:63; Kınacı & Yıldız, 2019:219–220; Yurdadoğ & Tosunoğlu, 2017:16):

- VAT exemption for the purchase of investment equipment of renewable energy resources domestically or abroad,
- Customs duty exemption for the import of investment equipment of renewable energy resources,
- Discount on renting, easement and usage of energy transmission lines (85% discount for 10 years),
- Discount on transmission system usage fee (50% discount for 5 years),
- Stamp duty and fee exemption on documents and transactions concluded within the investment period regarding power plants,
- Corporate tax reduction,
- Taking into account half of the depreciation period of the facilities,
- Insurance premium employer share support,
- Interest support,
- Investment site allocation (the Ministry of Treasury and Finance grants free use of immovable properties belonging to the Treasury),
- Unlicensed production permit,
- Additional support if domestic production parts and equipment are used in energy production facilities.

With the regulations made in recent years, significant tax advantages and incentives have been provided for renewable energy resource investments, especially solar power plant investments, in Türkiye. For example, T.R. The profits obtained from the facilities subject to the investment incentive certificate of the Ministry of Industry and Technology are subject to corporate tax at reduced tax rates, starting from the accounting period in which the partial or complete operation of the investment begins, until it reaches the investment contribution amount (Law No. 5520, art. 32/A; T.C. Sanayi ve Teknoloji Bakanlığı, 2024:6). In addition, by the Presidential decision dated 24.02.2022 and numbered 5209, various incentives were provided for solar energy-based electricity generation facility investments and wind energy-based electricity generation facility investments, provided that they operate within the scope of unlicensed activity and limited to the contractual power in the connection agreement. There is VAT and customs duty exemption, investment location allocation, stamp duty and duty exemption, and KKDF exemption in all regions for solar power plant investments. In addition, tax deductions ranging from 70% to 90% on a regional basis, investment contribution rates between 30% and 50%, insurance premium employer share support ranging from 6 to 10 years, and 10-year SSI employee share support and income tax withholding support specific to 6th region investments are offered (KPMG, 2023). With the "Regulation on Unlicensed Electricity Production in the Electricity Market" issued in 2011, buildings can produce their own electricity without obtaining any license, and if they supply the electrical energy they produce above their needs to the distribution system, they can benefit from the fixed price guarantee specified in the law for ten years (Yurdadoğ &Tosunoğlu, 2017:16).

7 Renewable Energy Based Smart Home Technologies

Today, in the digital age of Industry 4.0, smart buildings, smart facilities, smart factories, and artificial intelligence-supported engineering and technological tools have been adopted in every aspect of our lives (Bağcı, 2018:125). With the Information Revolution, widespread use of technology has not only caused differences in our standard of living and daily needs, but has also begun to change the technical characteristics of buildings, manifesting itself in building design and production. The idea of "Smart Home", which makes life easier, improves the quality of life, and offers a safer, more comfortable and more economical environment, has become widespread (Tomaş & Dostoğlu, 2020:487).

Smart homes are defined as homes that integrate many systems, manage them in a coordinated manner, manage the building environment autonomously in order to optimize user comfort, energy consumption, security and work efficiency, and use computer technology for this (Bulgurcu, 2020:2). Sustainable new generation buildings are architectural structures based on artificial intelligence, where the building is designed using different algorithms, is managed with holistic automation, and many different parameters are integrated with each other (Reinisch et al. 2011:2). Home automation systems are growing rapidly and are used to provide comfort, convenience, quality of life and security. These automation home systems are bluetooth based, voice based, GSM based, IoT based, and ocean based (Asadullah & Raza, 2016:31). Smart environments equipped with energy management systems in individual residences or buildings can minimize energy consumption through different algorithms that will control the needs and changing needs of users (Corno & Razzak, 2012:2130). For example, the irrigation system equipped with sensors in smart homes not only saves money but also makes irrigation easier. Thanks to the Internet of Things (IoT), it can connect to the weather forecast to see whether there will be precipitation and optimize its conditions accordingly (Tomaş & Dostoğlu, 2020:492).

Thanks to smart buildings using renewable energy resources, it is possible to switch from the traditional high consumption mode to low consumption and low pollution mode by adopting an architectural approach that will not cause environmental pollution, resource insufficiency and disruption of ecological balance (Tomaş & Dostoğlu, 2020:489). Smart homes are a sustainable practice that should be adopted to reduce carbon emissions in the housing sector and use renewable energy sources (AlFaris et al., 2017:272).

Smart home systems, which are designed using many technologies and systems, are quite costly. However, considering the cost-benefit analysis, it is supported by public authority for reasons such as providing energy efficiency, green passive design, contribution to the life cycle, environmentally friendly design and utilizing renewable energy sources (AlFaris et al., 2017:272). If smart homes are integrated with smart grid systems provided by local governments, it will be seen as a smart way to optimize energy performance and operate the energy systems of homes and cities in a smart and efficient way. Energy management systems provided in this way can automatically realize consumption practices and minimize energy consumption (Corno & Razzak, 2012:2130). Therefore, smart homes have many effects. Among these, environmental impacts can be summarized as follows (Bağcı, 2018:127):

- Lower levels of nature destruction due to the possibility of more production with fewer resources,
- Low level of emissions and waste due to focus on quality and efficiency in production,
- Evaluating risks in a virtual environment before investments are made,
- Significant resource savings and positive environmental impacts with the use of renewable energy.

7.1 Tax incentives for smart home technologies

Smart homes based on the use of renewable energy resources require personal capital expenditure, and although the system to be installed increases the value of the house, it also increases the costs of the house (maintenance, repair, insurance expenses). Therefore, regulations to seriously reduce costs need to be implemented (Çakmak, 2018:178). With the increase in environmental and economic problems, countries have determined various action plans, increased their investments and provided various financial incentives in order to benefit more from renewable energy resources. In addition to large-scale energy production from renewable sources, initiatives have been initiated in our country to use renewable energy sources in buildings, to allow households to produce their own energy, at least partially, and to sell the excess to the main grid (Yurdadoğ & Tosunoğlu, 2017:12). According to the regulation in the Income Tax Law No. 193, for the purpose of producing electrical energy based on renewable energy sources within the scope of unlicensed activities in accordance with the Electricity Market Law No. 6446, the installed power they install on the roofs and/or facades of the houses they own or rent is up to a maximum of 50 kW. The earnings of those who sell the surplus electrical energy produced from only one production facility to the last resource supply company are exempt from income tax (Law No. 193, Art. 9/9). In addition, expenses for thermal insulation and energy saving, which increase the economic value of the real estate included in the business, can be written off directly as expenses in the year in which they are made without being subject to depreciation (Law No. 193, Art. 40/7).

One of the most popular renewable energies used for buildings is solar energy (AlFaris, 2017:267). Many technologies have been developed to benefit from sunlight. Areas of use of solar energy include direct or indirect electricity generation, hot water production, space heating and cooling, process heat energy for industrial establishments and greenhouse heating (T.C. Enerji ve Tabii Kaynaklar Bakanlığı, 2024a). In Türkiye, which has a significant solar energy potential due to its geographical location, the total annual sunshine duration is 2,741 hours and the average annual total radiation value is calculated as 1,527.46 kWh/m2 (T.C. Enerji ve Tabii Kaynaklar Bakanlığı, 2024a). It has also been stated that in the 2024–2026 Medium Term Program, arrangements will be made to popularize the "Nearly Zero Energy Buildings" approach, which aims to achieve high energy performance and at the same time use a certain amount of renewable energy in public, commercial and residential buildings.

In Türkiye, the share of the residential and services sector in final energy consumption is 31% according to 2021 data (T.C. Çevre, Şehircilik ve İklim Değişikliği Bakanlığı, 2024). In 2022, natural gas with 48.3%, electricity with 17.1% and coal with 14.3% were the most consumed energy sources in households. In households, 65.3% of the total consumption consists of consumption for heating purposes, 14.1% for lighting and electrical appliances, and 11.9% for water heating. 76.3% of natural gas, which is the most consumed energy type in households, is consumed for space heating, 14.5% for water heating and 9.2% for cooking purposes. In electricity, lighting and electrical home appliances take the first place with 82.4% according to their intended use (TÜİK, 2024).

It can be seen that there is an intense energy consumption in buildings, especially for heating and lighting. Most of this consumption is met by fossil-based energies. For this, smart home systems are needed that will both provide energy efficiency and obtain the energy they use from renewable energy sources. Of course, it is obvious that this requires high investment costs at first. However, many devastating earthquakes have occurred in Türkiye and there has been loss of life and property; For this reason, it is known to control both public and individual building stocks and to make them comply with the rules to absorb earthquake shaking. Therefore, in the urban transformation process in Türkiye, in addition to earthquake resistance, both in the restoration of the existing building stock and in the new buildings to be built, it can be considered to transform the buildings into renewable energy-based structures. This will be beneficial in reducing costs. Thus, it will be a big step towards providing both energy efficiency and a green world, both earthquake-resistant cities and green cities.

8 Conclusion

With the increase in environmental and economic problems, countries have adopted various action plans, increased their investments and provided various financial incentives to benefit more from renewable energy resources. Financial incentive initiatives have also been initiated for smart home technologies, which have become common in recent years. However, these incentives are not yet at the desired level and are almost non-existent in Türkiye. The required electrical energy can be produced and stored on-site through systems such as small-scale solar and/or wind turbines and batteries to be installed in smart homes equipped with advanced technology. Therefore, through smart homes, it will be possible to switch from the traditional high consumption style to a low consumption and low pollution style by adopting an architectural approach that will not cause environmental pollution, resource insufficiency and disruption of ecological balance.

To ensure sustainability in energy, it is necessary to adopt and use renewable energy sources and low-carbon innovations, increase the energy efficiency of buildings, and implement the energy transition regarding energy use in buildings as soon as possible. In order to save money on electricity consumption and to fully combat climate crises, financial incentives to expand the use of renewable energy sources in buildings should be implemented as soon as possible. Financial incentives that can be provided for smart homes and systems that produce renewable energy resources can be listed as follows:

- VAT exemption for information systems in smart home technology installation,
- VAT exemption for purchases of solar panels and wind turbines to be installed in smart homes,
- Income/corporate tax exemption for a certain period of time for taxpayers operating in smart home design, architecture and construction businesses,
- Property tax exemption for smart home owners,
- Title deed fee exemption in smart home purchase-sale transactions,
- VAT exemption on smart home sales.

In addition to the tax incentives for individual homes mentioned above, more efficient energy and a more livable world will be possible by applying these tax incentives to structures such as workplaces, workshops, facilities and factories.

Bibliography

Akdoğan İ. & Kovancılar, B. (2022). Avrupa Birliği ve Türkiye'de Çevre Dostu Yenilenebilir Enerji Politikalarının Teşvik Türleri Açısından Değerlendirilmesi. *Manisa Celal Bayar Üniversitesi İ.İ.B.F. Yönetim ve Ekonomi Dergisi*, 29(1), 69–91.

AlFaris, F., Juaidi, A. & Manzano, F. (2017). Intelligent Homes' Technologies to Optimize The Energy Performance for The Net Zero Energy Home. *Agugliaro Energy and Buildings*, 153(2017), 262–274.

Asadullah, M. & Raza, A. (2016). An Overview of Home Automation Systems. 2016 2nd International Conference on Robotics and Artificial Intelligence (ICRAI), Rawalpindi, Pakistan, 27–31. doi: 10.1109/ICRAI.2016.7791223.

Bağcı, E. (2019). Türkiye'de Yenilenebilir Enerji Potansiyeli, Üretimi, Tüketimi ve Cari İşlemler Dengesi İlişkisi. *Research Studies Anatolia Journal*, 2(4), 101–117.

Bağcı, E. (2018). Endüstri 4.0: Yeni Üretim Tarzını Anlamak. *Gümüşhane Üniversitesi Sosyal Bilimler Enstitüsü Elektronik Dergisi (GÜSBEED)*, 9(24), 122–146.

Bayraç, H. N. & Çildir, M. (2017). AB Yenilenebilir Enerji Politikalarının Ekonomik Büyüme Üzerindeki Etkisi. *Uluslararası Yönetim İktisat ve İşletme Dergisi (ICMEB)*, 17, Special Issue, 201–212.

Bulgurcu, H. (2029). Bina Yönetim Sistemlerine (BYS) Giriş. Bulgurcu, H. (Editör), *Bina Yönetim Sistemleri ve Akıllı Binalar* (s. 1–14). Teknik Sektör Yayıncılığı A. Ş. ISBN: 978-975-8476-04-6

Christian Reinisch, C., Kofler, M. J., Iglesias, F. & Kastner, W. (2011). ThinkHome Energy Efficiency in Future Smart Homes. *EURASIP Journal on Embedded Systems*, 2011(104617), 1–18. https://doi.org/10.1155/2011/104617

Corno, F. & Razzak, F. (2012). Intelligent Energy Optimization for User Intelligible Goals in Smart Home Environments. *IEEE Transactıons on Smart Grıd*, 3(4), 2128–2135.

Çakmak, N. M. (2018). Gelir Vergisi Kanunu'na Göre Binaların Çatı ve Cephelerinde Yenilenebilir Enerji Kaynaklarından Üretilen Elektriğe Getirilen Vergi Muafiyeti. *Ankara Hacı Bayram Veli Üniversitesi Hukuk Fakültesi Dergisi*, 22(4), 173–196.

Çelikkaya, A. (2018). Dünyada Yenilenebilir Enerji Yatırımlarına Sağlanan Vergi Teşviklerinin Değerlendirilmesi. *Afyon Kocatepe Üniversitesi Sosyal Bilimler Dergisi*, 20(1), 357–384. Doi No: 10.5578/jss.67033

Çelikkaya, A. (2017). Yenilenebilir Enerjinin Teşvikine Yönelik Uluslararası Kamu Politikaları Üzerine Bir inceleme. *Maliye Dergisi*, Ocak-Haziran 2017 (172), 52–84.

Demir, N. & Baş, P. (2020). Avrupa Birliği'nin Enerji Sorunsalında Yenilenebilir Enerji Kaynaklarının Yeri ve Geleceği. *Mehmet Akif Ersoy Üniversitesi İktisadi ve İdari Bilimler Fakültesi Dergisi*, 7(3), 806–831. ISSN: 2149-1658.

Ecer, K., Güner, O & Çetin, M. (2021). Avrupa Yeşil Mutabakatı ve Türkiye Ekonomisinin Uyum Politikaları. *İşletme ve İktisat Çalışmaları Dergisi*, 9(2), 125–144.

EÜAŞ (2024). *2023 Yılı Faaliyet Raporu*. https://www.euas.gov.tr/raporlar

Güner, E. D. & Turan, S. E. (2017). Yenilenebilir Enerji Kaynaklarının Küresel İklim Değişikliği Üzerine Etkisi. *Artvin Çoruh Üniversitesi Doğal Afetler Uygulama ve Araştırma Merkezi Doğal Afetler ve Çevre Dergisi*, 3(1), 48–55. DOI: 10.21324/dacd.285523

International Energy Agency (2024a). *Energy Statistics Data Browser.* https://www.iea.org/data-and-statistics/data-tools/energy-statistics-data-browser?country=TURKEY&fuel=Energy%20 supply&indicator=TESbySource

International Energy Agency (2024b). *Energy Statistics Data Browser.* https://www.iea.org/data-and-statistics/data-tools/energy-statistics-data-browser?country=WORLD&fuel=Energy%20 supply&indicator=TESbySource

Kılınç Pala, P. B. (2024). Küresel Enerji Dönüşümü: Yeşil Enerji Kavramı ve Teşvik Programları. *Elektronik Sosyal Bilimler Dergisi*, 23(90), 599–610. ISSN:1304-0278

Kınacı, H. & Yıldız, F. (2019). Türkiye'de Yenilenebilir Enerji Sektörüne Yönelik Devlet Teşviklerinin Değerlendirilmesi. Taytak, M. & Şaşmaz, M. Ü. (Editörler), *Türkiye'de Mali Teşvik Sistemi ve Uygulamaları* (s. 205–230). Ekin Basım Yayın. ISBN: 978-605-327-864-1

KPMG (2023). *GES Yatırımlarında İndirimli Kurumlar Vergisi ve Uygulamada Dikkat Edilmesi Gereken Hususlar*. https://kpmgvergi.com/blog/ges-yatirimlarinda-indirimli-kurumlar-vergisi-ve-uygulamada-dikkat-edilmesi-gereken-hususlar/1276

KPMG (2022). *Enerji Sektörel Bakış Raporu*. https://kpmg.com/tr/tr/home/gorusler/2022/04/enerji-sektorel-bakis.html

KPMG (2016). Yenilenebilir Enerji: *Dünya ve Türkiye Uygulamalarına Bakış*. https://assets.kpmg.com/content/dam/kpmg/pdf/2016/03/tr-yenilenebilir-enerji-dunya-ve-turkiye-uygulamalarina-bakis.pdf

Oskay, C. (2014). Sürdürülebilir Kalkınma Çerçevesinde Rüzgâr Enerjisinin Önemi ve Türkiye'de Rüzgâr Enerjisi Yatırımlarına Yönelik Teşvikler. *Niğde Üniversitesi İktisadi ve İdari Bilimler Fakültesi Dergisi*, 7(1), 76–94.

Özbektaş, S., Şenel, M. C. & Sungur, B. (2023). Dünyada ve Türkiye'de Yenilenebilir Enerji Durumu ve Kurulum Maliyetleri. *Mühendis ve Makina Dergisi*, 64(711), 317–351.

Özen A., Şaşmaz, M. Ü. & Bahtiyar, E. (2015). Türkiye'de Yeşil Ekonomi Açısından Yenilenebilir Bir Enerji Kaynağı: Rüzgar Enerjisi. *Karamanoğlu Mehmetbey Üniversitesi Sosyal ve Ekonomik Araştırmalar Dergisi*, 17(28), 85–93. ISSN: 2147 – 7833.

Pak, R. B. & Özdemir, E. (2023). Küresel İklim Mücadelesi Ekseninde Türkiye'nin Yeşil Enerji Dönüşümüne Genel Bir Bakış. *Süleyman Demirel Üniversitesi YEKARUM e-DERGİ*, 8(2), 32–53. E-ISNN: 1309-9388, Erişim Adresi: https://dergipark.org.tr/tr/download/article-file/3316732

Pata, U. K. & Yurtkuran, S. (2018). Yenilenebilir Enerji Tüketimi, Nüfus Yoğunluğu ve Finansal Gelişmenin CO2 Salımına Etkisi: Türkiye Örneği. *Uluslararası İktisadi ve İdari İncelemeler Dergisi*, (Prof. Dr. Harun Terzi Özel Sayısı), 303–318. ISSN 1307-9832

REN21 (2023). *Renewables 2023 Global Status Report: A Comprehensive Annual Overview Of The State Of Renewable Energy*. https://www.ren21.net/gsr-2023/

Sabancı Üniversitesi İstanbul Uluslararası Enerji ve İklim Merkezi (2022). Türkiye *Yenilenebilir Enerji Görünümü Raporu*. https://iicec.sabanciuniv.edu/sites/iicec.sabanciuniv.edu/files/inline-files/Türkiye_Yenilenebilir_Enerji_Görünümü_Kitap__Türkçe_.pdf

Samancı, M. (2020). Yenilenebilir Enerji Yatırımlarının Arttırılmasına Yönelik Vergisel Teşvikler: Türkiye ve Seçilmiş Bazı Ülkeler Arasında Karşılaştırma. *Türkiye Siyaset Bilimi Dergisi*, 3(1), 55–69.

Sarıtunalı, H. N. (2021). Çevresel Güvenlik ve Enerji Arz Güvenliği Bağlamında Türkiye'nin Enerji Politikası. *Uluslararası Yönetim Akademisi Dergisi*, 4(2), 409–421. https://doi.org/10.33712/mana.913406

Steg, L., Perlaviciute, G., Sovacool, B. K., Bonaiuto, M., Diekmann, A., Filippini, M., … & Woerdman, E. (2021). A Research Agenda to Better Understand the Human Dimensions of Energy Transitions. *Front. Psychol.*, 12(672776), 1–11. doi: 10.3389/fpsyg.2021.672776

T. C. Cumhur Başkanlığı (2021). *Cumhurbaşkanlığı Genelgesi 2021/15*. https://www.resmigazete.gov.tr/eskiler/2021/07/20210716-8.pdf

T. C. Cumhur Başkanlığı, Strateji ve Bütçe Başkanlığı (2023). *Orta Vadeli Program (2024–2026)*. https://www.sbb.gov.tr/wp-content/uploads/2023/09/Orta-Vadeli-Program_2024-2026.pdf

T. C. Cumhurbaşkanlığı (2022). *5209 sayılı Cumhurbaşkanı Kararı*. https://www.resmigazete.gov.tr/eskiler/2022/02/20220224-29.pdf

T. C. Çevre, Şehircilik ve İklim Değişikliği Bakanlığı, Çevresel Etki Değerlendirmesi, İzin ve Denetim Genel Müdürlüğü (2020). *6. Türkiye Çevre Durum Raporu*, ISBN: 978-625-7076-05-0 Yayın No: 48. https://cevresehiriklimkutuphanesi.csb.gov.tr/Books/Book/a1c28ff7-0137-4d05-9446-71816276a732

T. C. Dışişleri Bakanlığı (2024). *Türkiye'nin Uluslararası Enerji Stratejisi*. https://www.mfa.gov.tr/turkiye_nin-enerji-stratejisi.tr.mfa

T. C. Enerji ve Tabii Kaynaklar Bakanlığı (2024a). *Rüzgar*. https://enerji.gov.tr/eigm-yenilenebilir-enerji-kaynaklar-ruzgar

T. C. Enerji ve Tabii Kaynaklar Bakanlığı (2024b). *Güneş*. https://enerji.gov.tr/eigm-yenilenebilir-enerji-kaynaklar-gunes

T. C. Enerji ve Tabii Kaynaklar Bakanlığı (2024c). *Jeotermal*. https://enerji.gov.tr/eigm-yenilenebilir-enerji-kaynaklar-jeotermal

T. C. Sanayi ve Teknoloji Bakanlığı (2024). *Yatırım Teşvik Sistemleri*. https://www.sanayi.gov.tr/destek-ve-tesvikler/yatirim-tesvik-sistemleri/md0103011615

T. C. Ticaret Bakanlığı (2021). *Yeşil Mutabakat Eylem Planı 2021*. https://ticaret.gov.tr/data/60f1200013b876eb28421b23/MUTABAKAT%20YE%C5%9E%C4%B0L.pdf

Tomaş, M. & Dostoğlu, N. (2020). Smart House with Artificial Intelligence. *Avrupa Bilim ve Teknoloji Dergisi*, (18), 486–493.

Tüzüner, S. (2007). İklim Değişikliği ve Enerji. *EMOENERJİ Toplumsal Haber ve Araştırma Dergisi*, 3, 6–9.

TÜİK (2024). *Hanehalkı Nihai Enerji Tüketim İstatistikleri*, 2022. https://data.tuik.gov.tr/Bulten/Index?p=Hanehalki-Nihai-Enerji-Tuketim-Istatistikleri-2022-53805

Uluatam, E. (2010). Yenilenebilir Enerji Teşvikleri. *Ekonomik Forum Dergisi*, 34–41. https://haber.tobb.org.tr/ekonomikforum/2010/10/034-041.pdf

Yurdadoğ, V. & Tosunoğlu, Ş. (2017). Türkiye'de Yenilenebilir Enerji Destek Politikaları. *Eurasian Business and Economics Journal*, *9*, 1–21.

193 sayılı Kanun (1950). *Gelir Vergisi Kanunu*, Kabul tarihi: 31.12.1960. https://www.mevzuat.gov.tr/mevzuat?MevzuatNo=193&MevzuatTur=1&MevzuatTertip=4

5346 sayılı Kanun (2005). *Yenilenebilir Enerji Kaynaklarının Elektrik Enerjisi Üretimi Amaçlı Kullanımına İlişkin Kanun*, Date Accepted: 10.05.2005. https://www.mevzuat.gov.tr/mevzuat?MevzuatNo=5346&MevzuatTur=1&MevzuatTertip=5

5520 sayılı Kanun (2005). *Kurumlar Vergisi Kanunu*, Kabul tarihi: 13.06.2006. https://www.mevzuat.gov.tr/mevzuat?MevzuatNo=5520&MevzuatTur=1&MevzuatTertip=5

The Effects of Economic Growth and Environmental Taxes on Green Technology Innovation

Burak Tuğberk TOSUNOĞLU[1]

1 Introduction

The rapid expansion of the global economy has introduced numerous challenges in achieving sustainable development goals. Economic growth is frequently associated with elevated levels of production and consumption. This growth trajectory often culminates in environmental degradation and the depletion of natural resources (Grossman and Krueger, 1995:350). Environmental degradation and climate change represent some of the most formidable challenges confronting the global economy. These issues imperil human health and income and productivity levels (Sharif et al., 2023:98). Environmental sustainability is central to contemporary economic growth policies, with the significance of green technology innovation gaining increasing recognition in this context. Green technology encompasses solutions designed to mitigate environmental harm and optimize the use of natural resources (UNEP, 2019). One of the paramount issues arising from climate change is its severe threat to human lives. The literature extensively documents the criticality of understanding the environmental impacts of economic activity. Nations globally are vying for economic development and progress, and with the expansion of the global economy, the demand for fossil fuels perpetually escalates. The continuous economic expansion profoundly influences climate change by driving energy-intensive behaviors that elevate atmospheric CO_2 levels and increase global temperatures (Wang et al., 2023:1).

Formulating sustainable development policies that account for the environmental costs of economic activities is one of the most significant challenges of our time. In this context, it is imperative to develop policies that mitigate the environmental sustainability impacts of economic growth. Among these policies, environmental taxes, incentives, and regulatory measures hold a

[1] Anadolu University, FEAS, Department of Economics, ttosunoglu@anadolu.edu.tr, ORCID: 0000-0001-9377-5136

prominent position (OECD, 2010:23–25). Environmental taxes are financial instruments designed to internalize the economic costs of environmental damage, thereby encouraging firms and individuals to reduce their environmental impacts (Bovenberg and Goulder, 2002:1471). These taxes can be applied to various environmental issues, such as carbon emissions, water pollution, and waste management. In addition to reducing environmental damage, environmental taxes have the potential to stimulate the development of innovative technologies (Jaffe and Palmer, 1997:610).

Green technology innovation refers to the development and dissemination of environmentally conscious technological solutions. Such innovations contribute significantly in various areas, including enhancing energy efficiency, promoting the use of renewable energy sources, and reducing environmental pollution (Rennings, 2000:319). Supporting green technology innovation is crucial for ensuring the sustainability of economic growth and achieving environmental objectives. By replacing traditional production methods, green innovation can minimize the environmental costs of economic growth and support sustainable development in the long term. However, the widespread adoption of green technology innovation depends not only on technological advancements but also on economic and political incentives.

The interactions between economic growth, environmental taxes, and green technology innovation are complex and multidimensional. While economic growth can increase environmental pressures, it can also provide the financial resources necessary for innovation (Porter and van der Linde, 1995:97–99). The prosperity associated with economic growth can raise environmental awareness and demand, thereby encouraging investments in green technologies. Environmental taxes, on the other hand, can direct firms towards more environmentally friendly technologies, thus fostering green technology innovation (Popp, 2002:160). Properly designed and implemented environmental taxes can promote innovation, making economic growth sustainable and helping achieve environmental goals.

This study aims to examine the effects of economic growth and environmental taxes on green technology innovation in OECD countries. The relationship between environmental taxes and economic growth will be analyzed within the scope of green technology innovation using patent data. The primary variable covered by the research objectives is the number of environmentally related patent applications (the share of environmentally related patents within total patent applications) according to the priority date under the Patent Cooperation Treaty (PCT). The research data spans the period from 1994 to 2020 and includes applications submitted to the European Patent Office. This timeframe has been selected based on the availability of comparable data. The findings of this study will provide significant insights for policymakers and will serve as a guide in achieving sustainable development goals.

2 The Impacts of Green Technology Innovation

Achieving economic and environmental efficiency in production processes is a priority for many businesses, which are increasingly adopting environmental innovation strategies or techniques to produce eco-friendly products. Green technology innovation (frequently referred to interchangeably by scholars as eco-innovation, green innovation, environmental innovation, and sustainable innovation) represents a strategy designed to minimize environmental losses through the efficient use of energy. Green innovation encompasses the development and implementation of practices specifically aimed at enhancing environmental quality. This form of innovation significantly mitigates the impacts of climate change, primarily driven by the emissions of greenhouse gases such as carbon dioxide (CO2) (Wang et al., 2023:2).

Despite extensive research, there is no universally accepted definition of green technology innovation. The prevalent view defines green innovation as the introduction of any new or significantly improved product (good or service), process, organizational change, or marketing solution that reduces the utilization of natural resources (including materials, energy, water, and land) and decreases the release of harmful substances throughout its entire life cycle. Moreover, eco-innovation is characterized as the production, application, or operation of a good, service, production process, organizational structure, or management or business method that is novel to the firm or user and results in reduced environmental risk, pollution, and resource use (including energy) compared to relevant alternatives over its life cycle. Eco-innovations include product, process, marketing, and organizational innovations that lead to significant reductions in environmental burdens. The positive environmental impacts can either be the primary objectives of these innovations or ancillary benefits (Hojnik & Ruzzier, 2016:32). Despite variations in terminology, all definitions incorporate an environmental component and reflect the two main outcomes of eco-innovation: reduced negative environmental impact and more efficient resource use.

Green technology innovation is crucial for achieving environmental sustainability objectives. These innovations exert various direct and indirect effects on the environment. By enhancing energy efficiency and promoting the use of renewable energy sources, green technologies reduce fossil fuel consumption and the associated carbon emissions. This represents a significant advancement in combating climate change and contributes to the conservation of natural resources (Stern, 2007:347). Furthermore, technologies that enhance energy efficiency yield both environmental and economic benefits by decreasing energy consumption.

Green technology innovation exerts extensive and profound impacts on the environment and plays a pivotal role in attaining sustainable development goals. These technologies substantially reduce reliance on fossil fuels by decreasing carbon emissions. The utilization of renewable energy sources (such as solar, wind, and hydroelectric power) minimizes greenhouse gas emissions in energy production. Concurrently, energy efficiency technologies optimize energy consumption, thereby mitigating environmental impacts. By enhancing energy efficiency, green technologies bolster economic growth. The implementation of energy-efficient technologies reduces energy costs, generating significant cost savings for both enterprises and consumers. These savings facilitate investments in other economic activities, thereby fostering economic growth (OECD, 2012: 55). This dual effect promotes energy conservation at both individual and industrial levels and supports the sustainable utilization of natural resources.

Recycling and waste management technologies play a critical role in preventing environmental pollution by reducing waste generation. These technologies optimize material usage and bolster the circular economy. Furthermore, green technology innovations provide advanced treatment systems to alleviate water and air pollution. Clean water technologies safeguard water resources, while air purification technologies enhance air quality. Green technologies also contribute significantly to the conservation of natural resources. This is evident in areas such as sustainable agricultural practices, water-saving technologies, and forest management. Additionally, green technology innovations aid in the protection of ecosystems and the preservation of biodiversity. This is achieved through environmental restoration projects and the conservation of natural habitats. However, it is crucial to acknowledge that the positive environmental impacts of green technologies are contingent upon various technical, environmental, economic, and social factors (Hannouf et al., 2020:24).

Green technology innovation has far-reaching and profound implications for economic growth. These technologies have the potential to harmonize economic growth with environmental sustainability, which is essential for achieving sustainable development goals. The relationship between economic growth and green technology innovation must be assessed through various lenses, including the creation of new employment opportunities, the enhancement of energy efficiency, and the stimulation of new market developments.

From an economic standpoint, investments in green technologies may initially incur high costs. However, in the long term, substantial economic benefits are achieved through energy savings and reduced operational costs. These technologies facilitate the alignment of economic development with environmental sustainability. Green technological innovation is recognized as a pivotal factor in fostering green economic growth. Such innovations have the potential to improve resource efficiency, mitigate environmental pollution, encourage the enhancement of industrial structures, and transform the nature of economic development.

Moreover, green technology innovations generate new employment opportunities and contribute to economic growth by increasing the overall employment rate (IEA, 2011:32). These innovations create job opportunities in sectors such as renewable energy, energy efficiency, and sustainable transportation, leading to both direct and indirect employment growth. For instance, the number of jobs in the solar and wind energy sectors is rapidly increasing, compensating for job losses in fossil fuel industries (IEA, 2019:32). These technologies facilitate the emergence of new occupational fields, particularly in renewable energy and energy efficiency. Renewable energy projects generate employment not only in energy production but also in related sub-sectors such as manufacturing, installation, and maintenance (UNEP, 2011:47).

Green technology innovations also stimulate the creation of new markets, thereby supporting economic growth. New products and services, such as renewable energy technologies, electric vehicles, and energy storage systems, are experiencing growing demand in global markets (World Bank, 2018:67). These emerging markets accelerate economic growth and offer a more sustainable growth model compared to traditional economies. Such technologies enable the development of new enterprises and business models. The expansion of green technology markets fosters a competitive environment that encourages innovation, thereby enhancing overall economic dynamism.

Green technology innovation necessitates considerable capital and human resources; while developing countries possess the requisite human resources, they often lack sufficient capital and advanced technology. In such contexts, the promotion and implementation of green technologies require robust policy support and refined market mechanisms (Si et al., 2024:3). The proliferation of green technology innovation is significantly influenced by public policies and incentives. Policy instruments such as environmental taxes, subsidies, and regulatory measures are pivotal in incentivizing firms and individuals to invest in green technologies (Portney and Stavins, 2000:289–290). These policies augment the cost-effectiveness of green innovations, thereby expanding their market penetration. Appropriately designed environmental taxes and incentives can catalyze the advancement of green technologies while concurrently mitigating the environmental costs associated with economic growth.

The social ramifications of green technologies are equally profound. By ensuring cleaner air and water, these technologies safeguard public health and elevate the overall quality of life within communities (WHO, 2018:5–6). Furthermore, they play a critical role in fostering environmentally conscious individuals, thereby enhancing societal awareness and responsibility (UNESCO, 2017:14–15). This heightened awareness contributes to the adoption of sustainable lifestyles and bolsters environmental consciousness.

In conclusion, green technology innovation exerts multifaceted and positive impacts on both economic growth and the environment. Factors such as the creation of new job opportunities, enhancement of energy efficiency, promotion of new market development, and increased competitiveness underscore the contributions of green technologies to economic growth. In this context, the support for green technology innovations is crucial for achieving a sustainable and balanced model of economic growth. Green innovation also serves as an indispensable tool in reaching environmental sustainability goals. Addressing the environmental, economic, and social dimensions of these technologies enhances the effectiveness of sustainable development policies. Public policies and incentives play a pivotal role in accelerating the adoption and dissemination of green technologies, thereby maximizing both environmental and economic benefits. Supporting green technology innovations is essential not only for ensuring a more livable world for present generations but also for securing the well-being of future generations. The integration of green technologies into the broader framework of sustainable development is imperative for fostering a resilient and thriving global economy.

3 Determinants of Green Technology Innovation

The growing body of literature on the factors contributing to green technology innovation has underscored the significance of economic growth and government intervention as key drivers of green innovation. Green technology innovation is critically important for sustainable development and environmental protection. In this context, academic studies on the factors contributing to green technology innovation have examined the impacts of various elements, such as economic growth, government policies, renewable energy investments, and environmental taxes.

The impact of green technological innovation on economic growth has been explored in various studies. Pu et al. (2022) indicate that green technological innovation supports green economic growth by enhancing energy efficiency and promoting clean production technologies, thereby reducing production costs. Ghisetti and Quatraro (2017) emphasize that green technological innovation boosts energy efficiency and economic growth. Chen and Yang (2024) find that urban green technology innovation significantly enhances urban green economic efficiency and reduces CO_2 emissions. Wang et al. (2023) assert that the presence of renewable energy, carbon taxes, and GDP in OECD countries, combined with green technological innovation and environmental taxes, has slowed the increase in CO_2 emissions and promoted green economic growth. This extensive examination of green technology innovation highlights the multifaceted nature of its determinants and the necessity for a holistic approach in policy-making to foster an environment conducive to sustainable and green growth.

Samad and Manzoor (2011) underscore the significance of economic growth as a determinant of green innovation within the context of diverse contributing factors. They posit that economic expansion fosters green innovations by facilitating larger markets, which can adopt substantial technological changes and enable increased investment in the development of green technologies. In contrast, studies by Shen et al. (2021) and Wang et al.

(2021a) contend that heightened economic growth targets might adversely affect green technology innovations. They argue that economic growth may impede green or eco-innovations because targets often prioritize quantity over the quality of growth (Sharif et al., 2023:100).

Beyond the roles of economic growth in influencing green innovation, the nexus between green innovation and environmental policy has attracted significant interest from researchers and policymakers. The transition toward green technology innovation, while imposing higher costs on the business sector, is predominantly facilitated through government intervention via environmental regulations. Robust and well-crafted environmental regulations are anticipated to spur innovative activities, especially among highly polluting firms, thereby enhancing productivity levels. A plethora of research emphasizes that environmental regulations exert a substantial and positive influence on green technology innovation by prompting businesses to seek alternative solutions to offset compliance costs. Van Leeuwen and Mohnen (2017) advocate for the implementation of environmental taxes to stimulate green innovation, whereas Hattori (2017) asserts that such taxes would only encourage innovation if the demand elasticity for polluting goods is low. Conversely, Acemoglu et al. (2012) highlight the importance of meticulously planning and promoting carbon taxes to avert any distortion or deterrence in green innovation practices and activities.

The dynamic interplay between environmental taxes and innovation is further elaborated upon in several studies, which suggest that environmental taxes may impose financial constraints on firms, potentially dampening their motivation to innovate (Aghion et al., 2012). This nuanced understanding of the determinants of green technology innovation underscores the complexity of fostering an environment conducive to sustainable and green growth, necessitating a multifaceted approach that integrates economic, social, and environmental objectives within coherent policy frameworks.

4 Green Technology Innovation in OECD Countries: The Relationship between Environmental Taxes and Economic Growth

The Patents in Environment-Related Technologies database provides the most up-to-date and comprehensive statistics for monitoring developments in environment-related technologies across OECD countries. These indicators enable the assessment of the innovative performance of countries and firms and facilitate the design of government policies related to the environment and innovation. Detailed search strategies have been developed to identify patents in environment-related technologies, utilizing over 200,000 classification symbols. These search strategies cover a broad spectrum of technologies related to environmental pollution, water scarcity, and climate change mitigation (OECD data explorer, environment-related technologies patents: https://data-explorer.oecd.org/). The data spans the years from 1994 to 2020.

For this study, data from 19 OECD countries with complete patent applications and environmental tax data for the years 1994–2020 were analyzed, and descriptive statistics were compiled. The countries included are Australia, Austria, Belgium, Czechia, Denmark, Finland, France, Germany, Ireland, Israel, Italy, Japan, Netherlands, Norway, Spain, Sweden, Switzerland, the United Kingdom, and the United States. The study incorporates data on environment-related technologies patents (GTI) as an indicator of green technology innovation, environmentally related tax revenue as a percentage of GDP (TAX), and GDP (constant 2015 US$) for the 19 countries from 1994 to 2020. The GTI data represents patent grants in environment-related technologies filed with the European Patent Office during the relevant years.

Tab. 1: Descriptive Statistics

Variable	Obs	Mean	Std. Dev.	Min	Max
gti	513	302.4466	589.7649	1	3918.66
tax	513	2.406413	.7965578	.65	5.35
gdp	513	1.88e+12	3.50e+12	9.28e+10	2.01e+13

On average, there are 302 patents granted for environment-related technologies, with the number ranging from a minimum of 1 to a maximum of 3,918. The average revenue from environmental taxes is 2.4% of GDP, with values spanning from a low of 0.65% to a high of 5.35%. GDP, in constant 2015 US dollars, averages 1.88 trillion USD, with a minimum value of 92.8 billion USD and a maximum value of 20.13 trillion USD.

Fig. 1: Annual Avereges of GTI, TAX, GDP.

Figure 1 illustrates the average values of patents granted for environment-related technologies, environmental tax revenues, and GDP over the years. From 1994 to 2000, there was a slight decline in the number of patents granted for environment-related technologies, followed by an upward trend. During this period, the average number of patents generally fluctuates between 100 and 200. From the early 2000s to 2010, the number of patents shows fluctuations without a clear increasing or decreasing trend. However, starting in 2010, a distinct upward trend in the number of patents for environment-related technologies was observed. Notably, after 2015, there is a rapid increase in the number of patents, with the average reaching up to 800 by 2020. This upward trend can be attributed to heightened environmental awareness and increased interest and investment in innovative technologies.

Figure 2 presents the annual changes in GTI for each country analyzed, highlighting the variations and trends in green technology innovation across the different OECD countries included in the study.

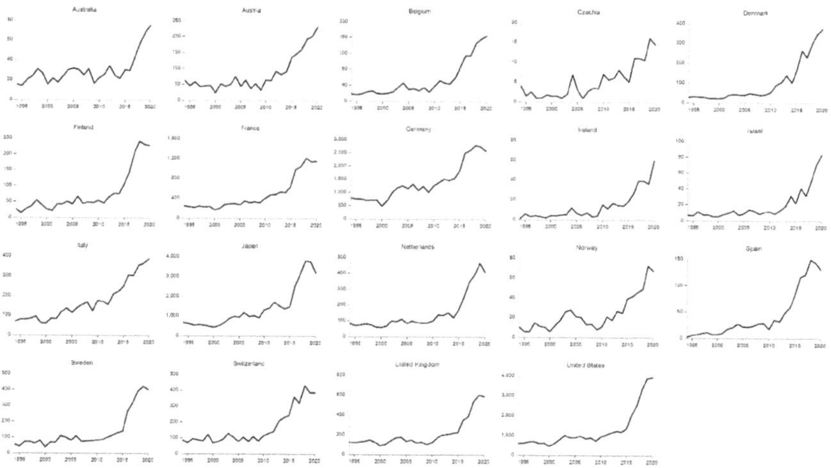

Fig. 2: GTI Trends by Country.

For most countries, a marked upward trend in the number of patents granted for environment-related technologies was observed after 2010. This trend is particularly pronounced in countries such as Germany, Japan, and the United States (Fig. 2). In contrast, countries like Belgium, Czechia, Denmark,

Ireland, Israel, Italy, Norway, and Spain exhibit lower numbers of patents in environment-related technologies, with the figures either remaining at low levels or following a stable trajectory over time. Significant increases in patents after a certain year can be attributed to factors such as the implementation of specific environmental policies, the enhancement of incentives, or the development of innovative technologies.

Figure 3 clearly illustrates the variations and changes in environmental tax revenues among different countries over time. Generally, while some countries exhibit increasing or decreasing trends in environmental taxes, others display a more stable pattern. This reflects the diverse environmental policies and tax practices of each country and provides crucial insights into how environmental taxes have evolved. Since the early 2000s, there has been a slight decline in environmental taxes, but in recent years, a more stable and narrower distribution has been observed. This may indicate that environmental policies and tax practices have become more consistent over time.

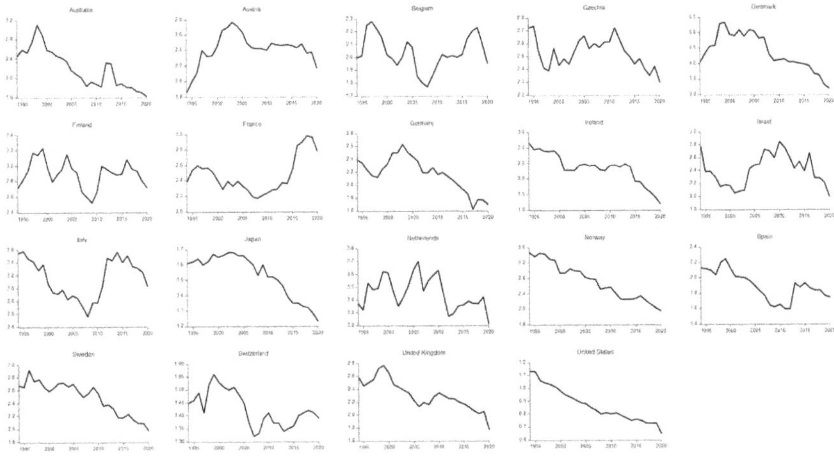

Fig. 3: TAX Trends by Country.

Figure 4 illustrates the GDP trends over the years for each country. It is observed that GDP has generally increased across all countries over time. Some countries, such as Finland and Italy, have experienced periodic fluctuations in GDP growth. The GDP growth rate has progressed at different speeds in each country, but the overall trend is upward.

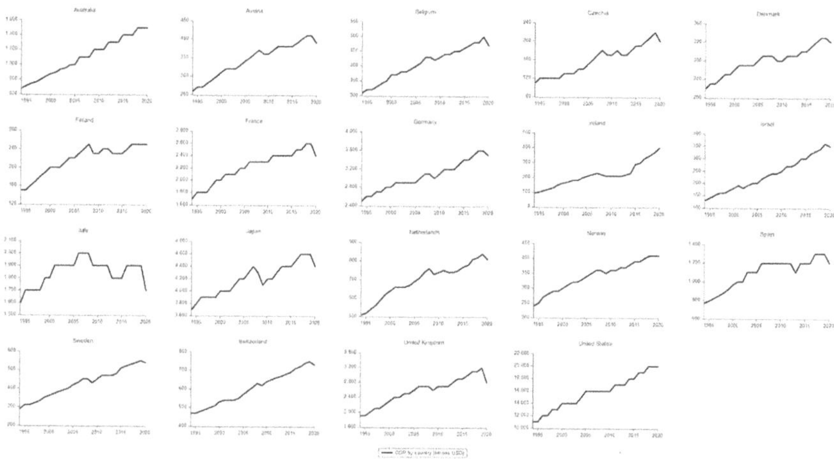

Fig. 4: GDP Trends by Country.

The correlation between economic growth and environmental taxes, which are considered determinants of green technology innovation in the academic literature, is depicted in Table 2 using data obtained from the respective countries. According to the correlation matrix, the correlation coefficient between TAX and GTI is -0.40. This negative relationship suggests that as environmental taxes increase, investments in green technology tend to decrease. In other words, high environmental taxes may adversely affect companies' propensity to invest in green technology, implying that raising environmental taxes might have a potentially inhibitive effect on green technology advancements.

Tab. 2: Correlation Matrix

	gti	tax	gdp
gti	1		
tax	−0.3991	1	
gdp	0.6124	−0.527	1

Conversely, the correlation coefficient between GDP and GTI is 0.61. This positive relationship indicates that as economic growth increases, investments in green technology also rise. This finding suggests that economically stronger countries or periods are associated with higher investments in green technology. It can be inferred that economic growth positively impacts green technology investments and developments. The direction of the relationship between the variables is also illustrated in the scatter plots (Figures 5 and 6).

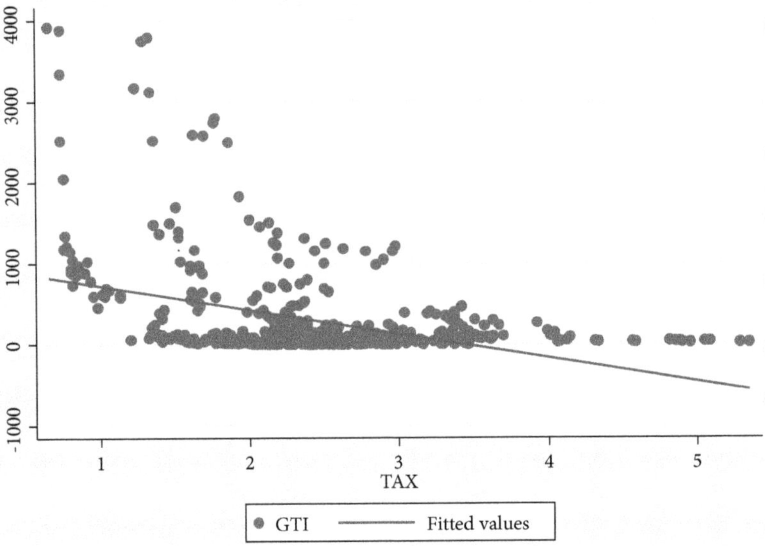

Fig. 5: Relationship between GTI and Tax.

5 Conclusion

The empirical analysis of economic growth and environmental taxes reveals their substantial influence on green technology innovations within OECD countries. The data indicates a notable correlation between these determinants and the advancement of environment-related technologies. Specifically, the correlation matrix demonstrates a negative relationship between environmental taxes (TAX) and green technology innovations (GTI), suggesting that higher environmental taxes may initially discourage investments in green technologies. However, as environmental taxes escalate, firms are incentivized to innovate to alleviate tax burdens, thereby catalyzing significant advancements in green technology.

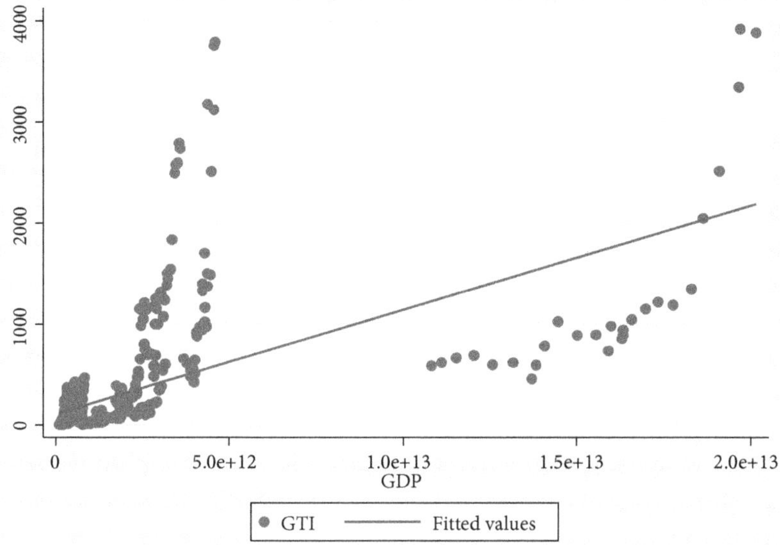

Fig. 6: Relationship between GTI and GDP.

In contrast, the positive correlation between GDP and GTI underscores that economic growth facilitates increased investment in green technology innovations. This relationship implies that economically robust nations or periods are more conducive to the development and adoption of environmentally sustainable technologies. These findings indicate that while economic growth directly enhances green innovation, the role of environmental taxes is more complex, necessitating a balanced approach to optimize their efficacy in promoting green technology.

Moreover, the temporal analysis identifies a clear upward trajectory in green technology patents post-2010, particularly in countries such as Germany, Japan, and the United States. This surge is likely attributable to heightened environmental consciousness and substantial investments in innovative technologies. Conversely, the persistently low levels of patents in other nations suggest a need for more robust policy measures and incentives to stimulate green innovation.

The development and dissemination of low-carbon technologies are pivotal for achieving carbon neutrality by 2050. Investments in low-carbon innovations are imperative, as extant technologies are insufficient to meet these ambitious targets. Therefore, it is incumbent upon governments to augment public R&D expenditures, prioritize low-carbon technologies in their fiscal agendas, and offer a long-term, stable perspective. Mitigating barriers to external financing and enacting supportive tax regulations for nascent firms are essential steps in facilitating access to capital for high-risk enterprises.

In summation, the synergistic implementation of green technology innovations and environmental taxes is essential for realizing both environmental and economic objectives. Public policies and incentives are instrumental in this process, underpinning the transition to a sustainable and balanced economic growth model. Policymakers must continue to address the challenge of reforming regulatory frameworks to foster the development of reliable and affordable energy sources while diminishing reliance on fossil fuels. The sustained emphasis on green technologies will be crucial in mitigating the environmental impact of economic growth and advancing a more sustainable global economy.

Bibliography

Arshian Sharif, Sinem Kocak, Hafizah Hammad Ahmad Khan, Gizem Uzuner, Sunil Tiwari, Demystifying the links between green technology innovation, economic growth, and environmental tax in ASEAN-6 countries: The dynamic role of green energy and green investment, Gondwana Research, Volume 115, 2023, Pages 98–106. https://doi.org/10.1016/j.gr.2022.11.010.

Bovenberg, A. L., & Goulder, L. H. (2002). Environmental taxation and regulation. In A. J. Auerbach & M. Feldstein (Eds.), Handbook of Public Economics (1st ed., Vol. 3, pp. 1471–1545). Elsevier.

Chen, S., & Yang, Q. (2024). Renewable energy technology innovation and urban green economy efficiency. Journal of Environmental Management, 353, 120130.

Ghisetti, C., & Quatraro, F. (2017). Green technologies and environmental productivity: A cross-sectoral analysis of direct and indirect effects in Italian regions. Ecological Economics, 132, 1–13.

Hannouf, M., Assefa, G., & Gates, I. (2020). From social hotspots to policies for successful implementation of environmentally better technologies? The example of social life cycle assessment of oil and gas technologies in Alberta, Canada. Environmental Science & Policy, 110, 24–33. https://doi.org/10.1016/j.envsci.2020.05.002

Hojnik, J., & Ruzzier, M. (2016). What drives eco-innovation? A review of an emerging literature. Environmental Innovation and Societal Transitions, 19, 31–41.

IEA. (2011). World Energy Outlook 2011. International Energy Agency.

IEA. (2019). Renewables 2019. International Energy Agency.

Jaffe, A. B., & Palmer, K. (1997). Environmental regulation and innovation: A panel data study. The Review of Economics and Statistics, 79(4), 610–619. http://www.jstor.org/stable/2951413

OECD. (2010). Taxation, Innovation and the Environment. OECD Publishing.

OECD. (2012). The Future of Eco-Innovation: The Role of Business Models in Green Transformation. OECD Publishing.

OECD Data Explorer, Environment-related Technologies Patents: https://data-explorer.oecd.org/

Pu, Z., Liu, J., & Yang, M. (2022). Could green technology innovation help the economy achieve carbon neutrality development–evidence from Chinese cities. Frontiers in Environmental Science, 10, 894085.

Rennings, K. (2000). Redefining innovation—Eco-innovation research and the contribution from ecological economics. Ecological Economics, 32, 319–332. https://doi.org/10.1016/S0921-8009(99)00112-3

Samad, G., & Manzoor, R. (2011). Green growth: An environmental technology approach. The Pakistan Development Review, 471–490.

Shen, F., Liu, B., Luo, F., Wu, C., Chen, H., & Wei, W. (2021). The effect of economic growth target constraints on green technology innovation. Journal of Environmental Management, 292, 112765.

Si, R., Wen, H., Wang, Y., & Cao, M. (2024). Does green technology innovation promote green economic growth? –Examining regional heterogeneity between resource-and nonresource-dependent cities. International Review of Economics and Finance. https://doi.org/10.1016/j.iref.2024.103406

Stern, N. (2007). The Economics of Climate Change: The Stern Review. Cambridge University Press.

UNEP. (2011). Towards a Green Economy: Pathways to Sustainable Development and Poverty Eradication. United Nations Environment Programme.

UNESCO. (2017). Education for Sustainable Development Goals: Learning Objectives. United Nations Educational, Scientific and Cultural Organization.

Wang, Z., Sami, F., Khan, S., Alamri, A. M., & Zaidan, A. M. (2023). Green innovation and low carbon emission in OECD economies: Sustainable energy technology role in carbon neutrality target. Sustainable Energy Technologies and Assessments, 59, 103401.

WHO. (2018). Air Pollution and Child Health: Prescribing Clean Air. World Health Organization.

World Bank. (2018). The State and Trends of Carbon Pricing 2018. World Bank.

www.ingramcontent.com/pod-product-compliance
Ingram Content Group UK Ltd.
Pitfield, Milton Keynes, MK11 3LW, UK
UKHW021014120926
8556IPUK00040B/1130

9 783631 923726